SOVIET UNION

PARADOX AND CHANGE

Robert T. Holt and John E. Turner

Editors

HOLT, RINEHART AND WINSTON

New York   Chicago   San Francisco   London   Toronto

Copyright © 1962 by Holt, Rinehart and Winston, Inc.
All Rights Reserved
Library of Congress Catalog Card Number: 62-18760
23720-1212
Printed in the United States of America

June 1965

The translation from *Komsomolskaya Pravda* on pages 177–178 is reproduced with the permission of the publishers of *The Current Digest of the Soviet Press*.

The report of the television quiz show on pages 188–189 is paraphrased from Irving R. Levine, *Main Street, USSR*, New York: Doubleday & Company, 1959, by permission of the copyright holders.

PREFACE

The contributors to this volume were, with one exception,[1] brought together by a trip to the Soviet Union in 1958. But this book is not a report of a visit; indeed, in many respects the book is more a product of our experiences after we returned from the Soviet Union. The genesis of such a volume requires a bit of explanation, which in a tongue more formal than English would be addressed quaintly, yet appropriately, "Dear Reader."

After our return from the Soviet Union, the members of the group were invited to speak before various audiences about our observations of life in this proletarian state. In toto, more than 500 presentations were given. A lively question period usually followed these talks. It became apparent after a few months that the same questions were being asked in varying forms by people of differing backgrounds. Certain aspects of the Soviet scene appeared to be especially puzzling to inquisitive Americans who have developed an interest in and a concern about the USSR. This book is an attempt to provide the lay reader with information that is relevant to the most significant of these questions.

Many Americans wonder how it is possible to write anything that is both detailed and accurate about the Soviet Union. Is not one of the purposes of the Iron Curtain to keep crucial data out of the hands of western analysts? Is it not the policy of the Soviet leaders to permit only certain information to filter through the Curtain—distorted information that is designed to mislead the western observer? Are not visitors to the Soviet Union carefully shepherded from place to place, being allowed to see only those things that serve the propaganda interests of the Soviet regime?

Although the Iron Curtain has for long periods obstructed intimate examination of the Soviet system, it has been translucent enough to permit the western observer a partial view of life behind it. The Cur-

[1] Mr. Victor Cohn was not a member of the travel group, although he has visited the Soviet Union on other occasions.

tain has always been more effective in keeping information about the outside world away from the Soviet citizen than in keeping information about the Soviet Union away from western journalists and scholars. Despite the obstacles to a free flow of information, specialists in Soviet affairs have been able to piece into meaningful patterns the vast amount of data available in Soviet newspapers, professional journals, and government publications. A great deal of what is printed cannot prudently be classified as propaganda, for the regime employs its press as a means of communicating with its functionaries in all sections of the country. Often, of course, the statistics are incomplete or incapable of being accurately interpreted. In investigating the dietary standards of the Soviet people, for example, it is possible to discover the number of tons of meat slaughtered each year, but it is difficult to determine whether this figure refers to live weight or to dressed-out weight—a matter that can affect estimates of meat consumption by as much as 30 per cent. Nevertheless, Soviet documents and newspapers provide valuable information on industrial development, deficiencies in agriculture, the changing composition of the Party, internal power struggles, and so forth. Skilled analysts can learn much from what may appear to be insignificant material. For example, a seemingly minor criticism in the press of a Party or state official may be the signal for a major shift in policy or the beginning of a large-scale purge.

Since 1955, the Iron Curtain has been raised to permit westerners who have been issued visas to visit the Soviet Union for short periods of time—a concession that has opened up new sources of information about life under Soviet rule. Although travel inside the country enables the student of Soviet affairs to gain new insights and to check his earlier conclusions against on-the-spot observation, the shortness of his stay and the inaccessibility of research sources render impossible the type of field studies that are so fruitful in other countries.

The foreign visitor in the Soviet Union, under the benevolent and overbearing guidance of Intourist, is somewhat restricted in the areas he is permitted to visit. Although Stalingrad was on our itinerary, the trip was cancelled at the last minute, purportedly because the canal locks were being repaired, but really because Premier Khrushchev was delivering an important address in that city. We were unable to see the new industrial cities of the Urals and Western Siberia—Magnitogorsk, Novosibirsk, Sverdlovsk; nor could we visit the ancient romantic cities of central Asia—Tashkent, Samarkand, Alma Ata. Despite some disappointments in negotiating the itinerary, however, we managed to travel in many sections of the Soviet Union—from Riga on the Baltic Sea to Irkutsk near the Mongolian border—from Leningrad in the north to Sochi on the shores of the Black Sea. By the end of our month's stay, we had traveled more than 10,000 miles within the borders of the USSR. While we were not always free to designate the places we desired to visit, once we had arrived at a destination we were permitted to roam about the city at will and to converse openly with the people whom we met.

Many foreign visitors would welcome an opportunity to live like a Russian—to share his quarter in a city apartment or in a collective farm cottage and to view the world from his social framework. However, many barriers ("barriers" is a better word than "restrictions") prevent such intimate social contact. The foreigner may elbow his way up to a bar in Kiev and drink vodka with the factory workers; he can stand with the Russians on a windy corner in Moscow, eating a hot *pirozhok* (meat pie) ; he may become part of the jostling crowd at a book kiosk in Leningrad; he can sit in a stadium with 100,000 Russians, watching a championship soccer match and even join the crowd in a resounding Bronx cheer; he may mingle with the more sedate at the Bolshoi; or he may stand silently with the peasants during an Orthodox worship service. But the western visitor who is eager to engage in more than surface activities is rarely able to penetrate vital centers of Soviet life. He will interview the trade union leader in the factory, but he will not be invited to share a meal in a restaurant or home. He will enjoy a cordial discussion with a professor at the University, but he is not likely to be invited to the professor's apartment to meet his wife and children.

There are probably two reasons why the Russian citizen is reluctant to enter into close communication with a foreign visitor. First, since the housing shortage is severe, he may feel uneasy about inviting western guests to his one-room apartment, where he shares kitchen and bath with other families. Second, when the Soviet citizen remembers that only a few years ago the personal contact with foreigners could be used as evidence of treason, he is understandably fearful of developing close ties with people from other lands.

Even though the student of Soviet affairs cannot surmount these barriers to intimate social relations, he can nevertheless fill in a number of gaps in his knowledge about the operation of the Communist system. Interviews with factory directors and officials in the regional economic councils provide information about the problems that have resulted from efforts to reorganize industry. Visits to selected collective farms point up dramatically the lack of mechanization and the inefficient use of manpower. Through discussions with officials of the ministry of justice, the foreign scholar can gain fresh insight concerning the penal system and the recent attempts at judicial reform. By visiting Soviet classrooms and interviewing school principals, he obtains a better view of the educational curriculum, teaching procedures, methods of control, and problems of motivation and discipline. The interviews that we had with officials in factories and farms, in the government and the school system, were not casual affairs. Many of them lasted three or four hours, and by working from a carefully developed interview schedule, we were able to ask the officials in different parts of the country the same questions and check their answers, one against the other.

Casual meetings with Soviet citizens in a park or on a street corner or at a collective-farm market gave us at least a sketchy notion of what some people are interested in and thinking about. A student may initiate a conversation in order to practice his English, and within a few moments he reveals his curiosity about the western world in a flood of questions on subjects that range from "rock 'n roll" and taxation to modern art and foreign policy. The master carpenter on a housing project may leave his work for a moment to inquire how long his American counterpart would have to work in order to earn enough wages to purchase a suit of clothes, and before the conversation is completed, he has commented on his own pay scale and living conditions. Such experiences provide a valuable (though admittedly incomplete) glimpse of Soviet life which is impossible to obtain without visiting the country itself.

We have incurred many debts in the preparation of this volume. Our greatest obligation is to the Louis W. and Maud Hill Family Foundation for financing our trip, and to its director, Mr. A. A. Heckman, who offered valuable suggestions at every stage of the project. The Hill Family Foundation was interested in supporting an endeavor that would provide the layman with background information about life and events in the Soviet Union. We hope that this book will help, at least in part, to discharge our responsibility.

We are also indebted to many people in the Soviet Union (these people must, of course, remain unnamed), who treated us so cordially and who gave so freely of their time to discuss a wide range of issues with us.

We also wish to thank Professors John Hazard, Sidney Hook, Val Lorwin, Alec Nove, Sigmund Neumann, Leonard Schapiro, and Robin Williams for reading and commenting on parts of the manuscript. Susan Linée and Jean Pearce cheerfully assisted with the typing.

Robert Holt would like to acknowledge the fact that he did some of the work on the final chapter while holding a fellowship at the Center for Advanced Study in the Behavioral Sciences. The quiet, scholarly setting of the Center provided a perfect atmosphere in which to engage in "speculative glances into the future" of the Soviet Union. John Turner made his contribution to the last chapter while on leave in Great Britain, under the sponsorship of the Fulbright Commission, the Graduate School of the University of Minnesota, the Winton Fund, and the Charles A. Weyerhaeuser Memorial Fund.

Nearly every scholar who writes about the Soviet Union must give special recognition to the editors and publishers of *The Current Digest of the Soviet Press*. All of the translations included in this volume are from the *Digest*. The usefulness of this publication, however, extends beyond its function as a translation service. The wide range of periodicals surveyed by the editors and their sensitive selection of articles for translation make the *Current Digest* a valuable medium for keeping abreast of Soviet developments, even for those who are skilled in the use of the Russian language.

Although we humbly acknowledge the assistance given to us by other scholars and by the foundations, responsibility for the material and the interpretation lies with the author (or authors) of each chapter.

R.T.H.
J.E.T.

Minneapolis, Minnesota
October 1962

INTRODUCTION

Robert T. Holt

They are brave men who will attempt a short book on the Soviet Union. A short book, unless it is very specialized, tends to be broad and sweeping. But how can one generalize about the Soviet Union? It is by far the largest country in the world—almost three times the size of the United States. It stretches from Big Diomede, only a few miles from Alaska, into the heart of Europe. It reaches south to the border of Iran and north to the Arctic Sea. Within its borders, one can find virtually every extreme of climate and terrain. The Russian plain stretches from the frozen tundra wasteland in the north through the great coniferous forests of the Taiga. To the south the taiga gradually gives way to the steppe that in turn melts into the deserts of Soviet Central Asia. Great ranges of snow-capped mountains rise to the east of the deserts—the Pamir, the Altai, and finally the Tien Shan, the "celestial mountains" that lie on the border of Sinkiang. Tea and citrus fruits grow in the subtropical valleys of the Caucasus; over 2000 miles to the northeast in Novoya Zenalya, the snow never melts.

The people of the Soviet Union are as diverse as the land itself. There are over 100 different nationalities; 60 different tongues are spoken. With this diversity, can one talk meaningfully about an "average Soviet citizen?" Can one say what he thinks about America, about Communism, about Khrushchev? The average Russian is about five feet four inches tall, weighs 140 pounds, is 55 percent female and always a little pregnant. In other words, Ivan Ivanovitch is every bit as fictitious as John Doe, his American counterpart. Any generalizations about the average citizen of the Soviet Union apply to a statistic, not to any flesh and blood human being. And in the absence of public opinion polls and a free press, generalizations about the average Soviet citizen are more risky than generalizations about the average American.

But this is not a *general* book about the land and the people in the Soviet Union. It deals with a number of *selected* areas of life. We like to look at it as a series of "depth soundings" that explores some, but not all, of the significant aspects of Soviet society that are of particular interest to the American people.

During the first 25 years of the Soviet regime, few Americans were interested in learning facts about that newly created proletarian state. Some sang its praises without knowing of what they sang; others were willing to let it remain a *terra incognita,* and, like the mapmakers of old, labeled the *terra incognita* as the place where the dragons dwell. Almost two decades ago, Winston Churchill characterized the Soviet Union as "a riddle wrapped in a mystery inside an enigma." Since that time we in the West have learned much about the Soviet Union. Indeed, our survival has depended partly upon how much and how quickly we could learn. Part of the riddle has been solved, part of the mystery understood, part of the enigma explained. What remains is not so much a riddle or a mystery or an enigma as an image of the Soviet Union as a land of paradox and change.

Perhaps one can say that the Soviet Union is a land of paradox because it is a land of change. It is a country that has been wrenched from an ancient order and turned at a ferocious pace into a twentieth-century industrial society. The old is very old and the new is startlingly new—symbolized by the peasant cutting grain with a hand sickle as a jet transport roars overhead.

The Soviet Union is a land that, while slowly emerging into the industrial age, was caught up in the convulsions of the 1917 revolutions and recast in the model of a proletarian state. It is a land hurtling forward to overtake and surpass the United States—the first nation to enter the age of space with Sputnik I—and yet a country that in Byzantine grandeur venerates the mummified remains of Nikolai Lenin.

There are other paradoxes of the old and the new and of the changing and the unchanging. One can see them in the history of powerful individuals, from the Kievian Prince Vladimir, who accepted Christianity in the tenth century and ordered the pagan idols to be hurled into the Dnieper River, to the Georgian despot of the twentieth century, who was toppled from the Soviet pantheon by his former underlings. There is the paradox of poetic justice that has made Stalin a victim of ruthless rewriting of history—a technique he himself used so freely to justify his position at the top of the Soviet pyramid of power.

Many of the questions that Americans ask visitors returning from the Soviet Union are testimony to this bewildering impression of paradox and change. How can a nation only a few years ago a backward land of decadent aristocrats, fanatic revolutionaries, and persecuted peasants be leading in the conquest of space? Is it possible that the Soviet Union can ever match the United States in industrial production? How can agricultural production, once one of the great strengths of Tsarist Russia, be a drag on the economic development of the Soviet Union today? Is there not a burning desire to throw off the yoke of dictatorship after all the years of oppression?

Some of the changes in Soviet society in the past 45 years are obvious to Americans. No one needs to be reminded of the growth of a large industrial complex out of a predominantly agricultural society or the rise of an atomic superpower from the humiliating surrender at Brest Litovsk. But other changes have been more subtle. Even when they can be recognized, their significance is difficult to fathom. Some of these more subtle changes are seen in the differences between the dictatorship of Joseph Stalin and that of Nikita Khrushchev. Let us begin our "depth soundings" into Soviet society by examining the classical features of Communist rule in the USSR and major developments since Stalin's death.

CONTENTS

Preface   v

Introduction, *Robert T. Holt*   xi

1
Soviet Politics: Old and New, *John E. Turner*   1

2
The Soviet City, *John R. Borchert*   35

3
Soviet Economic Growth, *Francis M. Boddy*   62

4
The Farm Problem à la Russe, *Philip M. Raup*   90

5
Soviet Science and Technology, *Victor Cohn and J. W. Buchta*   118

6
Soviet Education as "Training for Life," *Robert H. Beck*   138

7
Soviet Youth, *Thomas F. Magner*   163

8
The Soviet Airwaves, *E. W. Ziebarth and William S. Howell*   184

9
Speculative Glances into the Future, *Robert T. Holt and John E. Turner*   207

Bibliography   232

Index   237

1

SOVIET POLITICS: OLD AND NEW

John E. Turner

Professor of Political Science at the University of Minnesota, John E. Turner is a specialist in the field of comparative government. He is co-author of two books, The New Japan *(with Harold Quigley) and* The Soviet Dictatorship *(with Herbert McClosky). He has just completed a research project on the British Labour Party.*

On March 4, 1953, swarms of Moscow citizens hovered around wall newspapers pondering a startling item in *Pravda.* Joseph Stalin, revered leader of the Soviet Union for a quarter of a century, had suffered a brain hemorrhage and lay unconscious, unable to direct the affairs of state. Late the following evening the foremost Party and government officials issued a joint statement announcing to the Soviet people that "the heart of . . . [our] wise leader and teacher . . . [has] stopped beating." Stalin's political heirs, perhaps uncertain about how the masses would react to this news, warned the people against "disarray and panic" and urged them to pledge renewed allegiance to the Communist Party.

A few days later, on March 9, the new Soviet rulers stood on the reviewing stand in Red Square to pay their respects to the departed Stalin. The funeral ceremony, which had been arranged by a lesser member of the oligarchy, Nikita S. Khrushchev, featured eulogies by such stalwart Communists as Georgi Malenkov, Lavrenti Beria, and Vyacheslav Molotov. In solemn tones they expressed the grief allegedly felt by all the Soviet people over the death of the "great thinker" of

1

this era—the "great genius of mankind." After enumerating Stalin's virtues and achievements, Beria emphasized the need for the Soviet people to remain united behind the Party's policies and its new leaders. The great Stalin, he pointed out, had had the foresight to surround himself with able men whom he had personally trained to take over after his death. When the trumpetry was ended, a special guard of honor placed Stalin's body in the mausoleum alongside the remains of Lenin, where for several years it was to be viewed by long lines of devotees, pilgrims, and curious tourists.

Stalin's death marked the end of a spectacular and harsh epoch in Soviet history. Although the main patterns of dictatorship had already been formed in Lenin's day, they were extended and made more rigid under Stalin. In March 1953, his successors inherited this system of rule, as well as the difficult problems that had continually plagued it. Since the post-Stalin era has been influenced in large measure by the earlier decades of Communist rule, an analysis of developments in this period will be aided by a brief discussion of Stalin's rise to power and the essential features of the power structure that emerged. This background will bring into sharper focus the lines of continuity between the old and the new regimes and will enable us to place in better perspective the policies that have been introduced in recent years.

THE PATTERN OF STALINISM

Lenin's death in 1924 precipitated a bitter struggle for control of the Soviet system—a struggle for succession that resembled in some respects the contest that broke out after Stalin's death. The main contenders in this first skirmish were Leon Trotsky, a talented intellectual who was regarded as the "natural" successor to Lenin, and Joseph Stalin, who enjoyed strong support in the bureaucracy (*apparatus*) of the Communist Party itself. These two men sought power in a political organization that had been dominated from the beginning by its leadership and which had grown even more oligarchical after the Bolshevik revolution. An individual who could seize control of the Party's central organs was in a position to dominate the entire organization and through it to extend his hegemony over the principal domains of Soviet life. Stalin set about systematically to win control of the Party machinery, to isolate and then defeat his rivals, and finally to expand his influence in other realms of society.

Stalin's Rise to Power

Stalin's rise to power dates from 1922 when he became the Party's General Secretary, the chief administrative official in the Secretariat. This agency, which was responsible for the day-to-day conduct of Communist affairs, supplied the Politburo with the information needed to formulate the policies of the Party, and it served as the machinery that enforced the decisions of the Politburo. Although the Secretariat was initially conceived as a service unit for the Party's central organs, it gradually expanded the range of its activities—a development that naturally enhanced Stalin's status and power in the organization. As General Secretary he supervised the flow of information to the Politburo; he had access to personnel files, membership lists, and other Communist records; and he was in a position to screen candidates who sought admission to the Party. From this base of operations he was able to appoint his supporters to key offices in the Communist bureaucracy and to dismiss or transfer those whose loyalty he could not command. Stalin's work in the Secretariat kept him in close touch with Communist functionaries at all levels of the organization, thus giving him influence in many Party units that was denied to his competitors. Through his power over Communist secretaries in the local areas, he could influence the selection of delegates to the Party Congress, the body that formally elected the members of the Central Committee, the Politiburo, the Secretariat, and other important agencies. When Stalin eventually won a majority in the Central Control Commission, this victory not only gave him a voice in the conduct of the Party's purges but soon placed at his disposal the machinery for exposing Communist officials who might threaten his growing power.

During his final illness Lenin had become alarmed by Stalin's tactics, and in his famous *Testament*, which was not officially released to the Soviet public until 1956, he went so far as to advocate Stalin's removal from the post of General Secretary. Lenin was concerned, too, about the growing animosity between Stalin and Trotsky. Fearful that this enmity might degenerate into a fractional struggle that would weaken the Party, Lenin apparently hoped that his successors would establish some form of collective leadership, thereby minimizing the danger of schism.

Though Lenin had avoided designating any of his lieutenants as his successor, Trotsky as second in importance to Lenin appeared to be the leading candidate. In order to hold Trotsky in check, Stalin formed an alliance with two other prominent Bolsheviks who had long been associated with Lenin—Lev Kamenev and Gregory Zinoviev—and this entente, supported by the right-wing faction in the Politburo, dominated the Party Congress and the Central Committee from 1924 until 1926. Through their grip on the Party organization, Stalin and his fellow-triumvirs continued to handpick officials in the local areas, to dismiss or even arrest their opponents, and to prevent rival groups from communicating with rank-and-file members of the Party. When Trotsky and other renowned Bolsheviks protested against the policies and tactics of the new rulers, the Stalin clique launched a vigorous campaign against Trotsky and branded him a "factionalist" who was bent upon destroying the Party. Trotsky proved to be quite powerless against the men who controlled the Party apparatus, and within a few months his position in the organization had been seriously undermined, although he still enjoyed popularity in some Party circles.

With Trotsky effectively disarmed, the triumvirate—an alliance of political convenience from the beginning—soon split apart, with Stalin falling into open disagreement with Kamenev and Zinoviev. By 1925 he had become secure enough to abandon them entirely, and he entered into partnership with the rightist faction in the Politburo. Finding themselves outmaneuvered by Stalin, Kamenev and Zinoviev did an about-face and joined forces with Trotsky, becoming with him the leaders of the left opposition. They demanded a policy that would foster "world revolution" rather than jeopardize the future of the international proletariat by concentrating entirely upon the buildup of the USSR. They also called for the rapid development of heavy industry, centralized economic planning and control, the collectivization of agriculture, and the taxation of well-to-do peasants (*kulaks*) as a means of financing industrial development.

Those on the right, however, supported more cautious policies that had been introduced by Lenin himself in 1921. They favored the buildup of the Soviet Union as a proletarian stronghold, even if it meant neglecting the revolutions in other lands, especially since the USSR was not yet capable of providing significant support. They opposed the immediate collectivization of agriculture, contending that such a program would provoke widespread resistance among the peasants. The rights felt that the farmers could more easily be persuaded to support Bolshevism through concessions to private farming and the free market. In their view, forced industrialization at a rapid pace when the country lacked capital and technical resources would disrupt the economy and endanger the gains already made.

Stalin first opened his attack on the members of the left opposition. On one pretext or another they were gradually removed from their posts in the Party and the government, and some were subjected to reprisals by the secret police. Frustrated in their efforts to reach a mass audience through public meetings and the press, the leftists were faced with the dismal alternatives of either resorting to clandestine methods of opposition or of capitulating to Stalin's power, humbly confessing their errors, and begging for reinstatement in the Party. By the closing months of 1927, the remnants of the left opposition had been stripped of their power. In the Party Congress of that year they were unable to claim a single delegate. In 1929 Trotsky was banished from the Soviet Union, and Zinoviev and Kamenev, whose pleading eventually won them uncomfortable readmission to the Party ranks, experienced the terror of the Stalinist purge less than a decade later.

When the lefts had been rendered impotent, Stalin reversed his stand on economic issues and adopted the leftist domestic program in its most extreme form. He introduced emergency measures for rapid industrialization, collectivization of agriculture, and large-scale economic planning, all reflected in the first five-year plan. When his right-wing allies resisted these policies, Stalin cast them in the role of the right opposition and proceeded to undermine them by employing the same ruthless tactics that had proved so successful against the lefts. The final curtain on this political melodrama was drawn between 1936 and 1938, the era of the Great Purge and the Moscow "show trials," when all the old Bolsheviks who had ever opposed Stalin were sent to prison or executed. Soon thereafter Soviet propagandists began the task of falsifying documents and rewriting history in order to erase the memory of Stalin's enemies and to exaggerate his role in the development of Russian Communism.

Through his domination of the key organs of a highly centralized party, Stalin had succeeded by 1929 in defeating powerful and illustrious rivals; he had established himself as the acknowledged heir of Lenin, the supreme director of the Party and the state. On his fiftieth birthday in December 1929, he was showered with flowery tributes hailing him as an infallible leader in the march toward Communism. This signalled the beginning of the "cult of the individual," which grew to unbelievable proportions until Stalin's death in 1953. For more than two decades Stalin was able to rule without burden of public criticism or effective challenge by political rivals. Important policy matters were decided either by Stalin himself, or in consultation with Politburo colleagues who owed their positions to him. The Party's representative bodies met much less frequently, and even when they were called into session, the delegates voiced no criticism of official policy and cast their votes unanimously.

The first struggle for succession becomes relevant to an analysis of the post-Stalin contest when one realizes that Khrushchev, in defeating his rivals, has followed the main outline of Stalin's political strategy. It is important to recognize, too, that several features of the dictatorship erected by Stalin have been carried forward by the men who served their apprenticeships under that system. For this reason it will be instructive, before turning to the politics of the post-Stalin era, to describe briefly the major elements of the Soviet dictatorship, especially under Stalin: the official state ideology, the role of physical coercion and mass indoctrination, and the machinery of control.

Ideology and the Communist Party

Every large-scale dictatorship in the modern world strives to become an important industrial and military power. If a state is to achieve this objective, it must command a large measure of support from its citizens, upon whom it depends to operate the factories and farms, to serve in the armed forces, and to perform other roles that are required in a complex society. In seeking popular support, the dictatorship is influenced to some extent by democratic doctrine, claiming to be rooted in the masses and to govern in their behalf. The Soviet Communists, in seeking to legitimate their rule, have always leaned heavily upon the "proletarian myth" that is deeply embedded in Marxist-Leninist philosophy. According to this belief, "truth" resides in the working class, which is destined to inherit the earth and to rule in the new social order. The proletariat, however, is powerless to realize its destiny without effective leadership. Responsibility for leading the toiling masses to their utopia falls, therefore, upon the Communist Party, whose members are presumably gifted with insight into the laws of historical development. Since the "truth" that is embodied in the working class can be discerned only by the *vanguard* of the working class, the Party as that vanguard has earned the right to direct the revolution and the social reconstruction that is to follow. It must, of course, function in this role without hindrance from competing political organizations, which are regarded as agencies of the enemy. The will of the Party is believed to be identical with the will of the people; the Party's understanding of the laws of the social process enables it to accomplish for the masses what they are incapable of realizing for themselves.

The Party's exclusive mission and its pattern of organization were outlined by Lenin more than a decade before the Russian revolution. A party entrusted with the task of revolution, he contended, cannot be democratic in its structure, for endless discussion and wrangling over policy and tactics divert the attention of the members from Communist objectives and make it easier for enemies of the working class to find their way into the organization. The Party, Lenin believed, must be organized "from the top downward"; rank-and-file members must obey their leaders without question, and local Party units must give way to the decisions of the central organs. Opposition and factionalism within the Party cannot be tolerated because they weaken the solidarity of the movement. Indeed, Party members who challenge the decisions of their leaders are by definition purveyors of false doctrines, seeking to cast doubt upon Communist "truth."

This attitude toward conflicting viewpoints is one of the crucial differences between dictatorship and democracy. Democracy assumes that no single group in the society has a monopoly on truth. In the democratic view, there are usually several alternatives that may be considered in resolving a given social or political problem. It is assumed in a democracy that there must be a broad exchange of ideas if a healthy social climate is to be achieved and the best solution is to be identified.

Democracy recognizes the divergence of interests that is inherent in a pluralistic society, and it provides the machinery through which these interests can be articulated and conflicting viewpoints reconciled. In any modern social order, every sphere of life tends to develop its own elite—a group of specialists whose prized skills enable them to make claims upon the society. Elites emerge, for example, in business, agriculture, labor, education, science, religion, and the arts. In a democratic society, each of these elite groupings is permitted to compete for political power, and a wide range of views is expressed in the public forum. The open competition of many interests thus helps to establish a political balance, with no single group able to gain a monopoly of political power. Business executives are compelled to share power with trade unionists and farmers; Protestants find themselves working in political harness with Catholics and Jews; and government leaders are forced to trim their policies to meet the demands of organized interests. The existence of a variety of socio-economic groups, each striving to influence political decisions, not only creates an atmosphere of tolerance and restraint but also acts as a countervailing force against the power of the state.

In the Soviet Union a comparable equilibrium of social and political forces is not tolerated. On the contrary, all social formations are dominated by a *single political elite* that overwhelms its potential competitors and arrogates to itself the authority to make the crucial decisions in all fields of endeavor. The Communist Party does not permit non-Communist groups to compete with it in a free political market. Business executives, educators, religious leaders, trade unionists, and artists are forced to bow to the will of the political oligarchy, which uses the Party and the mass organizations to dominate the entire society. These political leaders determine what products will be produced in factories and farms, what studies will be included in the educational curriculum, what biological theory will prevail, what artistic themes will be expressed, and what literary styles will be acceptable. A single political elite, in short, seeks to impose its system of belief upon the Soviet community, dictating the standards of behavior in virtually every realm of life.

What forces prompt the dictatorship to fasten its controls over society and to regiment the behavior of its citizens? A fanatical movement like Communism, whose leaders claim to be infallible, endeavors to achieve uniformity—a prescription of the single-belief system—and imposes restraints designed to realize a monolithic pattern. Since unorthodox or "false" ideas are alleged to divide men's loyalties and disturb the ideological solidarity of the community, the regime usually attempts to direct the lives of its people in every detail, isolating them from contact with alien cultures and values. Thus official decisions must be enforced in virtually every area of endeavor, and elaborate controls are introduced into spheres of life that are considered in free societies to be self-regulating or to be beyond the scope of legitimate government concern. Additional controls are needed, too, when a dictatorial regime claims to represent the will of its people. In the absence of open discussion and genuine elections, the rulers are forced to erect a façade of democratic institutions, manufacturing consensus through mass indoctrination, manipulated plebiscites, and engineered demonstrations. The control system is thus designed to create a society of conformists who voice unanimous support for the Communist cause and its leadership.

Physical Coercion

In enforcing its controls over the life and thought of the people, the Soviet dictatorship has frequently resorted to physical force and the use of terror. The regime attempts to secure absolute obedience and conformity by creating an atmosphere of insecurity and fear; the aim is to discourage as well as to punish deviation. Primary responsibility for applying coercion falls upon the secret police apparatus, which has operated with ruthless efficiency throughout the decades of Communist rule. Nearly every economic establishment and social organization has its special unit of police who vigilantly watch for corruption and ferret out the disloyal, the unreliable, and the nonconforming. They compile dossiers on individual citizens, and, through a system of internal passports, supervise the movements of the population. An elaborate network of informers enables the authorities to investigate a person's most private affairs. During the Stalin era the police wielded extraordinary powers of investigation and arrest, and untold numbers of their victims experienced the dreaded knock on the door at night, imprisonment in some secret locale, prolonged investigation, and forced confessions. Such vague accusations as "counter-revolutionary," "class enemy," and "socially dangerous element" usually resulted in internment at a forced labor camp or even execution.

An ironical feature of modern dictatorship is the use of the people themselves to aid in the enforcement of terror. The Soviet regime admonishes all citizens to report irregularities to the proper authorities, to inform on their colleagues and neighbors, and to denounce all forms of "anti-Soviet behavior." The force of public outbursts and the enormity of the mass demonstrations serve to dramatize the overwhelming power of the dictatorship and the futility of resistance. The purpose of this mass participation is to produce a climate of hostility toward all citizens who violate Communist norms and to intimidate those who might be contemplating opposition.

While coercion and terror are everyday features of Soviet life, they are employed with varying degrees of intensity. A speedup in the number of arrests, greater severity of sentences, and increasingly bitter denunciations of certain groups in the press and on the platform often signal the onset of a purge. The purge usually begins in the upper echelons of the Party, and as it spreads downward, hundreds of regional and district Communist officials are removed from their posts or transferred to less desirable positions. As it gathers momentum, its scope is extended beyond the Party to other sectors of society, and before it recedes it has claimed as its victims important officials from nearly every field of activity—factory managers, collective farm chairmen, civil servants, artists, editors, and others who hold responsible posts. The purge casualties in the 1930s numbered in the millions, and many of the victims were arrested, imprisoned, or shot without benefit of elementary legal safeguards. The threat of purge breeds feelings of insecurity in broad sections of the population and serves as a warning to potential dissidents who may harbor doubts about the Party's leaders and their policies.

Mass Indoctrination

No dictatorship of course can rely entirely, or even primarily, upon physical coercion. Since the regime cannot function efficiently without the active cooperation of its people, it must generate at least a modicum of popular support. The Soviet dictatorship attempts to engineer con-

sensus among its citizens through an intricate system of mass indoctrination—control of the educational system, monopoly of the communications media, and regimentation of the arts.

A well-developed and rigidly controlled educational system is essential
in a dictatorship that seeks to develop industrial and military strength.
Trained, reliable functionaries are needed to manage the economic
enterprises, to staff the vast bureaucracy, to direct propaganda activities,
and to develop the country's material and human resources. Even
ordinary citizens must be given a minimum of schooling if the propaganda appeals are to reach them and if they are to be drawn into the
system of mass participation. The education of an entire population,
however, can become hazardous for a dictatorship, and therefore the
rulers seek to minimize the risks by regimenting the educators and
controlling the curriculum. In the Soviet Union great emphasis is placed
upon the indoctrination of future citizens with the essential Communist
virtues—love of country, devotion to hard work, obedience to authority,
knowledge of Marxist-Leninist doctrine, and unquestioning faith in the
wisdom of Party leaders. Far from being recognized as one who must
introduce students to a broad spectrum of ideas and knowledge,
the teacher is regarded as a propaganda agent who is expected to adjust
his classroom work to the requirements of the Communist line.

The indoctrination of the student population requires well-designed
control machinery, the main gear of which is the Communist Party.
While only about 20 percent of the members of the teachers' union
belong to the Party, these people are assigned to the key administrative
posts in the educational system. Many of the directives issued to the
schools are drawn up in Party councils, and important education reforms (including the one begun in 1958) are instituted by Communist
officials rather than by the educators themselves. Party representatives
have an important voice even in the selection of students for the universities. The significant decisions concerning the administration of
ordinary schools as well as of the higher educational establishments
are made in Moscow. The local authorities, in other words, have little
control over the educational curriculum, the allocation of school funds,
or the assignment of teachers.

The same pattern of control obtains in the field of mass communication. Instead of presenting an objective analysis of events, journalists,
editors, and broadcasters must rally the people to the support of the
regime. Since the newspapers, publishing houses, radio and television
stations, libraries, and bookshops are owned or managed by the Party
or the government, writers and commentators who desire to reach a
mass audience are forced into official channels and are required to

dwell upon acceptable themes. Similarly, artists, composers, and men of letters are herded into the barren pastures of conformity, where they are ordered to suppress their individualist urges and to employ their talents in creating "proletarian art," an artistic product that the workers and peasants can easily comprehend and one that will inspire them to meet their production quotas. With such tight controls imposed upon art forms and the media of communication, no access to a mass audience is legally open to the potential critics of the regime. If opposition is to function at all, it must do so informally, often in the darkness of the underground.

In full command of the instruments of persuasion, the Communist regime subjects the Soviet citizen to a heavy barrage of propaganda during all his waking hours. He is given stiff doses of propaganda in the classroom, in his newspaper, over the radio, at the cinema, on the stage, and in the concert hall. When he walks down the street or strolls through the park, it is impossible for him to escape the colorful banners and blaring loudspeakers calling his attention to the approaching Party Congress, the successes of the economic plan, or the "enemies" that must be conquered. Even the subway stations carry out propaganda themes, reminding the traveler of the various stages of Soviet development and the Bolshevik heroes responsible for this progress. In this atmosphere of stirring evangelism, an individual who entertains doubts may begin to suspect that he is out of step with the multitude—that perhaps even his friends and associates enthusiastically endorse the regime and its policies. Lacking the social reinforcement that might encourage him in his opposition, he is likely to keep his views to himself or even give them up and join the applauding throng.

The Machinery of Control

The ultimate responsibility for securing the obedience of Soviet citizens, whether through indoctrination or physical coercion, falls upon the Communist Party. Although it enrolls only about five percent of the population, its units are strategically arranged so that the organization reaches into every important domain of Soviet society. Government agencies, economic enterprises, trade unions, youth groups, and professional societies are structured to parallel the Party hierarchy and gear themselves to it, at every level of organization. Each establishment, whether located in a village, in a region, or in Moscow, has its Communist "cell" (primary organization) staffed by loyal Party members functioning under Communist discipline. Operating as a tightly knit core, these Party people are in a strategic position to control the policies of their respective institutions or associations and to report violations of official directives. In addition, the Party is largely responsible for selecting and assigning personnel to the important jobs in all fields and at every echelon of organization. Nearly all the plant managers and 90 percent of the collective farm directors, for example, hold Communist membership cards and are subject to the Party's dictates. By placing reliable functionaries in key posts throughout the society, the Party dominates the administrative agencies and social formations, integrating them closely with the center.

The power of the Party to decide what skills are needed, how many people will be trained in a particular specialty, and who will be assigned to a given job enables it to set the pattern of upward mobility in the Soviet Union, that is, to determine who will be permitted to advance professionally and economically. In designating those who are eligible for special training and preferred jobs, the Party is in a position to hold back individuals of questionable loyalty and to punish the nonconformists by interfering with their means of livelihood. By the same token, the Party's hold over the society is strengthened by the kinds of people it is able to recruit and reward with its favors. As one of the main thoroughfares for personal advancement, the Party naturally attracts the most ambitious, imaginative, and energetic elements of the society—those who are highly motivated toward power. Thus, through its capacity to bestow rewards and mete out punishment, it can draw the most talented people into the elite and put them to work in behalf of the regime. As in most societies, these people, enjoying the privileged status and material benefits that come with loyal service, are likely to develop a stake in the perpetuation of the system. In this way the Communist oligarchy develops a reservoir of talent and an important source of support, while at the same time depriving potential opposition groups of the leadership they would need to make their opposition effective.

Through mass indoctrination and the manipulation of rewards and punishment the regime seeks to place the stamp of obedience and orthodoxy upon the entire society. Such an ambitious goal, however, requires elaborate machinery for checking and cross-checking, especially in a system that tends to generate mutual fear and distrust. Within the Party structure, each Communist functionary operates under the direct supervision of the official immediately above him. In addition, the Party has certain organs, such as the Party Control Committee, whose agents check Communist activities at all levels and report directly to the central authorities in Moscow. The Party leaders also have at their disposal an organization of more than nine million rank-and-file Communists who have no effective voice in policy making, but who serve as watchdogs for the Party in their places of work.

Organized along the same lines as the Party is the government apparatus, from the ministry or state committee in Moscow down to the local
administrator or plant manager in the faraway town or city. Here
again the lower functionaries are responsible to their immediate
superiors, and such state agencies as the Commission of Soviet Control [1]
or the Procuracy [2] scatter their agents throughout the governmental
structure with orders to report directly to the Moscow officials. Aiding
in this investigative work are, of course, the *police* (the KGB), and
the *security agencies of the armed forces,* which overlap in their
functions but work through separate channels of authority. In this
way the regime has no need to rely upon a single source of intelligence;
each apparatus infiltrates the others, so that Party secretaries, state
administrators, police inspectors, and army officers can watch and inform on each other.

Until his death in 1953, Stalin was in personal command of this
sprawling network of distinct but interlocking hierarchies—the Party
apparatus, the government bureaucracy, the police agencies, and the
military establishment. Each group penetrated the others and scrutinized
their activities, reporting directly to Stalin and his henchmen. The
dictator sought to preserve his dominant position by pitting one group
against another, thereby encouraging a measure of rivalry among his
principal subordinates while keeping the strings of control in his own
grasp. High police officials and economic managers sat in Party councils
alongside men who had worked their way up through the Communist
apparatus. By frequent removals and appointments, Stalin reorganized
the several bureaucracies so that no single group would become permanently entrenched and thus be in a position to challenge his authority
or to circumvent his controls. To achieve the proper balance, he alter-
nated at various times his reliance upon these hierarchies. During the
purges of the 1930s, for example, the police were used to cleanse the
Party, the state administration, and the army, only to be reduced in
status when Stalin turned the fury of the purge against them. The
army's role was enlarged during World War II, but the transfer of
Marshal Zhukov to a post in the provinces at the end of the war signi-

[1] The Commission of Soviet Control is an agency of the central government
that is responsible for surveillance over the state administration, making sure
that the directives of the government are carried out. Through its army of inspectors it supervises the expenditure of public funds, audits financial records,
and investigates reports of irregularities.

[2] In many respects a separate branch of government, the Procuracy is a highly
centralized agency that supervises the enforcement of law in both the legal and
administrative fields. It acts as the state prosecutor in criminal matters and
conducts investigations of illegal activities at all levels of government.

fied the declining influence of the military. At the Nineteenth Party Congress in 1952, the appointment of leading officials from the economic and state bureaucracy to the enlarged Politburo-Presidium marked a recognition of their growing power. Especially during the last years of Stalin's rule, it was often difficult to discern which power group was playing a dominant role at any given time. With political and social control elevated to the rank of applied "science," Stalin's system of government represents the classical form of Communist dictatorship.

THE POST-STALIN POWER STRUGGLE

The unity of command temporarily collapsed in March 1953, creating a power vacuum and intensifying the struggle for succession that had begun even before Stalin's death. A dictatorship is vulnerable to such struggles because it usually lacks the legal machinery necessary for an orderly transfer of power. The stakes in the contest are enormously high; the losers, not permitted to function as a legitimate opposition, face the prospect of total defeat or even imprisonment or death. For this reason the internal battle for control becomes savage and often degenerates into a sheer struggle for survival.

Stalin's firm hold on the power levers had not prevented his lieutenants from trying to build up their own independent bases of strength. Malenkov, for example, had gathered support through his work in the Party apparatus and the state bureaucracy; Beria had collected a loyal following in the police agencies; Khrushchev had won influence among certain functionaries in the Party organization; and Molotov, Anastas Mikoyan, and Lazar Kaganovich had achieved prominence chiefly as government administrators. Preliminary skirmishing for advantage had been noticeable for several years, but with Stalin's death the would-be successors suddenly entered into the power struggle with renewed vigor. At the moment, however, and for several years thereafter, no single leader could muster sufficient strength to assume complete command. On the other hand, the several contenders could not risk an open struggle at a time of grave crises—unrest in the satellite countries, a tense international situation, emerging problems in the economy, and the unknown attitudes of the Soviet people. Stalin's successors decided, therefore, to display outward unity at the top ranks by adopting a formula of "collective leadership," which they hoped would conceal the internal struggle already developing behind the scenes.

At the outset Malenkov, like Trotsky in 1924, appeared to be heir apparent to the Kremlin throne. As early as 1948 he had begun to use his position in the Secretariat to dislodge his opponents and to install his supporters in vacant posts. In 1952 he had been chosen to deliver the Central Committee report to the Party Congress, an honor Stalin had always reserved for himself. When the Congress increased the size of the Central Committee and reorganized the Politburo into a larger Presidium, it is likely that both Malenkov and Khrushchev had managed to secure the appointment of some loyal regional Party secretaries and state administrators to these high Communist councils. Beria, on the other hand, had lost prestige during this early skirmishing. In 1952, for example, some of his henchmen were dismissed from their jobs, and a series of purges in his home territory of Georgia was apparently aimed at loosening his control. Again, only a few weeks before Stalin's death, the police apparatus that he supervised was the target of pointed criticism as a result of the alleged discovery of the "doctors' plot."

During the week following Stalin's death Malenkov boldly manuvered to extend his personal influence. The Soviet press featured him more prominently. *Pravda* printed a "doctored" photograph pointing up his close ties with Stalin and Mao Tse-tung, and congratulatory messages on his selection as Premier poured in from the provinces. Malenkov's political efforts, however, apparently alarmed his colleagues in the Presidium, and on March 14 the Central Committee approved his "request" to be released from his duties as First Secretary. It is not known whether Malenkov's resignation was forced or whether he voluntarily gave up his post in the Secretariat in return for the promise that he could remain as Premier. But, in any event, his removal as First Secretary proved fatal to his political career, for Khrushchev succeeded him in the vital office that Stalin had once used as a base of operations.

In the early days of the succession struggle, Beria too appears to have made a bid for power. A few days following the announcement of Stalin's death the two police agencies were merged into a single ministry and placed under his personal command. Shortly thereafter an official announcement declared that the doctors' plot, which had occasioned a charge of negligence in security matters against the police, had been a fabrication. In the three-month period from April to June, Beria proceeded to reorganize the police apparatus in most of the republics, placing his own men in key positions. According to Z. K. Brzezinski, a specialist in Soviet affairs, these tactics were proving so successful that some Communists in the satellite countries were suggesting that a Beria dictatorship might emerge. Beria's machinations, however, were extremely disconcerting to the other members of the Presidium, especially when he began to interfere in the affairs of the Ukrainian Party by launching an attack upon Party officials and engineering the dismissal of the Communist chief in that republic. Although reports of this episode are conflicting, Beria's rivals concluded that the ambitious police minister would have to be stopped, and in June 1953 they placed him under arrest. Six months later the regime announced that Beria and some of his henchmen had been shot for scheming to seize power by increasing the hegemony of the police organization at the expense of the Party. Beria's removal was the first in a series of actions designed to give the Communist apparatus more stringent control over the police.

The road was now cleared for an all-out struggle between the supporters of Premier Malenkov and the forces of First Secretary Khrushchev. Like Stalin in his contest with Trotsky, Khrushchev as First Secretary held an important advantage in being able to bid for the support of Communist secretaries in the lower echelons and to manipulate the Party apparatus. After the Beria episode, not only were the recent Beria appointees removed from the police agencies, but, in an extended purge, Party cadres were reshuffled throughout the entire country. During 1953 and 1954, many Communist functionaries in the regions of the Russian Soviet Federated Socialist Republic (RSFSR), the largest republic of the Soviet Union, were dismissed from their posts, and the impact of this shakeup was felt far down into the local units of the organization. Many of the officials assigned to the vacant positions were loyal followers of Khrushchev; indeed, some of the people who were placed in key offices had served under him when he was head of the Ukrainian Party (1938-1949) and while he was in charge of the Moscow section of the Communist apparatus (1935-1938 and 1949-1953). While this extensive reorganization was taking place, Khrushchev was making himself more widely known throughout the country and in some of the satellite states. Orders and medals were awarded to him, and he was hailed in the press as an imaginative Bolshevik leader who had helped Lenin and Stalin win victory in the civil war. By late 1954, he had emerged as the Party's leading spokesman, outlining his views on domestic and international problems in dozens of public pronouncements.

The rivalry between Khrushchev and Malenkov was exposed to public view in December 1954 and January 1955, when Khrushchev attacked the Premier for increasing the production of consumer goods to the disadvantage of military and other heavy industry. This point of view was, of course, attractive to army leaders, who had sustained a reduction of military appropriations under the Malenkov government. Supported by his allies in the military services and in the Party apparatus, Khrushchev was able to make his will prevail in the Central Committee, and a few days later he managed to bring about Malenkov's resignation as Premier. He then proceeded to take over the Malenkov policy of "consumerism," just as Stalin had adopted the domestic program of his rivals following their humilating defeat.

After Malenkov's resignation, Khrushchev tightened his grip on the central machinery of the Party. In July 1955, the number of secretaries in the Moscow headquarters was doubled, and three Khrushchev supporters were added to the staff. At the same time two of Khrushchev's protégés—one a member of the Secretariat and the other the secretary of the Ukrainian Party—were elevated to full membership in the Party Presidium. By the time the Twentieth Congress opened its deliberations in February 1956, many of the delegates who were to play an active role were regional secretaries and Moscow officials who owed their rapid rise in status to Khrushchev.

An analysis of the Congress proceedings provides a measure of Khrushchev's growing influence in Communist affairs. He delivered the opening speech, presented the Party report, and interrupted several other speakers to inject his comments. He even donned the robes of the theoretician to "bring up to date" Lenin's pronouncements on imperialism and revolution. And it was Khrushchev who astonished the delegates by launching the most devastating attack upon Stalin ever heard in the Soviet Union. The Congress increased the number of candidate members of the Presidium and enlarged the Central Committee and the Secretariat, thereby providing Khrushchev with important new posts in which to place men favorable to his policies. At the suggestion of the First Secretary, the Congress also established a special Bureau of RSFSR Affairs—an organ that immediately fell under Khrushchev's domination—to supervise Party organization in that huge republic.

But Malenkov, Molotov, Kaganovich, Nicolai Bulganin, and other influential Communists retained their seats in the Party Presidium, where they could challenge the First Secretary. In the closing weeks of 1956, the struggle for succession entered a new phase when these men made an indirect attack upon Khrushchev, using as their justification the issue of economic reorganization. The heavy demands upon the Soviet economy in the post-Stalin era had led to a proliferation of economic agencies, most of which were centered in Moscow. Factory managers complained that their local problems were frequently ignored and that their lack of authority to make administrative decisions compelled them to deal with many uncoordinated ministries in the capital. Responding to local pressures as well as to economic necessity, the new Soviet rulers began in 1955 to shift responsibility for the administration of many industrial enterprises to the republics. This industrial reorganization undoubtedly had the backing of Khrushchev, since the officials in the economic ministries in Moscow, who tended to support his rivals, would lose some of their authority. However, in the aftermath of the 1956 rebellions in Poland and Hungary and the internal economic crisis that had forced a lowering of targets in the five-year plan, some of Khrushchev's policies were called into question, and in December he was forced to concede that the powers of certain economic ministries should be extended rather than curtailed.

But before long Khrushchev began to maneuver for more extensive reforms that would diminish the power of the economic administrators and at the same time win support from Communist secretaries in the lower Party apparatus, who relished the prospect of greater authority, and from those factory managers who desired more leeway in carrying out their responsibilities. In February 1957, he convened the Central Committee in special session and secured approval for a program of economic reorganization intended to replace many of the economic ministries with regional economic councils. The essential features of his scheme were implemented by statute in May, and the Khrushchev regime began to transfer scores of industrial officials from Moscow to managerial posts in the provinces, where the regional Party function-aries could scrutinize their activities and exert somewhat more control over economic affairs.

Unwilling to accept defeat, Khrushchev's opponents in the Presidium took the offensive once again in June 1957. At that time Malenkov, Molotov, Kaganovich, and their allies, who had strong support in the state administration, managed to have the Presidium called into session, presumably for the purpose of arranging a celebration in Leningrad. Before the Presidium discussion had gone very far, they converted the meeting into an attack upon Khrushchev and demanded his resignation. With the aid of Marshal Zhukov, whose loyalty on previous occasions had won for him appointment to high Party office, Khrushchev and his friends succeeded in shifting the issue to the Central Committee, which was dominated by secretaries from the regional and central Party apparatus. After a week of bitter fighting, Khrushchev won a unanimous decision, and Malenkov, Molotov, Kaganovich, and some of their associates were stripped of their posts and denounced as an "anti-Party faction" who had conspired to seize control of the Party and the government. In another surprise development a few months later, Zhukov was accused of seeking to diminish the Party's controls over the armed forces, and he too was removed from Party and state office. In 1958, Bulganin suffered a similar fate and was listed as a charter member of the "anti-Party" conspiracy. He was followed in

1961 by the aged Voroshilov, who was humiliated at the Twenty-second Party Congress and forced to confess to disloyalty.

The downfall of these Communist leaders created a number of important vacancies in the Party's leading organs that Khrushchev again filled with his own followers, chiefly from the Secretariat and the apparatus in the republics. When the Twenty-first Congress was convened in January 1959, Khrushchev dominated the Presidium; more than three fourths of its members were also his subordinates in the Secretariat or in the Party organizations of the republics or regions. Of the men who had served with Khrushchev in the Presidium at the outset of the post-Stalin era, only Mikoyan remained by the end of 1960. As the Twenty-second Party Congress approached (October, 1961), the First Secretary reshuffled the Communist apparatus more vigorously and dismissed regional functionaries in several areas for their failures in agriculture or for sending in false reports. In filling these vacancies, Khrushchev, like Stalin in the earlier period, tended to give the nod to younger people—a new generation of functionaries who had entered the Party or the youth organizations during the war and who had reached administrative maturity in the years following Stalin's death.

The Twenty-second Congress provided another opportunity for Khrushchev to reorganize the Communist command so as to place his henchmen in important positions. The Central Committee was expanded into an even larger agency, and many of the new members elected to that body were functionaries from the provincial apparatus who had only recently been assigned to their posts. Similarly, the Secretariat was increased to nine members, and several of the younger leaders, who had had close association with Khrushchev, were entrusted with jobs in this agency. In order to place the "policies of relaxation" in more favorable light, the First Secretary and his colleagues bitterly assailed the "anti-Party faction," and demanded their expulsion from the Party. As at the previous Congress, but with greater impact, Stalin was singled out for biting criticism, and as a result his body was removed from the mausoleum and buried outside the Kremlin wall, near the graves of some of the minor saints and prophets.

Thus, in less than five years Khrushchev had successfully eliminated his formidable rivals, and he now stood in personal command of the dictatorship, simultaneously holding the posts of First Secretary, leader of the Presidium, chairman of the Bureau of RSFSR Affairs, and Premier of the Soviet government. As in the first struggle for succession, collective leadership, for all practical purposes, had given way to rule by a single leader. Even the "cult of the individual" showed signs of developing around Khrushchev, as Communist functionaries began to eulogize him as a "true Bolshevik," a "great leader and teacher," and a "loyal Leninist," and credited him with all sorts of achievements. Khrushchev, it appears, had been Stalin's most perceptive student.

POST-STALIN CONCESSIONS AND REFORMS

While struggling among themselves to fill Stalin's empty chair, the new Communist leaders were confronted by internal problems that demanded immediate attention. They could not, for example, be completely confident of the loyalty of the Soviet people, who had carried the burden of dictatorship for more than three decades. Although Soviet citizens have never been accustomed to voicing criticism of official policy and have, in any event, lacked effective channels to make their influence felt, the post-Stalin rulers nevertheless appeared uneasy about the temper of the masses—an anxiety that was probably reinforced by disorders in prison camps and by disturbances in some of the satellite countries. Fear of domestic unrest may have prompted Party leaders, shortly after Stalin's death, to issue the warning against panic and disarray.

The new regime also inherited a host of serious economic problems that had been developing since the 1920s. In the first place, the productivity of Soviet agriculture was lagging, reflecting the heavy state assessments that had been levied upon the peasantry and the meager amounts of capital that had been invested in the farms. Inadequate supplies of agricultural produce, coupled with chronic shortages of consumer goods, had resulted in depressed living standards that had no doubt affected the morale of the population. Then, too, overcentralization of the economy and the proliferation of state agencies had tended to narrow the range of decision making at the plant level and to erect bureaucratic impediments to the free flow of resources and supplies, thereby hampering efficient production. The problem of increasing labor productivity was made more difficult by the narrowly based system of wage incentives and by relentless pressures upon ordinary workers. Under the Stalinist policy of extreme wage differentials, for example, a relatively small group of skilled and "Stakhanovite" workers had been able to afford a style of living that set them apart from the majority of their fellows in the economic enterprises. Ordinary workers had always been subject to strict labor discipline, but more stringent measures were introduced in the late 1930s and during the war. Although some of these measures were not rigidly enforced after the war, compulsion remained a characteristic feature of the assembly line, stifling the enthusiasm of labor and inhibiting significant increases in productivity.

The Soviet Union, in other words, was experiencing the growing pains of a maturing industrial society. The economy had begun to level off so that spectacular growth rates no longer came easily, and further advances would have to be realized by combining the factors of production more efficiently. In comparing the relative performance of Soviet and American industry, Soviet economists and political leaders began to point out that labor productivity in the USSR was approximately one half that of the United States. If the Soviet Union was to achieve its economic objectives, it would need well-trained workers and a system of incentives to encourage them to increase their output. The development of a rational economic system requires an efficient labor force that is spurred on by the hope of adequate reward and personal well-being rather than by the fear of punishment.

Stalin's successors, then, were faced with the challenge of reorganizing the economy, readjusting the wage structure, strengthening agriculture, and improving living standards so as to stimulate greater production in factories and on farms. Such a program, if properly carried out, would have the additional advantage of enlisting the support of the masses and of dissociating the new regime from the brutalities and austerities of the Stalin era. These policies, however, would have to be introduced without weakening the position of the Communist Party and its leaders, for there was always the danger that in relaxing controls too quickly or too much the regime might unleash forces that would be difficult to contain.

Economic Changes

Economic concessions were first granted to the ordinary citizen in March 1953, when the new rulers announced extensive reductions in the retail prices of food and manufactured items. From time to time other price cuts followed. Shortly after Stalin's death, the regime also decreased the size of the 1953 state loan, thereby reducing the compulsory subscriptions ordinarily taken out of the worker's pay envelope. After a series of increases and reductions in subsequent years, the loan was formally discontinued in 1958. In addition, tuition fees for students in secondary schools and higher institutions, which the regime had imposed since 1940, have been abolished—an action undoubtedly welcomed by many low-income families. Throughout most of the post-Stalin era, the authorities have also increased allocations for new housing construction and housing repairs, and they have supplied the shops with more consumer items, thereby precipitating a significant rise in retail trade.

Probably recognizing the limited effectiveness of physical coercion in raising the worker's productivity, Stalin's successors have sought to entice him with more carrots instead of relying so heavily upon the lash of the whip. Attempts have been made to redress the disparity between high- and low-paid workers by reducing the excessive bonuses and salaries of upper-income groups, by adjusting piecework rates, and by raising the income scales of disadvantaged citizens. The regime, for example, has adopted a minimum wage that will be progressively increased under the current seven-year plan; it has reduced the direct taxes on low-income groups; it has shortened the work week in certain industries and has promised further reductions in the future; and it has increased retirement and disability pensions, especially for poorly paid workers and those in hazardous occupations.

Stalin's successors have also relaxed some of the harsh rules of labor discipline that had been in effect since shortly before the war. They have substituted voluntary recruitment methods, through the labor reserve training system, for the compulsory draft of younger workers; ordinary workers, however, may still be transferred involuntarily from overstaffed plants to factories that are short of manpower. In accordance with the policy of seeking to persuade rather than to compel workers to take jobs in undesirable locations, the regime offers wage supplements, travel grants, vacation benefits, and other inducements to citizens who volunteer to work in the underdeveloped areas of the country. Moreover, a worker no longer commits a crime when he changes jobs without permission or when he is absent from or late for work. While these concessions eliminate many of the Draconian wartime controls, factory workers are still subject to punitive measures. Plant directors, for example, have authority to impose fines upon a worker, to deprive him of bonus benefits, to remand him to the public ridicule of a "comradely court," or to dismiss him with an adverse notation in his labor record. The threat of losing social security benefits also encourages the worker to remain at his post. One of the distinctive features of the Khrushchev era is the renewed emphasis upon group pressure to keep the worker on his toes. This pressure is exerted through the Party unit in his factory, through his trade union, and through the system of popular courts, which operate independently of the regular court system.

In economic terms, consumer price cuts and rising wage levels represented an expansion in mass purchasing power. This increase has highlighted some of the deficiencies in agriculture, prompting Stalin's heirs to adopt measures for increasing productivity on the farms. In a bold attempt to realize this objective, they have appealed to the peasant's acquisitive drives by increasing the material incentives to produce. The tax structure has been adjusted to encourage farm laborers to work in the most "vital sectors" of the industry. From time to time the regime reduced the quotas of compulsory deliveries of farm produce to the state and eventually abolished them in 1958 in favor of a system of direct purchase by the government at higher prices. This policy has, of course, greatly increased the income of the collective farms, some of which is available for distribution among individual peasants on the basis of their work records. In recent years the regime has instituted a program of advance cash payments, under which the farmers are rewarded for their efforts in the collective fields without having to wait until the end of the year. As additional incentive, the collective farms have been given at least a nominal voice in planning their production schedules, and they have been permitted to purchase their own agricultural machinery from the defunct machine and tractor stations.

While increasing the rewards for peasant efficiency, however, the regime has at the same time tightened its controls over agriculture in an effort to preserve the collective farm system. Special tax assessments have been levied upon individuals who fail to join a collective, and steps are being taken to extend the collective principle to the development of common herds. Peasants who neglect their work in the common fields have been penalized by special tax levies and by curtailment of their private garden plots. Stalin's successors have also been successful in extending the Party's controls over agriculture, where the roots of Communist organization had heretofore been extremely tenuous. By merging the collective farms into larger units, the regime has been able to establish Party organizations on many more farms, and it has transferred thousands of Communist functionaries from the cities to the rural areas to help supervise agricultural operations. At the present time the percentage of farm directors who hold membership in the Party is the highest in Soviet history. The Party's control over agriculture has been further intensified since early 1962, when the regime drastically reorganized the industry as a result of chronic productions failures.

Legal Reforms

A surprising development in the post-Stalin era has been the regime's sponsorship of reforms in the legal system, apparently in an attempt to divorce itself from the brutality of previous decades. As one of their first official acts, in March 1953 Stalin's successors issued an amnesty decree applicable to certain categories of prisoners; other amnesties followed in 1954, 1955, and 1957. Although more favorable to criminals imprisoned for relatively common and lesser offenses than to those accused of "political" crimes, these amnesties opened prison gates for large numbers of inmates. The new regime has apparently recognized that the forced labor of millions of prisoners is not an efficient method of operation in a modern industrial economy.

After the downfall of Beria in the power struggle, the new Soviet rulers began to reorganize the police apparatus—for many years the symbol of Stalinist terror—and to decrease its authority. As a result the administration of the police establishment has been partially decentralized and placed under closer supervision by the Party. In September 1953, the Special Board of the ministry of internal affairs, which had broad powers to punish alleged offenders without a regular court trial, was abolished and its criminal cases were turned over to the regular courts. Many branches of police troops were shifted to the ministry of defense, and the economic enterprises that employed forced labor under police supervision were transferred to ordinary administrative agencies in the economy. After Khrushchev's rise to power, however, he and his lieutenants apparently felt that the weakening of the police apparatus must not be carried too far. At meetings of the Party Congress he has pointed out that the vast majority of police officials are honest and loyal devotees of the Communist cause and that the security agencies must be strengthened and closely linked with the working masses. On several occasions since 1959, the regime has hailed the police organization for its humane traditions, its dedication to the interests of the Soviet people, and its concern for "socialist legality." When its procedures became arbitrary, Soviet leaders now explain, the fault lay with "careerists" who had seized control of the police machinery and sought to exempt the security agencies from Party control.

Shortly after Stalin's death, the regime authorized the minister of justice to study the outdated criminal codes with a view toward their revision. The objectives of the revision, according to the minister, were to reduce the penalties for minor violations or to replace them with "administrative or public pressure" and also to increase the struggle against crimes "dangerous to society" (treason, sabotage, murder, robbery, and so forth). Encouraged by the post-Stalin relaxations and the emphasis upon "socialist legality," many legal specialists took advantage of the promise of legal reform to engage in a prolonged discussion in the press on the nature of Soviet law and the changes that were needed. They were able to exert such pressure for thoroughgoing revision that five years elapsed before draft proposals were presented for final action. Some legal scholars in the USSR, who have a deep understanding of foreign legal systems, strongly advocated a liberalization of Soviet criminal procedures more in line with western standards of jurisprudence. Many of these specialists criticized the doctrine of analogy,[3] the inferior role of the defense attorney, and the severe methods of investigation. In drawing up the draft proposals, they sought to enunciate important legal principles that would afford greater protection to the accused: a defendant shall not be arrested without the approval of the judicial authorities, he shall be entitled to counsel during the investigation as well as during the trial, he shall be presumed innocent until proved guilty, his confession shall not be accepted as proof of guilt unless corroborated by other testimony, and he shall not be punished unless convicted and sentenced by a court.

When these proposals were considered by the Supreme Soviet in December 1958, the authority of the courts to decide guilt and to impose sentence was upheld, the rule of analogy was formally abolished, the defendant was given some procedural guarantees, the age of criminal liability for minors was raised, the maximum term of imprisonment was reduced from 25 to 15 years, and parole was made easier. The deputies of the Supreme Soviet, however, refused to enunciate expressly the principle of presumed innocence and voted to deny the defendant the right of counsel during the pretrial investigation. Moreover, the codes as enacted enumerate many of the traditional "crimes against the state" that can easily be turned against individuals whose political reliability is suspected. In the new schedule of penalties, the death sentence has been extended to certain categories of offences, particularly those of an economic nature.

While relaxing some of the procedures and penalties that are enforced through regular Soviet courts, Stalin's successors have sought to control individual behavior by encouraging the mass organizations and "popular assemblies" to exert pressure upon potential offenders. Such methods are not new to the USSR, but there has been special emphasis placed upon them since 1955. The aim is to detect the "antisocial" citizen before he commits a serious wrong and to make him aware of group intolerance toward all types of forbidden behavior. Completely dominated by the Party, the mass organizations are ordered to censure errant members and to subject them to the hostility of their peers. Thus, instead of relying entirely upon the formal courts that enforce ordinary

[3] Under the rule of analogy, a person who has not violated any known law may nevertheless be punished by applying a law that covers a comparable act.

law, the Khrushchev regime depends to a great extent upon the social pressure of "public organizations" to enforce such vague prescriptions as the "elementary norms" of Soviet society.

In seeking to impose these social controls, the Communist rulers have established *militia assistance brigades* and *detachments* in factories, farms, schools, construction projects, research institutes, apartment houses, and elsewhere. Directed by reliable functionaries from the local Party organization, the government administration, the trade unions, and the *Komsomols*, the assistance units enlist members to help the regular police in patrolling the streets and to admonish citizens, especially young people, against wrongful behavior. Detachments of youthful *Komsomols*, who sometimes go to extremes in carrying out their assignments, have been active in the struggle against "hooligan-ism," seeking to impress upon offenders the importance of sacrifice and hard work.

The spotlight of public opinion has been focused upon citizens who lead a "parasitic" life. All the republics in the Soviet Union have enacted "antiparasite" laws that provide "justice by popular assembly," in violation of elementary legal principles. A citizen accused of avoid-ing "socially useful" work or of living on unearned income is brought before a general meeting of the residents of his area. No formal indict-ment is filed against the defendant, and he cannot claim the services of an attorney. If in the open balloting a majority of the general meeting votes against him, he may be exiled to a work settlement in a different section of the country (often in areas that are not attractive to volun-tary labor) for periods of two to five years. Only the executive com-mittee of the local soviet is entitled to set aside the decision, an un-likely prospect in most cases, since the committee is invariably under the Party's domination.

At the present time, public pressure on offenders is more usually exerted through the *comrades' courts*, which were used in limited areas of Soviet life until World War II and reintroduced on a wider scale in the post-Stalin era. These courts are established in economic enter-prises, in certain secondary and higher educational institutions, on col-lective farms, and in similar organizations. Composed usually of about 10 or 12 members elected by the workers in the particular enterprise or installation, they hear cases involving violations of labor discipline (absenteeism, tardiness, poor quality of work, negligence in the use of equipment, and so forth), the illegal use of state or public mate-rials, the shirking of "socially useful labor," neglect of children or aged parents, drunkenness and "bootlegging," abusive or foul language, transgression of residence regulations, minor property disputes, and similar matters. Proceedings may be initiated upon the recommend-ation of the local trade union, *Komsomol*, or soviet, the defendant's neighbors or fellow-workers, or the regular judicial authorities; but more often it is the plant manager who puts the machinery in motion. To provide the setting against which the accused may be publicly chastised for his "antisocial" behavior, the trial is held at his place of work or residence and in the presence of his fellows, who are permitted to ask questions and to make comments. A defendant who is found guilty may be given punishment ranging from a "comradely warning" to a fine or dismissal from his job. Here again he is denied the procedural safeguards that may be available to him even in the ordinary Soviet courts. He does not have effective channels of ap-peal, although the administrative authorities and local officials are entitled to demand a rehearing if they are not satisfied with the verdict. This system of punishment enables the plant manager or farm director to shift responsibility from himself to the mass organ-izations which, under the Party's firm control, can bring popular pressure to bear upon those who violate the official norms. Citizens are admon-ished not only to obey the law themselves but also to adopt an attitude of hostility toward "antisocial" acts committed by others. In some cases the trial proceedings have been recorded and then broadcast over the factory's radio facilities. That this subjects the accused to unbearable group pressure is suggested by a defendant who tried to get his case transferred from the comrades' court to a regular court: "You see, I am ashamed to appear before the comrades with whom I work. . . . Really it is easier to endure a stricter punishment than the stern court of the collective."

Ferment in the Arts

The post-Stalin changes in the economic and legal spheres have also been felt in the intellectual and artistic life of the USSR. Among the most imaginative and vocal elements in every society, the artists and writers strive to preserve the integrity of their calling and to secure a degree of freedom in selecting their themes and art forms. Since the 1930s the Soviet artist has been torn between the desire to express himself as an artist and the regime's demand that he serve as its propaganda agent.

Taking advantage of the political uncertainties following Stalin's death, Soviet writers and artists gave vent to their frustrations and began to criticize the restraints that bound them to politically acceptable themes and styles. Such restrictions, they pleaded, tended to stifle creativity and to encourage the development of standardized plots, stereotyped characters, and tiresome art forms. Deviating from the traditional descriptions of Soviet society as a happy brotherhood of workers and peasants eager to surpass their production quotas, writers timidly began to depict some of the frustrations and conflicts in Soviet life. In late 1954, however, the Party reasserted its authority over the rebellious writers and admonished them to follow its lead in their artistic work and to glorify the heroes of Communist production.

Another phase of the cultural "thaw" began in 1956, when Soviet intellectuals interpreted Khrushchev's attack upon Stalin as the omen of a more permissive attitude toward the arts. At this time political leaders were too involved with the power struggle, the effects of de-Stalinization, and the problems of economic reorganization to give much attention to the policing of intellectuals. With the victory of the Khrushchev faction in mid-1957, however, the Party was able to formulate a more consistent policy toward artistic life and thought. In a series of official pronouncements, Khrushchev himself set the stage for a tightening of Party controls by rebuking artists and writers who presented the "seamy side" of Soviet life.

Despite the admonition that art must serve the Communist cause, the voices of dissident artists can still be heard in the Soviet Union and, encouragingly enough, a measure of nonconformity appears to be tolerated. Although the intellectuals who seized upon the "thaw" to criticize the quality of Soviet literature have been publicly denounced, the chastisement has thus far been relatively mild, especially in comparison with the Stalin era when artists became special targets of oppression. In sharp contrast with the past, the new regime has also exhibited a more liberal attitude toward western literature, making available to Soviet readers a greater (though still restricted) variety of literary works by foreign authors.

THE POST-STALIN ERA: AN OVERVIEW

Stalin's death and the ensuing struggle for succession have ushered in important changes in the Soviet Union. The more significant of these changes reflect new developments and emerging problems in Soviet life; some of the reforms have merely removed the harsh restrictions that had been introduced during the wartime emergency; others have reinstated policies that Stalin had discarded during the most oppressive phases of his rule. Many of the changes have had the effect of reducing, at least temporarily, the severity of the dictatorship and are designed to make the Party and its leaders more popular with the masses.

Uniformed police, for example, though still conspicuous in great numbers, are apparently not as vindictive as they once were, and it is refreshing to see ordinary citizens occasionally argue with them in the streets. The people welcome the release of prisoners from the labor camps, the revision of at least some features of the criminal codes, the partial relaxation of labor discipline, and the denunciation of terrorist measures by leading Communist officials. Though still noticeably guarded in their conversations and actions, the people seem to breathe a bit more freely and no longer exhibit as much fear of being seen with foreigners as they used to.

In the economic sphere, many workers and peasants have more money to spend, and there is a wider variety of consumer items available to them in the shops and markets. As they observe vast programs of housing construction, especially in the major urban centers, they hopefully anticipate the day when they will be able to move from their crowded quarters into new (though poorly constructed, by western standards) apartments.

Local Party leaders and some factory managers applaud the new program of economic reorganization that presumably grants them more administrative discretion and permits them to deal directly with regional authorities instead of having to wrestle with so many economic agencies in Moscow. This "decentralization," does not give managers as much authority as most of them would like, however, for crucial decisions involving the establishment of plan goals, the supplying of equipment, and the financing of capital investment continue to be made by central authorities. The trend since 1959 has been towards a tightening of controls over these matters, suggesting that "recentralization" may already be underway. Be that as it may, the administrative shift of certain industries to the republics and regions has brought economic officials into closer touch with local problems and may have made some of them more aware of consumer pressures.

Perhaps one of the brightest spots in the post-Stalin era is the renewed vigor in the arts, with the promise of a freer cultural climate. Taking advantage of the political uncertainty, Soviet intellectuals, writers, and artists have not only called for greater autonomy of expression but they have also seized upon the new programs of cultural exchange to establish contact with their professional counterparts in other lands. Although the outbursts of the intellectuals have usually been curbed before the dangerpoint was reached, the writers' conferences have featured spirited debates that were unheard of during the closing years of Stalin's rule, and literary outlets now offer a more imaginative diet to the Soviet reader.

Despite the hopeful signs of the post-Stalin era, however, the essential features of the dictatorship remain largely undisturbed, and the political system continues to function in much the same way as before. This can be seen, for example, in the nature of the power struggle that broke out immediately after Stalin's death and soon degenerated into a typical Bolshevik battle for supremacy. Individuals and factions ruthlessly maneuvered for advantage, formed alliances when necessary, and then pounced upon their allies when collaboration was no longer useful. As in the first struggle for succession, collective leadership proved to be little more than a temporary political convenience and gradually gave way to one-man rule. Once again the leader who dominated the Party Secretariat was able to emerge as supreme ruler. Patterning his strategy after Stalin's, Khrushchev exploited his office to reorganize the Communist apparatus for his own purpose, removing his opponents and replacing them with people whose support he could command. Like Stalin, he increased the size of the central Party agencies and then "packed" them with reliable followers. With startling rapidity he gained influence in the provincial organizations of the Party and came ultimately to dominate the Central Committee and its Presidium—a position that enabled him to extend his influence into important areas of government and society.

In introducing reforms and granting concessions, Stalin's successors have carefully circumscribed them so that the basic power structure would be preserved. Collective leadership—rarely mentioned after Khrushchev had consolidated his strength—has not resulted in any significant transfer of power from the Communist high command to the lower units of the Party. While local Party meetings and elections are now held more regularly, the rank-and-file members are not free to challenge the regime's policies or the official slate of candidates, but remain under strict discipline as in the Stalin era. Collective leadership, it is now maintained, was never intended to weaken the role of the Party leader. The Party Congress, ostensibly the highest legislative organ in the Soviet Communist movement, wields no more power than it did under Stalin. It continues to endorse, without a visible sign of protest, all the policies submitted to it by the oligarchy, including such controversial matters as the economic plan and the attack upon the once-infallible Stalin.

Although the new Soviet rulers have become more consumer-oriented than preceding regimes, they have continued to place primary emphasis upon the development of heavy industry. Even when they hold out special promises to the consumer, the assumption is that planned increases in the production of consumer goods will be superimposed upon an expanding heavy industrial economy. Responsibility for directing the programs for economic development remains in the hands of top Party leaders. Under Khrushchev's program of economic reorganization, the key areas of decision-making are left to the central authorities. Indeed, with so many industrial managers transferred from Moscow to the regional economic councils, high Party officials are in a better position to formulate policies without being obstructed by powerful administrators, and, on the basis of these policies, to transmit directives to regional Party units that are equipped to scrutinize the activities of the economic councils. Similarly, the concessions in agriculture, while substantially increasing peasant income, have helped to reinforce the collective farm system and to accommodate extended Party controls in the rural areas.

While conceding some relaxation in the field of Soviet law and justice, Stalin's successors have attempted to keep the reforms within prescribed limits, to the disappointment of some of their own legal specialists. Despite the emphasis on "socialist legality," the new regime has displayed little interest in establishing the "rule of law." The Party and its agencies remain, as in the days of Stalin, above the law; no restrictions are recognized as binding upon the Communist organization, and the judicial authorities are still regarded as its agents. Although certain acts are no longer listed as crimes within the technical jurisdiction of ordinary courts, the Soviet rulers have placed renewed emphasis upon traditional controls exerted through organized social pressure and administrative action by factory and farm managers. Here again, of course, the Party plays a directing role, since the mass organizations and administrative personnel function largely under its control.

Thus coercion, though not as obvious as it was under Stalin, is still an important ingredient of the system. The limitations placed upon the police were at first interpreted by some observers as an indication that the new regime was making a sharp break with its Stalinist past. But the recent praise heaped upon police officials suggests that Khrushchev and his associates will not permit the downgrading to proceed to the point of weakness. Indeed, the entire schedule of "de-Stalinization" is apparently to be kept within acceptable bounds. Only a few weeks after Khrushchev's bitter assault upon Stalin at the Twentieth Party Congress, the regime warned that it would not tolerate Party members who, under the guise of criticizing Stalin, proceeded to cast doubt upon the "correctness" of Communist policies. Some people, the regime felt, were seeking to slander Stalin, while overlooking the "positive contributions" that he had made to Soviet development. Even while beating Stalin's corpse again at the Twenty-second Congress in 1961, Communist officials pointed out that the "cult of the individual" was not to be confused with the authority of the Party's leaders.

From this analysis of recent developments, it is clear that the Communist Party retains its pre-eminent position in Soviet society. The new Soviet rulers have shown no willingness to recognize the legitimacy of rival political organizations or to tolerate dissenting opinions on issues involving basic doctrine. Indeed, the Party appears to have improved its position in the power structure relative to such groups as the police, the government bureaucracy, and the military. Perhaps one of the most significant developments since 1953 has been the subordination of the groups that compete for power with the Party apparatus and the gradual elimination of the older, experienced leaders of these groups from the Party's high command. Thus, during the course of the succession struggle, the Party has been able to assert its authority not only over the intellectuals but also over the police, economic managers, and military officials. For example, since Beria's ouster, no police official has been granted a seat in the Party Presidium; police representation among the full members of the Central Committee has also declined, and at the present time the police apparatus is headed by a Party functionary, a former leader of the *Komsomols*.

Khrushchev's struggle with the economic bureaucracy can be traced to political differences that led to Malenkov's resignation as Premier in February 1955. The conflict, which raged for many months, was finally resolved in favor of the Party hierarchy in 1957, when the First Secretary pushed through his program of "decentralized" economic reorganization. The heavy concentration of economic bureaucrats in Moscow was partially broken up and many administrators were reassigned to the new regional economic councils, where they could be supervised by Khrushchev-appointed secretaries. When the "anti-Party faction" resisted these moves, its members were dismissed from the Party Presidium, thereby removing a number of state bureaucrats whom Stalin had appointed. In these encounters Khrushchev was forced on several occasions to turn to the army for support. In recognition for this assistance, Marshal Zhukov was appointed first as an alternate and later as a full member of the Presidium, the first professional soldier ever to be accorded such high Party status. However, when Zhukov attempted to use his new position to minimize Party controls over the armed forces, Khrushchev, who no longer needed the army as a counterweight in the power struggle, removed the Marshal from the Presidium and the ministry of defense and doomed him to obscurity. Khrushchev's choice as the new minister of defense was Marshal Malinovsky, who immediately stressed the importance of Communist controls over the military services. Malinovsky, however, was not assigned to Zhukov's seat in the Presidium, and the military establishment continues to be unrepresented in that body. Thus, during the years since Stalin's death, the Party apparatus, highly centralized in Moscow, has increased its power at the expense of other hierarchies. Indeed, Khrushchev's policy of using the Party-dominated mass organizations to keep the population in line may be designed to make his regime less dependent upon such power groups as the police and the army.

Even during a period of relaxed controls, the western visitor to post-Stalin Russia soon recognizes the signs of dictatorship. As soon as he crosses the frontier, he realizes that he is isolated from the outside world. Since only Communist news sources are available to him, he remains ignorant of world happenings unless he decides to get in touch with a western embassy. The curtain has been drawn so tight that few of the people he meets are even dimly aware of the Soviet veto record in the United Nations, and they are completely uninformed about the role of the USSR in Middle Eastern politics. Although impressive numbers of western periodicals have been placed in Soviet libraries, especially since 1954, only materials in the natural sciences are on open shelf, social science publications being less readily accessible to the ordinary reader. Policemen in red and black uniforms are stationed at the main entrances of libraries and radio stations, and an individual is permitted to enter only after he has shown his pass. Passes are also required for admittance to university buildings. The system of controls reaches far down into the educational system, where the Young Pioneers and the *Komsomols* are an integral part of each school and claim the loyalty of the overwhelming majority of students. Every educational establishment has an ample supply of Lenin statues and photographs of current Party leaders—reminders to students and teachers alike of their obligation to the Communist cause. While most of the people whom the foreign visitor meets casually in the street are curious about the West and fearlessly engage him in conversation, the inquisitive young intellectuals who hesitatingly suggest more serious discussion in a nearby park betray by their timid glances a fear that such intimate communion with outsiders might make them suspect. Such apprehension is probably reinforced by the oversupply of uniformed police who watch over all the hotels, libraries, intersections, and public gatherings. Regrettably enough, the Soviet dictatorship did not die with Joseph Stalin.

While present-day Russia bears many marks from previous regimes, the pattern of change nevertheless reflects the urgent problems of a more advanced era. Some of the more crucial problem areas, which have merely been outlined in this discussion, will receive more specialized treatment in other sections of this book.

In every modern society, of course, the pace of change is quickened in the metropolitan centers, where the imperatives of advanced technology make deep inroads into traditional life, even though features of the agrarian world continue to linger. It is in the urban communities of the USSR that one encounters evidence of subtle change—marks on the walls of the cities that enable one to find his way from one era of Soviet development to another. On the face of the Soviet city the lines of change are plainly visible, pointing up the advances over the past as well as some of the problems of the future.

2

THE SOVIET CITY

John R. Borchert

Professor of Geography at the University of Minnesota, John R. Borchert is especially concerned with urban and regional planning and the geography of the Soviet Union. Presently Urban Research Director, Upper Midwest Economic Study, he is the author of numerous publications on the geography of natural resources and land development.

A nation that aspires to rank as a great power in the twentieth-century world must become an industrial giant. Its industrial strength depends in part upon the vitality of its cities, whose inhabitants supply the manpower needed to keep the factories and the transportation system operating at full speed. To maintain industrial efficiency the city worker must be fed, clothed, and housed, and educational facilities must be set up to develop the technical and administrative skills demanded by an industrial age.

URBAN GROWTH

Although the movement of population from farms to cities began several decades before the Bolsheviks seized power, widespread urbanization is a relatively recent phenomenon in Russia, reflecting the accelerated rate of industrial growth under the five-year plans. As late as 1913, more than 80 percent of the Russian people lived in the countryside. Modern industrial development necessitated the reconstruction of the Soviet Union from an essentially peasant society into an urban society. This meant that the peasant had to be torn from his traditional surroundings and resettled in the city where he could be trained as a factory worker. The population of urban centers increased slowly during the 1920s, but the increase became especially marked during the 1930s after the programs of industrialization were well underway. By 1939 nearly one third of the Russian people lived in the cities, and today the proportion is close to 50 percent.

This urban growth is illustrated by the spectacular new cities and towns that have literally risen from fields and grazing lands. Magnitorgorsk, for example, at the foot of Magnitaya, a mountain rich in iron ore deposits, only 40 years ago was a sleepy little village of about 2,000 people and probably twice as many cattle and goats. Today the city has a bustling population of 284,000, and its modern steel mills stretch for nine miles along the Ural River. Novokuznetsk (Stalinsk, before the de-Stalinization) on the Kuznets coal fields in western Sibera —the largest known reserves of high-grade coking coal in Asia—is another new city. In 1926, 4,000 pioneers lived in this settlement in the valley of the Tom, where they had begun to carve nature's riches from beneath the earth's surface. In 13 years the population had swelled to 170,000, and today it numbers 380,000. There is also Karaganda in Central Asia, until the late 1930s an isolated, unmarked spot on an almost unexplored steppe. Today it is the home of 400,000 people.

Dramatic as their growth has been, the new cities and towns have accounted for only a small fraction of Soviet growth. By far the greater proportion of the new urbanites have crowded into the centers or accreted to the edges of the old cities. One tenth of the total growth of urban population since 1926 has occurred within a 100-mile radius of Moscow, in the heart of the section of the country known as the central industrial region. Since the Middle Ages this area has been the major center of Russian industry, markets, management, entrepreneurship, and the labor force. Moscow itself has grown from about two million people in 1926 to over six million today. Nearly all of the old, established cities of European Russia and the Ukraine have also absorbed their share of the nation's urban trek. Included among the cities that have been so affected are Leningrad, founded by Peter the Great in 1702 as his capital at the eastern tip of the Baltic, and the old river ports and trading centers of the middle Volga region.

Table 2-1 shows the trend of urban growth in two groups of cities: (1) the ten largest urban centers of European Russia and the Ukraine —the long-settled "hearth" of the nation; and (2) the ten largest cities of the outlying regions of the USSR—the lands of the Caucasus, Middle Asia, and Siberia.

TABLE 2-1

URBAN GROWTH IN THE SOVIET UNION

	Population 1926	Population 1959	Increase 1926-1959	Percent Increase 1926-1959
European Russia				
Moscow	2,029,000	5,406,000	3,017,000	149
Leningrad	1,690,000	3,321,000	1,631,000	97
Donetsk (Stalino)-				
Makeevka	253,000	1,057,000	804,000	318
Kiev	514,000	1,104,000	590,000	115
Kharkov	417,000	934,000	517,000	124
Gorky	222,000	942,000	720,000	324
Kuibyshev	176,000	806,000	630,000	358
Odessa	420,000	667,000	247,000	59
Dnepropetrovsk	237,000	660,000	423,000	178
Kazan	179,000	647,000	468,000	261
Total	6,137,000	15,184,000	9,047,000	147
Outlying Regions				
Baku	453,000	971,000	518,000	114
Tashkent	324,000	912,000	588,000	181
Novosibirsk	120,000	886,000	766,000	638
Sverdlovsk	140,000	779,000	639,000	456
Tblisi	294,000	695,000	401,000	136
Chelyabinsk	59,000	689,000	630,000	1,067
Omsk	162,000	581,000	419,000	269
Erevan	65,000	509,000	444,000	683
Karaganda	—	397,000	397,000	—
Novokuznetsk (Stalinsk)	4,000	377,000	373,000	9,325
Total	1,621,000	6,796,000	5,175,000	319

Source: *Narodnoe Khozaistvo SSR* (1959), Moscow, 1960.

As the table indicates, urban growth has been significant throughout the Soviet Union. The greatest percentage growth has taken place in the outlying "frontier" regions, but the greatest numerical growth has occurred in the old centers of European Russia. The table reflects the fact that, under the influence of the planned economy, there has been a gradual shift eastward in urban population and growth. Two thirds of this urban growth, however, has occurred in the old, established cities of the west. The expanding population has, in effect, made all the cities in the Soviet Union "new" cities.

In the light of these trends, it becomes evident that the cities are the places from which to view at close range the changing complexion of the Soviet Union. They are the centers of economic and political power; they are the clearing houses for the nation's supplies and information. They represent, in other words, the most important frontiers of the USSR. But before we can study the "new cities," we must examine briefly the way of life of the people who descend upon the city from the countryside.

The Soviet Union had at the outset a small urban and industrial base in relation to its population. The growth of cities involved the farm-to-city migration of million of peasants, who had limited knowledge of modern sanitation, technical skills, and urban ways of life. Within two generations the peasants have provided half or more of the population of the cities, and they have brought with them the imprints of their earlier life.

THE SOVIET VILLAGE— SOURCE OF THE URBAN FLOOD

From the villages of the Soviet countryside comes the flood of new city people. These rural villages, with their high birth rates, have served as a vast well, maintaining relatively constant populations themselves while pouring out a steady stream of emigrants to the cities. Since 1958 the quickening pace of the migration to the cities has for the first time caused the rural population to drop to less than half the national total.

The opportunity to observe a truly rural Soviet village at close range has come to comparatively few western visitors thus far. The farm villages that most visitors see in detail lie within the commuting or delivery range of a major city, perhaps 10 to 20 miles out. This does not mean that these villages are especially rigged "showplaces"—they are merely the most convenient to display since they are within easy driving distance from the city. But such villages are likely to have had their rural way of life diluted by their proximity to an urban center, where the peasants journey daily to market or to work.

The typical farm villages are far from the big urban centers. The foreign visitor can see hundreds of them as he travels the long distances between major cities. He can observe the clusters of houses and barns and the roads and fields spread out beneath his plane. And fascinating vignettes of village life can be caught as he looks through the windows of his train. From such experiences he is eventually able to breathe life into the image of the countryside that he has formed from studying the ponderous statistics published by the ministry of agriculture.

One or two streets lead through the village, but they are hardly streets in our sense of the word. Usually they are simply an open swath, perhaps 100 feet wide, with a blanket of grass or weeds that provides the running space for geese or forage for a few goats. Footpaths mark the sides of the street, while the roadway lies at the center. A few villages may be fortunate enough to have a cobblestone roadway; a rare village may be pierced by a blacktop trunk highway. But most often the roadway, like the footpaths beside it, is a twisting, rutted, pitted strip of bare earth that shows the distinctive color of the region's soil: pale gray in the village that stands among the infertile soils of the north, black in the rich agricultural areas of the Ukraine, red in the rainy subtropics of the Black Sea coast.

The buildings hug the earth, leaning in various directions and pitching and sagging with every tiny hump or depression on the land surface beneath them. Few show any influence of the level or the plumb line. Windows and door frames form parallelograms and trapezoids, but seldom rectangles. Some are painted, while others are colored by a coating of blue or yellow stucco. The cottages are small, having only one or two rooms; and plumbing is unknown. Sanitary facilities are primitive. There may be a creek or spring at the edge of the village, and it is not uncommon to see peasant women doing the family laundry at the water's edge on a summer morning. A well may be located at the center of the village, with well-worn paths stretching to every cottage.

Each cottage stands on a plot of ground about the size of an American suburban residential lot. Attached to the cottage or adjacent to it is a shed in which to store firewood and to house the family pig, a goat, or some poultry. There is a tiny garden plot on which potatoes and vegetables and perhaps a few apple trees are grown to supplement the family food supply. The peasant cottages are indeed simple dwelling places.

Apart from the cottages, there are a few other structures in the village. Somewhere there is a general store that looks much like any cottage and is stocked with the simplest of necessities. A church may still be standing from prerevolutionary days, but it is likely to be used as a storehouse today. Other larger structures postdate the revolution— the big collective barns and sheds, a medical and first-aid station, a school, a library stocked with Soviet books, magazines, and news-papers. Always there is the drafty, sparsely furnished headquarters of the collective, where a few trained technicians work on production charts, technical journals, or report forms.

Life in the village is a simple combination of hard work and relax-ation. The peasants report for assigned duties with their brigades in the collective fields or pastures, or they plod to their tiny private plots to stake out the goat or the cow, to scythe hay, or to dig potatoes. Fun and enjoyment are wherever they might be caught—in quiet reflec-tion in the open fields or in the squat shelterbelt, along the brook on a summer day, or along the footpaths in the deep snow of winter; at the weekly cinema or a wedding celebration; a family game of dominoes; pondering pictures of Moscow's traffic and skyscrapers in a magazine; an opportunity to see and touch, perhaps even to buy, a new model radio or a bicycle on display at the district fair.

For centuries the peasant village has been the basic unit of Russian settlement, although the picture is changing today. Here is where the majority of the Soviet people were born and grew up, living together in cramped housing and carrying the burdens of rigorous farm work, often with manual tools. These are simple and compact communities where collective effort is employed to accomplish a task and where the villagers have shared the same experiences for centuries. It is from the vantage point of the village that most Soviet citizens have viewed the changes that have come to their country, mostly, though not entirely, since the revolution—the rise of public education and the spread of literacy, technological advances and the increasing government propa-ganda, bureaucracy, and scientific research. The greater part of today's Soviet urbanites have come from the rural villages. They have brought with them to the cities their meager belongings, their aspirations, and the view of the world that they gained in their peasant surroundings.

MOSCOW, THE SOVIET METROPOLIS

Moscow is the place where most foreign visitors are introduced to the urban side of the Soviet Union. It is also the biggest single mecca for immigration from other sections of the country. The reasons for this are not hard to find: Moscow is the showpiece for much Soviet advertising and propaganda; it is a city of great historical tradition; and it is the center of government, business, education, and the hub of the nation's transport and communications system. It has combined the functions and traditions of New York, Washington, Chicago, and Boston in one metropolis. It is truly the heart of the Soviet Union.

Moscow provides a wealth of opportunities to gain insight on Soviet cities and the Soviet system.

The pattern of Moscow resembles in many ways that of many other large European cities (see Map I between pp. 96 and 97). At the center is an ancient riverside fortification that is surrounded by concentric rings of growth and rebuilding. Each ring is a geographic region of the city today. But it is more than this: the ring is also a monument to a distinctive era in the economic history of the metropolis and it reflects in its own way the position of Moscow in the broader geographic patterns of the nation.

The National Symbol

The ancient fortification at the center of Moscow is the Kremlin. Its 64-acre grounds are smaller than those of some state capitols in the United States and it houses only a minute part of the vast government administrative offices in the city. The Kremlin is an unusual, striking, and from some vantage points, charming museum of Russian culture and politics. But it is mostly a symbol—the symbol of the power center of the Russian empire, past and present.

The Kremlin's hilltop site is a monument. The old fortress stands on high ground on the outside of a wide meander of the Moscow River. The land drops sharply to the river on the south and falls away slowly to the west toward another meander in the same twisting stream. At the base of the long slope toward the east the tiny river Yauza enters the Moscow. Here in the year 1147 a Russian prince chose the site for a military outpost. To the north lay the forest lands and peasant villages he intended to protect. Not far to the south, in the partly wooded margins of the treeless steppe, lived his Tatar enemies.

Parts of the Kremlin walls are a monument to Prince Dimitry Ivanovich, who enlarged the fortification to approximately its present size and built the first walls of stone in 1367. Most of the brick walls one sees today are monuments to Grand Duke Ivan III, who erected them nearly five centuries ago.

The turrets and tower gates are reminders of the Kremlin's growing importance in the subsequent centuries as Moscow came to command the growing overland trade between Asia and northwestern Europe, and Ivan the Terrible went from the Kremlin to Kazan in 1552 to crush Tatar control with one of the largest land armies ever assembled up to that time. This victory, and those that followed, opened the lands of the middle and lower Volga, the Urals, and Siberia to Russian settlement.

There is a story, perhaps apocryphal, that after his great victory

Ivan commissioned an architect to design a cathedral. It was to be the most beautiful building in the world and have a tower to commemorate every Russian victory. When the building was completed Ivan had the architect's eyes burned out so that he would never be able to design a more beautiful building. That cathedral is St. Basil's on Red Square.

The Kremlin is indeed a symbol of the ancient origin, the endless turbulence, and the durability of the Russian nation. It is also a symbol of the long history of Moscow as the center of Russia's political and economic life.

The Lifted Face

"Ring" streets circle the Kremlin in the fashion of many European cities. The most important of these is the Sadovaya. This wide boulevard that lies a scant mile from the Kremlin marks the location of an eighteenth-century wall and moat that passed into oblivion after the Napoleonic invasion of Moscow in 1812. This was the most recent and outermost wall to enclose the old city. Other concentric ring streets lie between the Kremlin and the Sadovaya, marking parts of the thirteenth- and fourteenth-century "Chinese" wall, remains of which can be seen in downtown Moscow, and the sixteenth-century "White" wall.

Between the Kremlin and the Sadovaya is central Moscow, the section of the city that has experienced the most face-lifting as a result of post-revolutionary reconstruction. Here is a city of asphalt streets, masonry buildings, well-kept little parks and flower gardens, and broad squares. The buildings are a mixture of the old and the new. There are eighteenth- and nineteenth-century, three- and four-storey buildings of brick and stone in a variety of architectural styles. Most of them once served as offices, stores and shops, townhouses of merchants, and apartments of the bourgeois class; a few have always been theaters or museums. These were the good buildings of prerevolutionary Moscow.

Mingled with the old are many new buildings that have arisen since the revolution. There are a few large functionally designed office buildings dating from the five-year plans of the prewar period—for example, the central telegraph office and the tall house of the USSR Council of Ministers. There are the pretentious solid blocks of eight-and nine-storey apartment buildings along Gorky Street and many other more modest postrevolutionary apartment houses. There are three massive "wedding-cake" skyscrapers, symbolizing the extravagant monumental architecture of the postwar Stalin period, and there is the handsome new home of Radio Moscow in the contemporary western style.

Central Moscow contains the heart of the city's bus, tram, and subway systems. Radical lines converge at Red Square and nearby Sverdlov Square. The central area is probably the starting point or destination of the majority of Moscow's nine million daily public transit trips.

A great variety of activities take place around this center of the city's circulation system. A block on either side of the subway hub are the city's two largest department stores, including the much publicized GUM. The central area embraces most of the restaurants, theaters, museums, specialty shops, half of Moscow University, many institutes, and the Lenin Library. Here are the "home offices" of most of the business enterprises of the Soviet Union and the foreign embassies. Five of the eight major hotels are also situated in this area. The ornate new Pekin Hotel and the older but mammoth Moscow Hotel receive Communist dignitaries from every part of the world. The busy old showplaces of Tsarist Russia—the Metropole, the National, and the Savoy—which entertain thousands of western guests each year, are a bit threadbare now, perhaps symbolic, in the Soviet view, of an obsolete capitalist past.

Although shops and offices occupy the street floors of nearly all buildings, most upper floors are used for apartments. Even in the skyscrapers two-thirds of the space is given over to apartments. Central Moscow is, more than anything else, a residential district, and for two important reasons. The need for floor space for retailing and wholesaling activities in the central area is slight in Soviet cities because of the paucity of consumer goods. At the same time, there is strong pressure from the most affluent and educated people for living space in the heart of the city. There have been neither the facilities nor the mood for a mass "flight to the suburbs."

At night central Moscow is the brightest part of the metropolis, though even it is dark by the standards of any western city. Street lights are closely spaced. Bright red stars glow from the Kremlin towers and the pinnacles of the skyscrapers. A scattering of electric signs shine from the rooftops and marquees, announcing the names of the principal hotels, restaurants, and shops, or urging citizens to buy ice cream and to subscribe to the government loan. The din of traffic and the endless shuffle of thousands of pedestrians continues after nightfall along the walks and intersections.

Central Moscow is the cosmopolitan heart of the nation. It is *the* Moscow of Muscovites, foreign visitors, and propaganda photographers. Its buildings and smooth streets show the best in urban development that Tsarist capitalism and Soviet Communism have had to offer in

Russia. To the visitor who arrives from the West it is massive, interesting, and drab—obviously a changing mixture of the ancient and the new. To the peasant or townsman from Moscow's hinterland it is, patently, by far the biggest, brightest, busiest, and richest city he has ever seen.

The Emergent Slums

Beyond the Sadovaya lies the second major zone of Moscow, extending from half a mile to one and a half miles outside the great ring boulevard and to the inner belt of railway trackage that girdles the city. This zone is the home of perhaps a million Muscovites. Although historically it is not as old as the central zone, physically this section of Moscow is older, for it has had lower priority for redevelopment.

Here were the expanding outskirts of the city in the eighteenth and early nineteenth centuries—the homes of workers, the neighborhoods of various crafts and trades, the colonies of immigrants from the provinces. Here were the factories erected close to the labor supply as the industrial revolution crept into Tsarist Russia; and here were the homes of workers who fought in the uprisings of 1905 and 1917.

It is in these expanding outskirts that the municipal and central government authorities found the land for botanical and zoological gardens, and here are the many smaller parks and squares, where Communist leaders later established the spacious Gorky Park of Culture and Rest—a center of amusement, concerts, lectures, and exhibits for the "enjoyment of the workers."

Industry is very important in the second zone, but it is light industry that requires no railway trackage, for this part of the city was largely built up before the railroad era came to Moscow. The factories are poorly lighted congested dens of workers (mostly women), benches, tools, and machines. Often a factory is found crowded in a basement of an apartment or shop. While the buildings are old, the machines are usually first-rate.

The workers' hands move quickly, maintaining a tradition of Moscow labor that is centuries old. The workers are responding to a piecework system, for they need all the money they can earn, and they hold compulsory membership in a union that has no economic bargaining power. These industries make clothing and light house furnishings as well as assemble light metal goods and mechanical or electrical products—radio parts, mechanical pencils, clocks, and a multitude of other items.

Much of the old residential character also remains in the second zone today. There are many blocks of cobbled streets and many more blocks of log or rough timber houses—one-or two-storey, crowded, multifamily flats. Neighborhood baths partly compensate for the lack of even nineteenth-century plumbing in these houses. In 1960 a Soviet economic journal reported that ". . . only in the next four or five years are all living quarters expected to be connected with the water supply system" in Moscow.[1] Meanwhile, forests of television aerials sprout from the pitching and sagging roofs.

Apartments of postrevolutionary vintage, four to eight floors, and other substantial houses of the Tsarist age are scattered among the wooden buildings and factories. These more substantial buildings dominate the main thoroughfares. But behind them, in courtyards in the centers of the blocks, lie clusters of cottages and wooden tenements. Devoid of paint and plumbing, these dwellings face in no particular direction, but lean and sag and pitch, often depending for their support upon masonry buildings surrounding the court. They are separated by uneven patches of bare earth.

These are slums, yes, but in another sense they are typical dwellings of the rural peasants transplanted to an urban setting. They are sometimes stacked upon one another in two-storey cabins. Though removed from a winding village roadway, the dwellings crowd around a central courtyard or press against a city street. The people who live in these houses do not walk to work in fields or pastures; they walk instead to a nearby factory or ride the public transit to a more distant one. But these are the same simple, crowded housing conditions one finds in the villages. As if to hold a bit of the village atmosphere, the residents fill their windows the year around with potted plants and flowers. The greenery softens the harsh, austere surface of the neighborhood and serves as a reminder that the Soviet city has been swollen in two generations by a gigantic migration from the countryside.

The rows and clusters of cabins and shacks, whether designated as slums or transplanted peasant housing, are marked by the government for eventual elimination. For many years, Soviet propaganda and advertising showed only the new and the reconstructed; slums were officially unrecognized. Nevertheless, the slums could not easily be disguised, and in recent years the regime has devoted a great deal of attention to the housing problem. Slum clearance is emphasized on billboard posters and is dramatically portrayed in "Panorama," the Soviet version of "Cinerama." Areas of new housing have increased substantially in the postwar period, and inroads have recently been made upon the slums. The slums, which once so dominated urban housing that they could not be "seen" by official photographers, have now

[1] *Gorodskoe Khozyaistvo Moskvy*, Number 8, 1960, page 27.

become small enough in the total picture to receive recognition by the government.

The Ring of Steel

A belt of busy railway tracks girdles the second ring at an average distance of about two miles from the Kremlin. Here was the ragged edge of built-up Moscow in the last 30 years of the nineteenth century, when the railway net of European Russia was constructed. This is where the railway builders encountered the barrier of the pre-existing city. Hence, it is in this section that the visitor today encounters the first zone of major railway trackage and associated land uses as he moves outward from the city center. This, again, is a pattern repeated in many other large, old European cities.

Radial lines enter the railway belt from every direction. Their sprawling, garish passenger terminals stand in a ring one or two miles from the heart of the city. The stations are joined to one another by the "Big Circle" subway line, and radial subway lines link most of them with Sverdlov Square at the city center.

The sights are similar at every station. Waiting for the trains are swarms of citizens of every age—businessmen, peasants, ordinary soldiers, military officers—pushing or jostling or wrestling with unwieldly burdens of string bags, battered suitcases, or squirming children. Some sit on their luggage eating bread, apples, tomatoes, or meat pies; others crowd around a kiosk to buy a drink of pink lemondade or an "Eskimo" ice cream sandwich. The crowd finally swarms through the gate to the open platform and into a long line of modern, green, steel coaches. There they can relax and take off their shirts or put on pajamas for the journey. The space in the coach is reserved, for almost every train is filled. The Soviet population today is much more mobile than it used to be, and the railroads carry 80 percent of the intercity passenger traffic.

Most of the trains run long distances. The destinations, which are marked on the sides of the coaches in European fashion, comprise a fascinating gazetteer of place names—cities to the west in Europe, far to the south along the Black and Caspian Seas, to the distant mountains of Middle Asia, to Siberia, to China, and to the Arctic region: Murmansk, Vladivostok, Peking, Tashkent, Tblisi, Odessa, Berlin, and many more.

Freight trains enter and leave on these same lines, bringing products of the whole country to the capital. Trainloads of pulpwood, paper, and lumber are brought from the northern forest; grain, fruit, and fish roll in from the steppes, the subtropics, and the seas to the south. Carloads of steel and industrial equipment arrive from the other major manufacturing regions of Leningrad, the Ukraine, the Urals, and smaller centers in other parts of the country.

A belt railway ties together the radial lines that converge at the outer edge of the second ring. At several points the belt widens into very large marshalling yards. This industrial zone embraces old plants dating from Tsarist times that originally stood on the outskirts of the city early in the railroad era of the nineteenth century, as well as other large factories and electric power stations that have been built since the revolution. The land that remained open in the trackage belt in the 1920s, when the first five-year plan was promulgated, has all been utilized. The most important parts of this industrial zone lie on the east and southeast sides. Here can be found the great electrical equipment plants, the ballbearing plant, the huge automobile plant, and the largest electric generating stations.

A port has been built in the southeast part of the city, where the Moscow river cuts through the belt railway zone. Barges tie up here to unload logs and lumber, sand and gravel. The vista is reminiscent of any major industrial complex—a broad reach of river with strings of barges; vast storage yards for construction materials and machinery; a tangle of railway tracks; a horizon latticed by smokestacks, high-voltage transmission towers, power lines, and gas reservoirs, with open patches of sandy wasteland, isolated shacks, and flat buildings.

The visitor is forbidden to photograph this scene of factories, bridges, and railway yards. One is tempted to risk a photo anyway, for this is a fascinating and little publicized side of Moscow. Another look at the landscape, however, convinces one that there is no point in risking a picture, since these elements make similar pictures the world over. In parts of the city nearer the Kremlin, the visitor sees Moscow as the Washington, New York, or Boston of the USSR. Here in the belt railway zone, however, Moscow appears as the Soviet Chicago.

Advancing Walls

Beyond the belt railway zone lies the third ring of Moscow. Covering more than 20 square miles, it provides the place of residence for probably more than two million people, and the place of work for tens of thousands. More than any other section, this is the "new city." Most of the construction in this ring has taken place since the revolution. Here the walls of Soviet Moscow advance like the massive, cold, inexorable glaciers of the Ice Age across the north Russian plain. This is an area of cranes and bulldozers, partly finished walls, new blocks, beleaguered farm villages, and ditches and mounds of dirt.

The spectacular advance follows a few main thoroughfares that lead from the city. They are the widened, repaved *chaussées* of the Tsarist and capitalist era—the coach and pedestrian routes to the provincial cities, to St. Petersburg, to the favorite country places of the nobles and merchants. Among the more prominent of these routes today are the Mozhaisk highway to the west, the Leningrad highway to the northwest, the Yaroslavl highway (now Peace Prospect) to the north, the Kaluzhsakaya highway to the southwest (now the route to the main airport), and the roads between the extensive remnants of forest east of the city.

Ten- or twelve-storey apartment buildings are rising along these main arteries and along new, major, cross streets. Practically all of the construction has taken place since 1945, a significantly large part since Stalin's death. At some time in the postwar period the decision was apparently made to abandon temporarily the program of slum clearance and housing redevelopment in the older, pre-existing parts of the city and to concentrate instead upon large-scale new housing construction an outlying open land. Except along the Sadovaya few new apartment buildings are situated inside the belt railway zone, but the construction program in the outer ring is gigantic, measured against any standard. In just one section apartments have been built in the past five years to house 300,000 people.

The effect of this decision to concentrate on building was, of course, to speed up the housing program. Cheap land that was easy to clear was exploited for rapid development, and the existing slums and old districts were left to provide housing, albeit substandard, on a temporary basis. The housing program de-emphasized expensive and time-consuming redevelopment, postponing such activity for a future, hopefully more affluent, generation of taxpayers—a policy that has been followed in every western metropolis during its critical period of rapid growth. This fact suggests that there may be such pressing problems associated with rapid urbanization and modern technology that men are forced to similar decisions regardless of their differing political and social philosophies.

The new apartment houses are each a block long and accommodate at least 100 families, usually more. The open space surrounding each building is used today for decorative landscaping and playgrounds, but it could be sacrificed to provide parking space if an automobile era comes to the USSR. The typical apartment contains two or three rooms plus a very simple kitchen and bath. The amenities are few, but they represent a great advance over the peasant cottage or the nineteenth-century urban flat.

The space is designed to meet the official national standard of nine square meters (about 100 square feet) of housing space per person. The apartments are equipped with electricity, water, and gas, since pipelines now tie Moscow to the distant natural gas fields of the middle Volga and the western Ukraine. There is no provision, however, for private telephones in many of the buildings. By day these buildings frown heavily upon the boulevards below; at night their lighted apartments have a brightness, warmth, and color that, in Moscow, is refreshing and unusual.

These tall buildings are constructed without the steel or reinforced concrete skeletons familiar in the West, for there are higher priority uses for steel. This new construction depends upon bearing walls, which, of course, restrict the range of design possibilities. Many apartment buildings are assembled from big, three-meter-square prefabricated members that include doors, windows, and plumbing, and these are hoisted into position by the large electric cranes rising like a forest above every major construction project. Once in position the panels are welded together at a few points. Within the past year, architectural journals have reported that whole apartments have been prefabricated and assembled into buildings in the same way. While the finished product appears massive and solid, western architects have observed that, in the event of a major shock, these structures would seem hardly more stable than a child's house of blocks.

As it projects outward along the main highway, the advancing wall of new apartments gradually surrounds and envelops vast enclaves of older and different developments. In one sense, it is a "pincers" advance, in which pockets of rural villages, slums, and blight are surrounded and subsequently liquidated. In another sense, the advance is creating a spectacular "false front" along each thoroughfare. This front is presented to the visitor, who arrives in the city via a major highway. But behind the new buildings lie many unsightly blocks that await improvement.

In addition to the growing residential areas in Moscow's third ring, there are bands and scattered patches of industry along the railroad lines radiating from the city. They are mixtures of foundries and machine works, wood and metal fabricating shops, brick plants, truck repair stations and motor pools, and scores of others. In many cases planning appears haphazard, with elaborate new apartment houses crowded close to noisome industries or railway yards.

On the other hand, there are extensive public recreational lands in the third zone. Here are forests and meadows that remain from estates of Tsarist times—notably the dense 2500-acre Izmailovo forest on the city's eastern edge, the 1500-acre Sokolniki Park, and the adjoining 5000-acre forest preserve in the outskirts to the northeast of Moscow. Such breathing space is especially important for the Soviet metropolis, for the population density within the city is five to ten times as great as that of most American urban residential areas.

Perhaps the most important of the "greenbelts" is the big Lenin Hills reserve high above the Moscow River near the southwest edge of the city. The site of the spectacular new skyscraper campus of the science faculties of Moscow University, the grounds are devoted extensively to recreation fields and experimental plots for agronomic and botanical study.

The "new city" of the third zone is an important and interesting place to watch. The effort to mass-produce housing for millions of new urbanites ranks with such spectacular Soviet undertakings as the building of the steel mills of the Urals and west Siberia or the big dams of the middle Volga. The housing projects are different, however, and perhaps more important because they represent "consumer" goods. The great new heavy industrial developments can ultimately be used either for military purposes or to raise the level of living for the individual citizen. Housing can be used only to raise the level of living. The size and persistence of expenditures for new housing may be the first large-scale indicator of some change in the goals of the Communist regime.

Tables 2-2 and 2-3 indicate that in the past the Soviet Union has scarcely kept abreast of its urban housing needs. But there are also indications that the housing boom is only now getting under way. In the post-Stalin era, the nation is, for the first time, building new housing fast enough to reduce the shortage—an important trend that bears watching.

New housing construction has been most significant in the postwar period, and the pace has greatly quickened in the post-Stalin years (Table 2-2). In recent years, for the first time since the inauguration of the five-year plans, urban housing space is rising faster than urban population (Table 2-3).

The Suburbs

The Kazan and Yaroslavl stations are two of the busy main-line rail terminals in the belt railway zone. They face wide, bustling Komsomol Square, one of the busiest traffic centers in Moscow, located about one and a quarter miles northeast of the Kremlin. Two subway lines

TABLE 2-2

HOUSING CONSTRUCTION IN THE USSR, 1918-1960
(Excluding collective farms)

Period	Total housing built (millions of square meters)	Average new housing built per year (millions of square meters)
1918-1928	42.9	4.3
1929-1941 (first three five-year plans)	122.9	9.4
1941-1945 (war)	49.8	9.8
1946-1950 (fourth five-year plan)	102.8	20.6
1951-1955 (fifth five-year plan)	151.7	30.3
1956-1960	327.6	65.5

Source: *Narodnoe Khozaistvo SSSR* (1959), Moscow, 1960; and *ibid*, (1960), Moscow, 1961.

TABLE 2-3

URBAN HOUSING SPACE AND URBAN POPULATION, 1913-1960*

Year	Urban housing (millions of square meters)	Urban population (millions)	Sq. meters of housing space per person
1913	180	24.7	7.3
1926	216	26.3	8.2
1940	421	60.6	7.0
1956	668	87.0	7.7
1960	958	103.9	9.2

* Source: *Narodnoe Khozaistvo SSSR*, Moscow, 1959 and 1960.

cross at this point—the radial line to Sverdlov Square in central Moscow, and the "Big Circle" line. Bus and train lines converge from the whole northeast quadrant of the metropolis. All through the day and far into the night more than a quarter million commuters swarm through the gates of these two stations. They work in many parts of

Moscow, traveling there each day from their homes in little-known out-lying or recently annexed suburban communities of from 40 to 100 thousand inhabitants—Khimki, Babushkin, Perovo, Rublevo, and others smaller or more distant. They ride the hard-seated electric trains that rumble every two or three minutes from Komsomol Square to the north and east suburbs. They are the largest division of Moscow's army of suburban commuters.

Other commuters pour through the stations that serve the suburbs in the west and the south; still others ride buses. These people live in dozens of towns and villages within a 20- to 40-mile radius that have been pulled into Moscow's employment market. The electric railways and bus lines have helped to alleviate the housing shortage in Moscow by enabling workers to live in the surrounding towns.

The busiest place in any Moscow suburb is the railway station. Here the frequent electric trains discharge their passengers from the city, and every few minutes scores of people cross the platforms. Arriving passengers may pause briefly at a shop to buy food or drink on the way home and then diverge into the maze of streets leading from the depot.

One or two streets are probably blacktopped; a few more might have a rough cobblestone pavement that recalls the days before the revolution. The others are unsurfaced and probably ungraded. Blacktop or dirt footpaths follow the edge of the streets. Between the paths and the roadway, grass or weeds cover the ground and provide a grazing area for the suburbanite's family goat.

Many blocks are lined with cottages standing in uneven rows behind high, irregular hedges or wood fences. They are set in quiet, shady surroundings among damp beds of shrubbery and flowers in summer. One can picture them as unpainted, dark, warm oases on a bleak plain in winter. Perhaps a goat or some poultry wander in the yard or huddle in an attached shed. Other blocks are open and broken into dozens of small vegetable and potato patches.

Still other blocks are lined with two-storey houses. Elsewhere a block or two of apartment buildings rise above the cottages and trees. Each apartment building is five storeys (the legal maximum for a walkup) and measures about 30 by 70 feet. A building probably contains nine or ten thousand square feet of living space and houses about 90 or 100 people, if it conforms with official standards of 100 square feet per person. If one assumes that there are three persons per family (there are likely to be more), 30 families probably live in this small building. One can count 30 TV aerials on the roof. One wonders how many bathrooms there are.

Aside from the crowded conditions, which exist everywhere in the country, how is living in the suburbs? The sights and smells tell the story. Gas pipe lies in small piles here and there along the streets, as the local soviet prepares to supply the suburb with natural gas. The hallways of many apartment buildings reek of wood smoke, for wood is the fuel for heating and cooking. Water hydrants stand at one-or two-block intervals along the streets, but there is no running water in many buildings and hence no sanitary sewer. In Moscow a 1958 survey showed that 39 percent of the apartments had bathrooms; 10 percent had running hot water.[2]

There is, however, a sprinkling of garages and private autos. Although probably not more than one family in 400 owns an automobile in metropolitan Moscow, the ratio is clearly higher in some suburban districts. The inhabitants of these areas are "upper middle class" Soviet citizens who often live in dwellings of one to three rooms that have the amenities of a centuries-old peasant village.

Industries have grown in the suburbs, too. Metal fabricating and engineering works hide behind guarded concrete walls, with only their long gables and skylights visible to the passerby. Elsewhere big, sprawling brick and cement factories appear across open fields and along the broad, open swaths of railway land. Thousands of suburbanites ride the buses that go to the gates of these local plants.

New industries and new apartments are rising on the edges of many Moscow suburbs, adding to the visitor's impression of the entire metropolis as a vast, growing collection of construction projects. They remind one, too, that urban growth has involved not only the movement of country people to the city, but also the extension of the city commuting pattern into the country.

The Countryside

Beyond the suburbs lies an indefinite region known to Muscovites as the "Moscow countryside." It is a land of low relief and long, gentle slopes, where just a slightly elevated swell commands a panorama of land and sky. The occasional small streams run with the steadiness provided by the moist, cool summer climate of the North European plain. Broad, flat marshes and meadows follow the stream courses. In a thousand years of agricultural activity, peasants have cleared the trees from roughly half of the gently rolling uplands. The clearings are occupied by pastures and fields of grain and hay in rotation. The remaining birch, oak, and pine forests form the ever-present back-

2 T. Sosnovy, "Town Planning and Housing," *Survey*, Number 38 (1961), p. 177.

ground. They will spread again, to within about ten miles of the city's edge, for all of this land is a "greenbelt" zone under Moscow's master plan. Log cottages, thatch roofs, and widely scattered herds of dairy cows blend with the landscape in this quiet, rustic countryside.

To one who comes from a land that is subject to greater aridity, greater seasonal extremes, or greater relief, the Moscow countryside seems drab. But Muscovites find beauty in the marshes and meadows, in the verdure of the forest floor, and in the closely spaced columns of white birch and red pine trunks that support the forest canopy. Like people everywhere, they discover beauty in the land they know. An emotional attachment to the land finds expression in the works of many Russian writers, while the same feeling comes with less eloquence but ample conviction from other citizens. As our car left the edge of the metropolis, the official guide remarked, "Gentlemen, we are now entering the Moscow countryside. I think it is the most beautiful in the Soviet Union." He was serious, even though he has just returned from several days amid the magnificent mountain and ocean panoramas of the Caucasus Black Sea coast. The attachment of urbanites to the bucolic landscape may be another reflection of the fact that most of these city people have either emigrated from the country and the small towns themselves or have peasant parents or grandparents.

The nearby countryside, too, exhibits signs of change. A new freeway slices through woods and fields. Buses and trains bring more and more people to picnic in the woods and meadows. The increasing number of paved roads leading from the metropolis and the gradual rise in living standards have introduced the greatest scourge of the countryside—the motorized, picnicking family. Along the highway that follows the ancient road and footpath to Zagorsk, the historical monastery town, one sees occasionally the unmistakable rumpled, soggy newspapers or empty bottles blemishing the roadside woods. A cartoon in an issue of the Soviet humor magazine *Krokodil* depicted two bears moving into a woodland glade after the departure of a family of picnickers in their four-door "Pobeda." The bears show obvious disgust as they bandage a broken birch sapling, nurse trampled wild flowers, and sweep up discarded papers and bottles.

Even the Moscow countryside feels the impact of urbanization.

THE OUTLYING CITIES

Besides Moscow and its suburbs there are about 174 cities in the Soviet Union with more than 100,000 inhabitants. No more than half a dozen of them are wholly new cities. The others are old, established places. Like Moscow itself, the other cities have had a relatively large accretion of immigrants during the past three decades. All have many of the same elements one finds in Moscow—an old core that has usually had at least a little facelifting; new apartments; blocks and courtyards of simple cottages; suburbs and countryside. But the "mix" of these components is different in the smaller cities. (See Map II between pp. 96 and 97, which shows the major cities and industrial regions of the USSR.)

For one thing, there has been far less facelifting in the central parts of many smaller cities. Central Leningrad has comparatively little new construction. Even before the Bolshevik revolution, the city was a showplace of eighteenth- and nineteenth-century European architecture. Its splendid government office buildings, palaces, and churches were monuments to the huge amount of construction capital that was poured into the Tsars' city of St. Petersburg for two centuries. Only maintenance and repairs were necessary to keep it a showplace.

In other older cities, there commonly is a cluster of three-, four-, or five-storey buildings within a block or two of the busiest intersection. In architecture the buildings are suggestive of a 70- or 80-year-old business block in a small city of the American northeast or middle west; but the brick walls of the Soviet buildings are covered with a drab skin of yellow or green plaster.

These buildings in prerevolutionary times housed the main hotels, department stores, banks, and business offices of the city. Today a department store—perhaps recently revived—again occupies one of these large buildings. The main hotels are threadbare museums of nineteenth-century furnishings and plumbing, not unlike the oldest respectable hotel in a small American city. They accommodate a swelling stream of Soviet and foreign visitors, industrial traveling men, and miscellaneous delegations. Another building—in Rostov-on-Don it is a former bank—might house the city Palace of Pioneers, a center for the sparetime activities of Communist youth. Perhaps a few more old buildings are now used for city government offices and bureaus, while still others help to relieve the ubiquitous housing shortage.

Somewhere near the old heart of the city there is likely to be a vast new paved plaza or park adjoined to a few spectacular new government office buildings and, perhaps, a hospital or regional university. These civic centers are symbols of the new regime. Some of them, however, are only partially completed, and often they are merely small drops in a sea of old buildings and streets that await redevelopment.

The broad main streets leading from the city center are lined with one- or two-storey masonry buildings. Like most of the older buildings and some of the new ones, these seem to roll and pitch with slight undulations in the terrain. The walls have a homemade appearance. "These are Russian cities; Leningrad and Riga are European cities," a Russian told us. "What do you mean—'European city'?" we asked. Without hesitation the Russian replied with gestures. He moved his hand forward in a perfectly straight line and said, "European city." Then he pulled his hand back to his chest and put it forward again in a waving motion and said, "Russian city."

In contrast with Moscow's completely repaved central district, the smaller cities still have many cobbled or brick streets. It is not uncommon to see water or sewer mains being laid at the edges of the central district. Redevelopment has come more slowly to the old cores of the outlying cities, for, unlike Moscow, they are neither international show windows nor centers of sprawling government headquarters.

The older outlying cities differ from Moscow in still another respect. A greater proportion of the housing appears to consist of small cottages —timber or brick—accommodating one or two or three families. As city populations have grown, the pressure for increased housing has been greater than the government could meet with the portion of tax income it was willing to allocate to this need. At the same time, however, the pressure was too great for the government to ignore. As a result, private individuals have been permitted to build their own houses, often with aid of a government loan. An individual can obtain the right to use a small city lot and to purchase building materials from the local housing authority. The site on which he builds and the number of families who dwell in his house must, of course, conform to the controls of the housing and planning authorities. The location of his house must fit the general patterns of the city's growth and the extension of its utilities and public transport facilities. There is no "suburban explosion." Once he has permission, the individual puts down footings of timber or masonry and builds his cottage. It is a simple place, with two or three rooms, sometimes less, and without running water and modern sanitation; it is not quite level or plumb. Such a house reminds one of the peasant cottages of the countryside. Indeed, the rows of similar cottages, the unpaved streets and footpaths, and the widely spaced water hydrants give the whole neighborhood the appearance of a peasant village.

Private dwellings form a substantial part of the total housing picture in Soviet cities, accounting for perhaps one fourth of the total urban housing floor space in the USSR today. Under the early five-year plans, between 1926 and 1940, two thirds of all the nation's new urban housing was built privately. During and since World War II, the proportion has varied between one fourth and one third.

In 1960 one third of all new housing was privately constructed. The rapid progress in state housing construction has led to a move to end all private building in the cities, but the most recent Soviet statistics do not yet reflect that policy.

It is clear that the use and construction of private, cottage-type urban dwellings is most important today in the outlying cities. Consequently, the old, partly reconstructed cores of those cities are often surrounded by vast "villages" of tens or hundreds of thousands of people.

These "village" sections of the cities are more primitive than they are untidy or unpleasant. They are reminiscent of small American towns of the nineteenth century. The cottages often stand among grassy yards, vegetable gardens, or a scattering of fruit or shade trees. But many neighborhoods are devoid of paved streets, sewers, or water mains.

Table 2-4 indicates the housing space available in Moscow and in 23 major outlying cities. The figures dramatically show the impact of 30 years of five-year plans under Stalin upon the housing supply of these metropolitan centers. Forced-draft industrialization, Communist philosophy, dictatorship, and wartime devastation are all reflected.

In three decades the average floor space per person dropped slightly. In 1956, after ten years of postwar recovery, it was the lowest since the five-year plans began, and it was far below the announced national standard of 99 square feet per person. The average floor space per resident had fallen drastically in cities with the best housing, while the average for those with the worst housing rose slightly. Thus the net effect of the revolution, hampered by the war, had been to lower the average level and narrow the spread between the best and the worst.

Some spread remained, even under Communism. Furthermore, the government appeared to be permitting the gap in housing standards between Moscow and many of the smaller cities to widen. In the postwar period up to 1956, approximately half of the total new housing in all 24 cities was in Moscow. Yet Moscow had only 28 percent of the total population of those cities. Meanwhile, as the table shows, housing standards held relatively constant or improved somewhat in early postwar years in certain outlying cities, notably in some of the constituent republic capitals (Kiev, Baku); in traditionally influential Leningrad; in certain centers of heavy or defense industry (Donetsk, Chelyabinsk, Sverdlovsk, Omsk, Gorky); and in traditional cultural and economic centers that have had relatively small industrial growth (Odessa).

TABLE 2-4

HOUSING SPACE IN SELECTED SOVIET CITIES*

City	Approximate average square feet of housing space per inhabitant: 1926	1940	1956	1960	Approximate population of city 1960
Moscow	89	75	80	108	6,208,000
Leningrad	138	89	87	99	3,445,000
Kiev	107	87	86	109	1,174,000
Baku	74	68	69	92	1,038,000
Gorky	68	73	73	90	1,003,000
Kharkov	86	87	84	103	976,000
Tashkent	68	76	66	88	971,000
Novosibirsk	61	66	65	87	963,000
Kuibyshev	85	68	66	85	863,000
Sverdlovsk	70	76	76	97	832,000
Donetsk (Stalino)	41	76	79	112	749,000
Chelyabinsk	74	68	68	94	733,000
Tblisi	106	98	94	98	724,000
Odessa	121	99	98	108	696,000
Dnepropetrovsk	96	85	85	104	707,000
Kazan	90	73	68	84	693,000
Perm (Molotov)	61	72	69	88	678,000
Rostov-on-Don	81	91	88	101	645,000
Volgograd (Stalingrad)	64	75	72	102	632,000
Omsk	74	66	67	91	630,000
Saratov	80	77	75	91	622,000
Minsk	86	83	69	85	570,000
Erevan	68	74	68	85	558,000
Alma Ata	66	63	63	87	508,000
AVERAGE	81	78	76	95	

* This table portrays 30 years of change in the amount of housing space per capita in 24 large Soviet cities. To give the figures meaning, keep in mind: (1) the Soviet official standard is nine square meters (approximately 100 square feet) per person; (2) the average is four persons per dwelling unit (above our actual national average). The average new urban single-family house in the United States in 1960 contained about 300 square feet of floor space per person; the average new apartment contained approximately 210 square feet per person. Source: *Narodnoe Khozaistvo SSSR*, Moscow, 1959 and 1960. *Statistical Abstract of the United States, 1960*, Washington, 1961.

Table 2-4 indicates one reason for the pressure that had built up for a more liberal policy in the last years of Stalin. Housing, one of the most basic consumer goods, was in extremely short supply, even in the centers of highest living standards. Inequities among cities were persisting or even growing slightly. Major war damage remained unrepaired. The western part of the USSR housed about 40 percent of the nation's population. Less than two decades ago it was still a huge battlefield in the war against the Nazis. As late as 1958 many Soviet cities still showed scars of the war.

Note the sharp increase in housing space that came in the post-Stalin period. The rate of new construction is the highest in Russian history. The present national standard of floor space has been reached or surpassed in one third of the cities. Variations among the cities are less than they have ever been, and war damage has virtually disappeared.

There are also differences in the kinds of industry found among the outlying cities. The cities on the coal and iron ore fields have great steel furnaces and smelters; urban centers on the edge of the northern forest are noted for their lumber and paper industries; the cities in the Urals and Siberia embrace the major ordinance industries; and the cities beside the great dams on the Volga and Dnieper are important for their electrochemical and electrometallurgical industries. The countryside also varies from the forests and pastures of the north through the dusty grain fields of the steppe to the barren plains and irrigated fields of the desert; from the flat plain of western Siberia to the mountains of the Middle Eastern and Chinese borderlands.

THE HANDWRITING ON THE CITY WALL

Although this sketch of the Soviet city is incomplete, perhaps it depicts the major elements of the physical setting in which the foreign visitor meets and interviews his Soviet hosts. In examining this setting, one is immediately confronted by a number of basic facts about the Soviet Union.

The visitor is surrounded by hundreds of thousands of people who earnestly go about their daily affairs—living, working, studying, playing. As he talks with many of these ordinary people he comes to feel that, despite decades of tyranny and turmoil, the basic human values have survived in their hearts.

The city also shows constant change. The influence of the work and the ideas of the past can be seen on every side in the appearance and location of places of residence, trade, and industry. But the new city has emerged from the old city. And a new city and newer ways of living and thinking will continue to emerge from the building and the technologic changes now in progress.

In the Soviet city there is continual, rumbling evidence of the country's growing industrial capacity. Technologic growth along western lines and accompanying increases in material wealth have produced problems and invite solutions that are already familiar in the West. A volume of geographical articles on satellite cities of the great metropolitan centers appeared in 1961.[3] The authors mention some interesting problems connected with urbanism—the crowding of industry in already congested central cities; time-consuming commuting distances for workers; urban "sprawl" resulting from families shifting their year-round residence to what were once summer houses outside Moscow; the need to preserve open space in the new "greenbelt" zone around Moscow. What comes through is the fact that plans have yielded repeatedly to unforeseen forces of technologic change, complex social interactions, and unavoidable expediency.

Promises made by the regime to improve the housing situation are not always carried out. Despite the announced goal of improved material wellbeing for the masses, the regime deferred the improvement of housing or even the maintenance of current housing standards in order to pour its investment resources into other types of development.

Inequalities in housing standards between major cities have also been permitted. For example, vital industrial cities such as Kuibyshev or Novosibirsk are considerably less well housed than Moscow. Likewise, within any single city today, there is a vast range between the best and the worst housing. This problem will not be solved easily or quickly. To bring the entire nation up to the emerging Moscow standards will take many years. In the meantime, the material desires of the maturing urban population are likely to rise even higher, thus placing even greater pressure upon the authorities to allocate more resources for housing.

The wide range in the age, condition, and desirability of housing facilities is likely to continue to exist for many years to come, however. This variation in housing accommodations stimulates competition among socio-economic groups for the better facilities and the high social status they bring—outward evidence of stratification in a society that set out to become classless.

The housing in a Soviet city also reflects the rural origin of a major portion of the urban population. It reminds the visitor that millions

[3] *Goroda Sputniki*, Moscow, 1961; English in Soviet Geography, Number 3, 1962.

of Soviet citizens now living in urban centers evaluate their housing not against the standards of the West, nor even against prerevolutionary standards of Russian cities, but against the standards of the rural peasant village.

Finally, the spectacular housing boom in the Soviet cities since the death of Stalin reflects the fact that the system does respond to pressure for change. It is capable of altering priorities and modifying goals. It can adopt "western" approaches to problems for the same economic reasons that have led to their adoption in the West—for example foresaking slum clearance for faster, cheaper development of open, outlying land during a period of rapid urbanization.

The trends in urban growth and development and the problems associated with them will continue as long as industrialization persists. Nikita Khruschev has promised no letup in the industrial development at least until the Soviet Union surpasses the United States. But promise is not the only ingredient of performance. Whether or not the other ingredients can be supplied raises a whole new set of questions. To be sure, answers to many of these questions are suggested figuratively by the "handwriting on the wall." However, one can and must probe more deeply into the economic, political, and social structure of the USSR.

3

SOVIET ECONOMIC GROWTH

Francis M. Boddy

*Professor of Economics at the University of Min-
nesota and Associate Dean of its graduate school,
Francis M. Boddy is the coauthor of* Principles
of Economics *(with Fred Benham) and of* Applied Economic Analysis *(with others); he is co-
editor of* Savings in the U.S. Economy *(with
Walter W. Heller and Carl L. Nelson).*

Nikita S. Khrushchev, an inveterate speech-
maker, never misses an opportunity to "say a few words." At important gatherings he often holds forth for six or eight hours. He has the
rare distinction of having been the before- and after-dinner speaker on
the same occasion. The Moscow press reported that one of his speeches
to the 1961 Party Congress continued through the morning *and evening*
sessions of the Congress.

Khrushchev's speeches are characterized by repetition. Certain
themes—often expressed in the same, tired phraseology—are repeated
over and over again. Perhaps the most persistent theme in Khrushchev's
talks and writings is the prophecy that the Soviet economy will, within
a little more than a decade, catch up with and surpass the United
States in man-hour productivity and in total production. In a television
address to an American audience in September, 1959, Khrushchev
asserted:

The United States is at present the richest and economically the most
highly developed power. The figures for your country represent the highest
ceiling in the capitalist world. You must bear in mind, however, that the

62

average annual rate of industrial expansion in the Soviet Union is about three to five times higher than in your country, and for this reason within the next ten to twelve years we shall surpass the United States both in physical production and in production per capita of the population, while in agriculture this will be accomplished much earlier.

Khrushchev has made similar boasts to the neutralist nations. In February 1960, for example, he told an Indonesian audience:

The peaceful economic competition between us and the United States can be visualized . . . as a long-distance race. The United States is still running ahead of us, and this is not surprising. They had an earlier start. To speak figuratively, it already runs under great tension, as if its breath were running short. A young and strong runner, the Socialist Soviet Union is slowly catching up with it and will soon leave it behind.

Are such statements propagandistic fantasy or is there a serious prospect that the Khrushchev regime will be able to achieve its objective? If such a forecast had been made by Joseph Stalin, it would have been brushed aside as unrealistic nonsense. Even in the middle 1950s, few westerners believed that the Soviet Union stood any chance of equaling American production in the foreseeable future. But these attitudes were suddenly changed when the Russians launched Sputnik I into outer space and sent Gagarin into orbit around the earth. Many people gained a new respect for the capabilities of Soviet science and began to reappraise the official claims of economic growth in the USSR.

In 1959 the Central Intelligence Agency estimated that the Soviet economy had grown at the rate of about seven percent annually during the previous eight years—a rate of growth twice that of the United States during the same period. On the basis of carefully evaluated evidence, it was predicted that the USSR could maintain a growth rate of six percent per year through 1965. An economy that grows at a rate of seven percent per annum will double in about ten years; an economy that grows at a rate of only three percent per year will double every 24 years.

This testimony indicated cause for alarm. In the period from 1955 to 1960 the annual growth rate of the American economy had been less than three percent, reflecting the impact of two recessions during that time. In the face of these unfavorable reports, the joint economic committee of the United States Congress held a series of hearings and published the views of specialists who had studied Soviet and American economic growth. When the new administration came to power in

1961, it listed as one of its major objectives the stimulation of economic growth—an explicit response to the Soviet challenge.

To be sure, there is cause for concern, but for how much concern? Does the USSR have a chance to overtake and surpass the United States during the next decade? in the next 20 years? by the turn of the century? In trying to answer these questions, let us look first at some of the detailed studies of growth rates in the Soviet Union.

GROWTH RATES IN THE SOVIET ECONOMY

The discussion of Soviet growth rates falls naturally into two parts: (1) the growth of industrial output in areas where Soviet production effort has been concentrated and (2) the growth of total output.

Estimates by G. Warren Nutter, submitted to the joint economic committee of the Congress in 1959, indicate the following average annual rates of growth of the civilian output of Soviet industry in three recent periods: 1928 to 1940, 7.4 percent per year; 1940 to 1950, 5.1 percent per year; and 1950 to 1955, 7.7 percent per year. As for industrial output, in a supplemental statement submitted to the committee in 1960, the CIA estimated that the average annual growth rate in Soviet industrial production from 1950 to 1959 was 10 percent per year, and that the projected rate of growth from 1959 to 1965 would be 8.6 percent per year.

The growth rates for the gross national product of the Soviet economy, that is, the total value of all goods and services produced, were estimated by Morris Bornstein to be between six to seven percent per year from 1950 to 1955, and between seven to eight percent per year from 1955 to 1958. Another estimate gives an annual rate of growth in gross national product from 1950 to 1955 of somewhat over five percent per year. The CIA estimate is a growth rate, from 1950 to 1959, of seven percent per year.

While these western estimates indicate a rate of growth in the Soviet economy that is somewhat more than twice that of the American economy during recent years, they are substantially below the rates of growth claimed by the Soviet Union in official statements. Soviet leaders claim a rate of growth of eleven percent per year for industrial output, and eight percent per year in national income. Furthermore, they claim to have met these targets during the first two completed years of the new seven-year plan (1959 and 1960).

The gross national product of the United States (in 1954 dollars, that is, corrected for changes in price levels) increased from 1947 to

1960 at an average annual rate of about 3.5 percent, and from 1955 to 1960 at about 2.3 percent per year.

While there is general (but not unanimous) agreement that the Soviet economy has been and is growing at a rapid rate, it is also true that the total output of the Soviet economy was in 1960 only about half that of the United States. Thus, differing estimates as to the future growth rates of these two competing economies can give widely varying answers to the question, Can the Soviet economy catch up with and surpass that of the United States? An optimistic view is that the growth rate of the United States economy will rise above its recent levels and that the Soviet rate will decline substantially. This view would postpone for many years the date on which the Soviet objective could be reached or would make it impossible to achieve it, depending on the magnitude of the changes in growth rates. On the other hand, the maintenance of recent high growth rates by the Soviet Union and a failure of the growth rate in the United States to rise above existing levels would bring the date relatively close. It should be recognized that even if the present levels of the Soviet gross national product are far below those of the United States, sustained rates of growth in the Soviet Union higher than those of the United States means that inevitably the total output of Soviet production will eventually surpass ours.

If one looks at data reported during the past five years by the Soviet Central Statistical Administration in its annual reports on plan fulfillment, some interesting rates of growth can be computed for the output of groups of products. Taking the median index for each group of products to represent that group, one can assign the following average annual rates of growth in physical output from 1956 to 1960, by product class groups (Table 3-1).

TABLE 3-1

Class	Average rate of increase, in percent per year
Food	7.5
Clothing and textiles	6.9
Household goods and supplies	13.0
Fuel and power	13.2
Industrial materials	8.2
Machinery	6.7
Transportation equipment	11.7

Over the same period of time, the total physical movements of goods (freight shipments) by rail, highway, river, and pipeline increased at the rate of 9.3 percent per year.

These separate indices, then, support the conclusion that the Soviet economy has been growing at a rapid rate in the most recent years: in industrial production by about nine to eleven percent per year, and in total output by about seven to eight percent per year.

But predictions based solely on extrapolations from the past are notoriously unreliable. Whether these rates of economic growth, or something similar to them, can be maintained in the near and more distant future is an open question. One can get an idea of the complexity of the problem by examining the factors that determine rates of growth in any economy. The consideration of these factors, one at a time, may make it possible to arrive at some reasonable judgement on this question.

THE DETERMINANTS OF ECONOMIC GROWTH

At any one time the upper limits on economic output are set by three sets of conditions: (1) the quantity and quality of available natural resources, capital goods, and manpower; (2) the levels of scientific, industrial, and agricultural technology; and (3) the efficiency of the organizational structures at all levels in the economy. The maximum potential rate of growth of an economy is set by the factors that limit the long-run growth of each of the above conditions. (For a short period of time, however, output could be increased significantly over and above these limits by such policies as increasing the length of the work day, reducing the maintenance of capital, neglecting the education and training of new workers, or overexploiting natural resources.)

Let us examine these three sets of conditions and see if any one of them is likely to circumscribe the industrial growth of the USSR in the next few decades.

Natural Resources

The land area of the Soviet Union is almost three times that of the United States, and somewhat larger than the combined territory of Canada, the United States, and Mexico. Indeed, one sixth of the land area of the entire world lies within the Soviet borders.

Virtually every raw material necessary to run a large-scale modern industrial economy is to be found in this vast land mass. Soviet reserves of a number of important mineral and nonmineral resources are among the largest in the world. Rich deposits of coal are distributed widely throughout the country. Petroleum reserves are probably sufficient to meet Soviet needs for a long time. These fuel resources are complemented by a great potential for hydroelectric power production—a potential three times that of the United States, although (like the United States to some degree) the location of much of this underdeveloped power is far from the areas of prospective need.

The Soviet Union is also well endowed with metallic ores. Although much of the iron ore is not of superior quality, Russian technologists have developed economical methods of processing these ores to concentrate the iron content. Other metals important in producing steel alloys are also available. The Soviet Union is the world's largest producer of manganese and one of the largest producers of nickel.

In only one important sector, agriculture, does the natural resource base seem to be deficient. Some of the land area of the Soviet Union is useless for agricultural production because it is permanently frozen. Almost all of the Soviet Union lies north of 45° north latitude (the latitude of Minneapolis, Minnesota, and of Bangor, Maine). In the areas south of the permafrost, lack of sufficient rainfall, short growing seasons, and other climatic handicaps severely limit the amount of land that can be effectively planted. Even this limited area is, in general, much less naturally productive than the agricultural land in the United States. Since the Soviet economy follows a policy of agricultural self-sufficiency, the limited resource base for agriculture is a matter of critical importance. The attempts to overcome this deficiency are discussed in detail in Chapter 4.

This brief survey suggests why many experts on the Soviet economy conclude that the Soviet Union compares favorably with the United States in the variety and richness of its raw material base, except in the agricultural sector. The currently developed and prospectively available natural resources probably set no restrictive limits upon nonagricultural production in the USSR in the foreseeable future. In agriculture, however, the Soviet leaders are struggling to break through the limits set by the quantity and quality of agricultural land resources. This limitation will very likely restrict agricultural output for a long time to come and may act as a restraint upon the nonagricultural sector as well.

Manpower

The Soviet Union had, in 1961, a population of about 215 million persons, about one fifth larger than that of the United States. It was, however, a badly balanced population. Because of severe war losses, women outnumber men by some 20 million, and there is an especially small number of people in the 10 to 19 year age group, reflecting the low birth rates of the war and early postwar years.

The total labor force in the Soviet Union is about 110 million persons, about 45 percent greater than the American labor force. But the number of men in the Soviet labor force is only some five percent greater than in the United States. Although the mature working age population (25 to 64 years) of the Soviet Union is 22 percent greater than that of the United States, the number of males in this age group is roughly the same in both countries. The number of women workers in the Soviet Union exceeds the number of men workers by more than three million. Whereas the women make up less than one-third of the labor force in the United States, they comprise over 55 percent of the workers in the Soviet Union.

Although the Soviet Union has a male population of working age of about the same size as that of the United States, it has managed to develop a larger labor force because of the extraordinarily high participation of female labor and the greater numbers of young people (in the 15 to 24 age group) who work in factories and on farms.

Through the early 1960s the segment of the population in the 15 to 19 age bracket is expected to grow somewhat less rapidly than the comparable group in the American population, but demographic projections to 1965 do not imply any inability of the Soviet Union arising out of a labor shortage to meet the goals of the 1959 to 1965 plans.

With so many women and young people already in the labor force, any further increases in the labor supply will come primarily from population growth. Short-run increases (or decreases) can be brought about, however, through changes in military call-up and changes in the assignment of students to secondary and advanced educational institutions.

The level of education and training of the Soviet population has been pushed up at rapid rate by a heavy commitment of resources to formal education and by a great emphasis upon on-the-job or work-related training. But in spite of the very great advances, the average level of education of the Soviet citizen is far below that of his counterpart in the United States. In 1959 over half the population over 15 years of age had not completed elementary school (seven years), and only a little more than 15 percent had completed high school, technical school, or higher education. Nevertheless, an appreciation of basic scientific and technical information, as well as considerable amounts of more general knowledge, has been diffused through the population, particularly in the growing urban centers.

The growth of Soviet economic activity and the expansion of national output will make heavy demands on Soviet manpower if the planned rates of growth are to be achieved. But a continuation of the present rates of natural growth in population and a still further movement of labor out of the agricultural-rural sector into the industrial-urban sector will probably furnish the required industrial labor force. Moreover, the maintenance or further development of present programs of formal and on-the-job training is likely to establish at least the minimum levels of skills required in the working force. The transfer of substantial numbers of workers from agriculture to urban employment can be carried out, according to Soviet economists, without interfering with goals for agriculture. At the present time there are far too many workers inefficiently employed in agriculture. Withdrawing from the rural areas these labor reserves that currently have a low level of productivity may force a better use of labor, making the workers who remain on the farms far more productive. Under such circumstances, the output of the agricultural sector of the economy might actually increase, despite the lower labor input.

To make these shifts and to maintain and raise the level of industrial skills will necessitate expanded investment of resources in urban housing, education, and training programs. This the Soviet Union will be able to do if the Communist leaders decide to continue along their present course.

Thus, despite the relatively low educational level, the manpower situation in the Soviet Union does not appear to be a limiting factor in the carrying out of the current seven-year plan, nor does it appear likely to restrict continued long-run expansion of the Soviet economy, especially if industrial training programs are expanded and enriched.

Capital Goods

Early in the Soviet period, a decision was made to concentrate the major industrial effort on the development of electric power and on the rapid development of heavy industry. The first effort went into the "electrification drive" put forward by Lenin in 1920. With the development of the first formal five-year plan in 1928, the drive to develop a heavy industrial base for the Soviet economy was clearly set forth. The following four five-year plans, and the current (1959 to 1965) seven-year plan continued this emphasis. These plans direct a large percentage of the total resources of the economy (some 25 percent or so) into the production of factories, machinery and equipment, power stations, transportation equipment, mines and mineral processing plants, and the like. These products are the capital equipment for future production and are achieved at the cost of consumer goods, which could have been produced instead.

These capital goods, moreover, have been largely designed to produce still more capital goods. In other words, there has been a strong and steady drive to develop the basic industries that, in turn, lead to the development of still more of the same basic industries. This emphasis on the use of current inputs to produce the means of producing still more future inputs has led some observers to christen it the "input-input" system.

Why was such a rapid and costly industrialization drive a basic economic policy of the Soviet leaders? First, they believed that only by creating the base for economic and military power could the USSR protect its very existence in a hostile world. Second, they believed that the building of capital goods would be the shortest path to economic development. Third, given the availability of manpower and technology, the development of natural resources and the creation of new industrial capital would build up the elements that were relatively in very short supply.

In the early years of Communist rule, when the economy was badly broken down from the effects of the war and the revolution, the problem of somehow accumulating the financial capital to carry out such a program was a critical one. External financing, by loans, investment, or by gifts from foreign countries, ran the danger of foreign influence and control and besides was not likely to be feasible in view of the political position of the Soviet government. Internal financing, on the other hand, would mean a ruthless restriction of current consumer output in order to devote resources to the industrialization program. The second alternative was chosen, and the burden was laid particularly heavily on the agricultural population. By means of harsh, forced collectivation, control was achieved over the peasants. This control was then used to exact from the farmers the bulk of their output, under a system of compulsory deliveries to the state at very low prices.

The farmers' deliveries were then processed by the state and sold to the rising industrial population of the cities at very high prices, with the "profit" used by the state as a major contribution to the financing of the industrialization drive. By making food supplies available in the cities (even at the very high prices) the regime was able to make the money-income incentives of the city workers really effective, and by the price-spread was able to finance much of the industrial expansion.

By virtually any economic measure, the drive for the accumulation of capital goods (and for the building of industry to produce capital goods) has been a striking success. By the end of the 1950s steel production (but not capacity) approximately equalled that of the United States. The basic material for heavy industry exists, a heavy machinery industry has been built up, and there is a capability in some areas for mass-producing machine tools—a development that makes possible considerable savings in time and money. The existing stock of capital goods in the Soviet Union is of relatively recent construction; hence the replacement of depreciated and obsolete capital takes less of the current output of capital goods than is the case in the United States, leaving more as a net increase to current stocks.

Capital goods, however, are still the relatively scarce resource in the Soviet Union. The continued use of all available capital equipment is greatly emphasized, while the retirement of obsolete equipment and its replacement by more modern machinery are neglected. In some Soviet industries much of the equipment is outdated, and older factories have a jumble of old and new machines. But if during the next several decades the rates of capital accumulation in the Soviet Union continue at present levels, and if investment in military production does not absorb an inordinate amount of this new capital, the stocks of capital goods will not be a major bottleneck in the Soviet drive to catch up with the United States in industrial production.

Technology

Ten years ago most Americans, including some experts on the Soviet Union, would have argued that the low level of Soviet technology would significantly impede economic growth. The recent pioneering efforts of the USSR in exploring outer space, however, have clearly demonstrated that in certain high priority areas Soviet technology ranks with the best in the world.

In the process of becoming industrialized, the Soviet Union has had an advantage in being able to borrow extensively from the developed technology of the western world. The first phase of the borrowing took place before and during the first and second five-year plans, when American, British, and other western engineers and technologists went to the USSR to help construct factories for the production of machinery and equipment. The next step was to introduce the new equipment widely into the production process in both industry and agriculture and to train the workers in the operation and maintenance of the machinery. A new stage has now been reached in which modern technology has been introduced on a large scale throughout industry, and Soviet specialists have developed advanced techniques in some fields on their own.

Industrial technology requires major investment in capital equipment. The continued emphasis on investment in the Soviet Union has spurred the development of better technology, especially in heavy industry, which has absorbed much of the capital investment. In certain industries, such as iron ore processing, electric power, machine tools, aircraft, Soviet technology seems to be on a level with the West, and even more advanced in some respects. Heavy industry generally appears to be not far behind western standards in technical know-how, although in practice the operating technologies are further behind because of a less general leveling upward of industrial practices to the standards of the best establishments. In light industry, on the other hand, both the widespread knowledge of modern technology and its use in current operations are far behind western standards.

Since technology is, by its very nature, free to flow from the countries of its origin, and since Soviet leaders are engaged in a massive effort to inform themselves about technological developments throughout the world, there is no reason to suppose that a lack of knowledge of modern technology will handicap the Russians. The widespread dissemination of this information to scientists, research institutes, and technicians in industry is being pushed by strong governmental measures. The adaptation and introduction of advanced technology are conditioned by the required investment in the accompanying physical capital and in the training of construction, operating, and maintenance personnel. Since the Soviet Union is devoting great effort to both of these areas, one may expect the levels of technology in use to continue to rise and to contribute substantially to economic growth for some time to come.

Another aspect of technology, however, is that of developing organizational methods for operating huge, complicated industrial establishments and for coordinating the operations of these industrial complexes with the rest of the economy. Here the Soviet Union faces the problem of developing its own technology, for the managerial techniques of the West, geared to a capitalist economy, may not transfer directly to the Soviet scene. In operating a system of centrally controlled planning, the Communists have experienced great difficulty in devising appropriate indices to measure the performance of managers and to guide the efficient operation of the plants and industrial complexes. The widespread use of piecework wage rates bonus-incentive systems at all levels has shown the power of the income motive, but to be truly effective, these systems must be based on measures of economic effectiveness that truly reflect the achievement of the desired production. At present the incentives to innovate are particularly weak; the risk involved to the manager and to the enterprise in the introduction of new methods is a significant factor in slowing down the use of better methods and equipment.

In considering the determinants of economic growth, then, it would appear that the natural resources, manpower, capital goods, and technology available in the USSR do not impose, at present or in the near future, severe restrictions upon the ability of the economy to grow at a substantial rate. There is a clear restraining factor, however, in the problem area of agriculture. The ability of the farms to expand total output—especially to increase the production of meat and dairy products—and to provide the raw materials that are badly needed in industry may be held back by the natural factor of limited resources and by the organizational problems of collective and state farms.

CAPITALISM AND SOVIET COMMUNISM

If we take the view that in the economic race between the Soviet Union and the United States the basic resource factors (except for the deficiency in Soviet agriculture) are about equal, the outcome may be determined largely by the relative efficiency with which the two economies can be managed. Here, of course, direct comparisons are difficult because of the striking organizational differences between the two systems: one is a mixed-market economy, the other is, basically, a centrally planned state socialism. Nevertheless, both the US and the USSR come up with answers to essentially the same questions. Each of them has to make decisions concerning:

1. Who shall use the available natural resources? For what purposes? How intensively? At what locations?
2. How much of current resources shall be directed to the production of investment goods—and of what kinds?
3. How shall the remaining available capital goods and labor supply be used? What goods and services shall be produced for current consumption?
4. How shall the output for current consumption be distributed to the consumers?
5. How shall resources and output be allocated between private or personal consumption and public or group consumption?

The distinctive characteristics of capitalism and Soviet Communism can be illustrated by the location of the decision-making power in the economy and by the forces that determine how these decisions are made.

Features of Capitalism

1. Ownership and control of natural resources, capital goods, and personal labor lies with individuals or firms owned by individuals. These are the private property rights of a capitalistic society. Such rights may be temporarily (or permanently, except for labor) assigned to other persons by mutual agreement. This is the *right of contract*.

2. The organization and fundamental direction of the economic processes of production, exchange, and consumption are accomplished by the market system. This is, first of all, a system for the collection and dissemination of *information* as to current supplies and demands and market prices; and it is, secondly, a system of processes and institutions by which the exchanges of the goods and services are arranged for and accomplished. Under capitalism the market system is not directly planned nor are the prices fixed by the government or by any organized groups, but arise spontaneously and react freely to the economic actions of all the individual persons or firms in the economy.

3. The income of each individual and firm is determined basically by the market valuation of the contribution of that individual's (or firm's) labor, or of his other owned resources, to the economic output of the system.

4. Hence the economic incentives that lie behind economic decisions are (a) income for the owners of resources, (b) profits for the business firms, and (c) individual desires and satisfactions for the consumers.

In modern western capitalism generally, and in the United States, government has become an important economic sector. For defense, and for a variety of other governmental activities, the governments purchase large quantities of materials and products and hire large numbers of employees through the markets. In addition, governments of capitalist countries plan their policies of taxation and expenditure, as well as their monetary policies, in such a way as to promote full employment of resources and stability in overall economic conditions. In carrying out these activities, however, the governments have generally acted through the markets and have not used direct controls or "fixed" the market results.

In spite of the governmental effects, and in some cases controls, on the free market, however, a basic characteristic of western capitalism is the dominant role played by the free market in directing the whole economic process.

Features of Soviet Communism

1. All natural resources and all capital goods are owned collectively, that is, by the state; and the direction of their use, as well as the use of the labor of all individuals, lies with the state.

2. The organization and direction of the economic processes of resource use, production, and distribution is directly controlled by the state, although each consumer is permitted to choose, to a large degree, how he shall spend his income for the goods or services available to the consumer.

3. The incomes of individuals come solely from payments for personal contributions to the production of goods and services, and the rates of payment are determined by the state. No individuals are permitted to own or to receive the income from natural resources or capital goods (except for the "private plots" permitted to the farmers), or to hire other individuals for productive or income-earning activities.

4. The market processes and institutions are firmly and centrally controlled by the state, and the forces of supply and demand do not control market prices or economic decisions. Rather, prices and economic decisions conform to the central directive—the economic plan of the state. In the actual operation of Soviet Communism, this complete economic control and direction by the state is somewhat tempered by the economic and political necessities of permitting some degree of individualism, particularly in the agricultural sector, and permitting some freedom of choice to consumers. Some small areas of private property exist (for example, the small "private plots" allotted to the collective farmers and private ownership of some livestock). Moreover, in recent years the collective farms have been freed from the system of compulsory delivery of their produce to state agencies at state-set prices, and they may sell their output directly in consumer markets if they wish. But these are minor exceptions. The basic pattern is centralized state control over all significant economic decisions.

From this brief sketch of the two economic systems, the primary differences are apparent. First, the contrast of individual versus state ownership and control over resources; second, the contrast of a free-market system versus central planning as a means of organizing the economic life of the society.

In a mixed-market economy there is no overall economic plan that directs each individual or firm in its economic activities. Decisions on who shall make how much of what for whose consumption are decentralized. The quality and quantity of production in a given firm or industry are determined over time by the interaction of the forces of supply and demand. The future plans for a firm are made by the management as it estimates future demand for its products in relationship to anticipated costs. The resources needed for production are bought at a price determined by the market; the products produced are sold at a price determined by the market.

In the Soviet Union, on the other hand, the plans for each operating unit (the *enterprise*) are handed down from above. The resources needed for production are sent to the enterprise at a fixed price according to the plan—management does not (in theory, at least) have to procure them. Finished products are distributed through the marketing outlets according to the plan at a price set by the plan. The plan for a firm is a segment of the plan for an industry (before 1957) or for an area (after 1957) that, in turn, is a part of the master plan for the entire economy.

To the uninitiated observer of these two different economic systems, the planned economy, in which all important decisions are centrally made by relatively few men, may seem to be the model of rational and efficient order; and a free economy may appear as a disordered array in which hundreds of thousands of entrepreneurs are making independent decisions, with only disorder and inefficiency as the inevitable results. But reality may be quite the reverse. The market mechanism in a free economy is an integrating force of great power, providing the entrepreneur with the information necessary to make rational decisions concerning the most efficient use of resources in his firm.

When in a free market system the economy is running along at something like full employment; when general economic conditions are relatively stable, so that decision-makers have reason to be confident of their future plans; and when free competition is the dominant characteristic of the market relationships; then the economy has, in its market system, an operating process that leads to an efficient allocation of resources that, in turn, produces a maximum of desired products and services.

In fact, of course, and in spite of the effort of governments to maintain the desirable conditions, the system works far from perfectly. Unemployment obviously signals failure to achieve as much output as can and should be produced. Monopoly is neither fully prevented nor perfectly regulated when it does arise. And the rapid changes in technology and in consumer and governmental demands keep the system continually off balance. Nevertheless, free-market system achieves a very high degree of economic efficiency and preserves the highest levels of individual human freedoms.

Part of the job of the designers of a planned and centrally controlled economy is to develop incentives and mechanisms that will achieve the efficient allocation of economic resources to achieve *their* economic objectives. What they need, therefore, is a plan or set of plans that will do for their economy what the market largely does for western economies. The complexity of the problem of detailed allocation of all economic resources by a central plan may be illustrated by a vastly oversimplified example, using a very simple "economy," and posing the problem arising out of a single planned change for the coming plan period.

AN ILLUSTRATION OF THE PLANNERS' PROBLEM

One way to illustrate the difficulty of allocating resources in a planned system is to set up an input-output table for a simple economy (Table 3-2). This simple hypothetical economy consists in its entirety of five sectors (metal, machinery, fuel, agricultural products, and labor). The table shows the number of units of the products (outputs) of each sector required by each of the other sectors.

Across the top of the resulting table are listed sectors that consume the products of each producing sector. For example, the figures in the machinery column (reading down) show the units of output of each of the producing sectors that are consumed during the year by the machinery sector in the creation of its output. In order to make 200 units of machinery, it takes 65 units of metal, 25 units of machinery, 5 units of fuel, 10 units of agricultural produce, and 200 units of labor. The same sectors as producing sectors are listed down the side (except

TABLE 3-2

A SIMPLE MODEL OF AN ECONOMY

Producing Sectors	Consuming or Using Sectors					Total Output
	Metal	Machinery	Fuel	Agric.	Households	
Metal	10	65	10	5	10	100
Machinery	40	25	35	75	25	200
Fuel	15	5	5	5	20	50
Agriculture	15	10	50	50	525	650
Labor	100	200	100	550	50	1000

that the output, labor, is used as a title instead of the title of the consuming units, households). One can read across a row and find in each column the disposition of the output of that sector. The disposition of the total output of 50 units of fuel is shown by the figures in each column in the row labeled "Fuel."

An input-output table can be constructed on the basis of past records of actual operations of the economy or from knowledge of the technical and engineering requirements of the available techniques for producing each product.

We can show the basic problem of a planner who is concerned with setting future production targets in each sector by looking at this table. (The establishment of such goals is, of course, one of the things the Soviet economic plan does.) Suppose that the planners decide to increase next year the amount of machinery to be made available to the household sector by 20 units. Since the total machinery output is 200 units, this is an increase of 10 percent in the total output of machines. This increase in production will require a 10 percent increase of all of the products needed to make machines: 6.5 units of metal, 0.5 units of fuel, 1 unit of agricultural produce, and 20 units of labor, *plus* 2.5 additional units of machinery (it takes machines to make machines). Thus the other units of inputs into the machine sector will have to be increased by an additional 1.25 percent. But this is only the beginning of the computations. The additional units of metal that are required to make the additional units of machines will require increased inputs into the metal sector of the economy. Thus we can see that a change in just one column in the table requires a change in many other columns. If our planners were trying to set new goals for each of the products used by each of the other sectors, there would be hundreds of computations to make in this simple five-sector economy.

While even this simple illustration seems complex enough, the problem of Soviet planners is unimaginably more complex. Our five-sector input-output table must be replaced by one containing thousands of sectors. (A thousand sector table would have one million entries, although many would consist of zeros.) The computational problem would be impossible if it were not for the development of high-speed electronic computers. Even these, however, could not effectively handle an input-output model that would recognize the need to break down the calculations to particular enterprises within the product classes and economic sectors. In many respects, however, the computational problem is the easy one. It is even more difficult to get the information needed to construct such a table, particularly in a rapidly changing economy where technological developments and increased labor productivity are constantly modifying the input-output relationships. Estimates have to be used, and errors in estimating even a few of the required input-output relationships will generate errors through the system. Inaccuracies of this sort will result in nonfulfillment of an output plan or in a waste of resources or both.

As the planner runs through the computations of the input-output requirements necessary to fulfill a specified final output list, he may well find bottlenecks in the form of shortages of plant capacity, of raw materials or fuels, or of labor. This would call for a recasting of the plan to allocate more resources to break these bottlenecks by increasing investment in the critical areas, which will mean that lower output goals must be planned in the final-goods sectors. Sometimes, indeed, it may not be feasible to provide the inputs called for by a plan, and the goals may have to be adjusted to bring them within the limits imposed by resources and technology.

After the major outlines of the problem of economic decision-making in a planned economy have been laid out, there still remains the question of what administrative structure is to be established to carry out the plan that has been decided upon.

THE ORGANIZATION OF THE ECONOMY

The administrative organization in a planned economy may be set up in various ways. Two obvious alternatives are to use a functional or a geographic division. All firms in a given industry (or related group of industries) may be put under the same top management, or the country may be divided into regions, with every firm in a given region under central direction. The Soviet Union has tried both of these approaches. Until 1957, the former approach was used; since 1957, the latter. A brief sketch of the old organizational system and a review of the reasons why it was changed will point up some of the major difficulties in running a planned economy.

The highest executive body in the Soviet Union is the Council of Ministers, a group roughly comparable to the cabinet in most western countries. Until 1957, there were a large number of industrial ministries in the Council. For example, there was a ministry of heavy machine building, another for ferrous metallurgy, another for the coal industry. All firms in a given industry, no matter where they might be geographically located, were under the direction of the minister. He had the power to issue orders to all plants and organizations within his jurisdiction. Thus each major industry was organized in a huge horizontal monopoly, with a minister in Moscow as the responsible executive official.

Under the Council of Ministers was a kind of economic general staff known as "Gosplan." Gosplan was responsible for drawing up the economic plan for the entire economy. The basic outlines of plans involving the allocation of resources to the armed forces and other government services, the apportionment of investment goods of all kinds, the allocation of consumer goods, and the specification of types and quantities to be produced were determined by the top leaders in the Party. Gosplan was to take these outlines and translate them into explicit terms—to specify how certain resources were to serve certain ends at certain times. Production targets were established for every firm in every industry. Supplies, sources of supplies, amounts of labor, prices of products, and distribution of products were all contained in the economic plan.

This system of organizing the economy had two notable advantages for the regime in the 1930s and 1940s. First, it placed the entire economy under the direct control of the dictator, enabling him (along with his top advisers and confidants), to set the priority of economic goals and to see that they were carried out. Secondly, it proved very effective in the first stages of the industrialization drive when the object was to develop quickly a few major industries. But in the late 1940s and early 1950s, serious problems arising from the overcentralization of decision-making while the economy was growing increasingly complex began to appear.

Three specific problem areas can be identified. The first was that of interindustry supply. The central plan provided for the distribution of the products of any one ministry to the other ministries that had need for them. These other ministries, in turn, redistributed these products to their various producing units. Many problems arose under this arrangement. If an automobile factory failed to receive the necessary amount of electric wire needed to build automobiles, the manager could not legally go to the manager of the plant producing the wire, even if it were only a half mile away. Rather, he would go up his chain of command, eventually to the ministerial level. The minister in charge of automobile factories (or probably someone in his office) would contact the ministry in charge of plants making electric wire in an effort to get delivery on the wire. But what was a major problem to the manager of the auto factory, who saw his assembly lines idle for lack of wire, was likely to be only one of many items on the notepad of the minister in Moscow. Before the manager's complaint passed through the labyrinth of bureaucracy (and par for the course was six months to a year), he would have experienced considerable delay and frustration.

While waiting for his case to be handled by the central authorities, the manager might consider two extralegal or illegal solutions. His auto plant could set up facilities for manufacturing wire, usually at high cost. Or the manager could resort to *blat* (illegal bribing or bartering or the use of "influence" to get the needed supplies). A group of operators called "pushers" (*tolkachi*) who were experts in cutting red tape and getting illegal deliveries grew up outside the official organization. (A genus of the same species evolved in wartime Washington to "expedite" at a price the delivery of scarce supplies.) As the number of firms and products rapidly expanded in the USSR, these kinds of supply problems were magnified enormously.

A second problem had to do more generally with the allocation of the factors of production. Any given pattern of production in a given economy at a given time uses up factors of production in a given ratio. As changes in products are introduced, there is a change in these ratios. In a market economy, the changed demands are quickly reflected by changes in price, and adjustments can be made. But in the Soviet system of centralized planning, prices do not serve this function. The old planning mechanism was too cumbersome to adjust rapidly to changes in the relative scarcity of the factors of production that occur because of changes in products or in the way they are produced. Under such conditions, it was difficult to employ the factors of production in their most efficient combinations.

The third problem area is perhaps just an illustration of how centralization can rapidly become overcentralization. In a centralized decision-making system, there is a tendency for officials at the intermediate and lower levels to avoid responsibility and to buck all decisions up to the top. Problems that could be solved much more adequately closer to the production units were pushed up the chain of command to the central authorities, who either resolved them without considering all the relevant data (ignoring, for example, unique local conditions) or delayed in making a decision.

Not long after Stalin's death penetrating criticisms of the operation of the economy began to appear. At the Twentieth Party Congress (1956), a number of speakers lashed out at the industrial ministries and at economic bungling in general. By the end of 1956, it had become apparent that some downward revisions in the goals of the sixth five-year plan were necessary, and quotas were modified accordingly.

Then dramatically in early 1957, Khrushchev pushed through a program of economic reorganization. Most of the old industrial ministries were dissolved (the notable exceptions being those for transportation, power, fuels, and some branches of industry, particularly heavy industry) and the economy was reorganized on a regional basis. Just over 100 economic regions were established and virtually all of the industry in each region came under the control of an economic council (*sovnarkhoz*). In other words, most of the great horizontal monopolies were broken up and replaced by a series of vertical monopolies based on a geographical division. Planning remained centralized under the direct control of the Council of Ministers, but the reorganization did bring about a decentralization of the structure for controlling the execution of the plan, as well as for the preliminary preparation of the plan for the next period. Some Soviet economists suggested that the development of the "regional approach" to economic planning and administration was a natural outgrowth of recent historical developments.

The transfer of movable equipment to the new industrial areas east of the Urals in the face of the advancing German armies in World War II gave an additional spurt to these developing industrial complexes. The reconstruction of the transferred plants and their integration into the existing facilities of the new areas had be done quickly and on the spot, under the war conditions of the time. This forced and purely temporary decentralization of major decisions had two important consequences. It gave a large number of planners and managers the experience of decentralized operations and decision-making, and it demonstrated the operational advantages of such a basic structure of organization.

At the end of the war, power and control were again centered in Moscow and the lesson seemed lost. But after the reconstruction period from 1945 to 1950, industry resumed its rapid growth trend. The emerging rapid expansion and growing complexity led the regime to consider the use of a wider degree of geographical decentralization in the control structure and to use areas or districts, rather than industries or industry groups, as the organizational units for operational control.

Some American observers have suggested that, in addition to the managerial reasons for the shift, there may have been internal political reasons for Khrushchev's decision. The dismemberment of most of the economic ministries in Moscow and the assignment of large numbers of the former ministry executive and staff personnel to the some 100 newly formed councils of the national economy could have been a power play on his part to reduce the influence of the economic apparatus in Moscow in his struggle to remove possible polictical opponents and to firmly establish his complete personal control, which was based largely on his position in the Party apparatus.

For whatever reasons the decision was made, however, it has had the effect of partially solving some problems and raising other problems to new importance; and it certainly led to a great rise in the morale and feeling of effectiveness of operating managers in the Soviet Union.

As Khrushchev's reform has worked out thus far, the new organization seems to have contributed to the easing of a number of problems that had plagued the economy. First, it has increased the speed of making certain economic decisions at the intermediate and lower levels. The managers of the factories are in direct daily contact with *sovnarkhoz* officials in the region, who in turn have wider contacts higher in the administrative hierarchy. Second, within a given economic region, the problem of inter-industry supply has been alleviated. If, for example, an automobile factory needs more electric wire, the *sovnarkhoz* can expedite delivery if the wire factory is in its area. Third, some flexibility in the allocation of capital has been introduced at the regional level. Specific decisions for some plant expansion are not tied as closely to the central economic plan as they were previously, and the local councils may reassign and modify to a degree the original allocations. This means that if probable supply problems can be estimated at the local level, some local action can be taken to take care of this difficulty before it seriously hampers production. Fourth, there has been some reduction in the amount of wasteful long-distance transportation of commodities, since there is greater pressure now to use local, rather than distant, sources of supply.

All four of these improvements, it should be noted, derive from one basic consequence of the reorganization: the increased discretionary power that is given to economic managers at intermediate and local levels. Managers are less closely tied to plans made by remote bureaucrats and are somewhat more able to solve local administrative problems on the basis of their skills, initiative, and detailed knowledge of the local situation.

While the economic reorganization has contributed to the alleviation of some problems, difficulties of a different sort have already begun to emerge, and these pose a threat to the efficient operation of the economy. The first and most significant of these problems is the pressure to achieve economic self-sufficiency (*autarky*) that seems to develop within a region. As is perhaps the case in any vertical monopoly, there is a natural desire on the part of the regional authorities to free themselves from dependence upon outside supply sources over which they have no effective control. The *sovnarkhoz* in the city of Moscow, for example, experienced difficulty in getting shipments of polyethelene from a factory in Stalingrad, which is, of course, under the jurisdiction of another *sovnarkhoz*. The solution of the Moscow *sovnarkhoz* was to allocate capital for a new polyethelene factory within its own economic region. The overwhelming factor in this decision was the supply problem in Moscow; little thought was given to the question of whether Moscow was the best location for such a plant, or whether, in terms of the entire economy, this was the best use of capital. This tendency toward self-sufficiency may, of course, lead to serious supply problems of an inter-regional nature. A local *sovnarkhoz*, for example, may prefer to hoard certain supplies in anticipation of shortages rather than to ship them to a plant in another economic region, particularly if it is receiving no important supplies from that region.

The program of economic reorganization may also bring about some modification in the general pattern of control in the Soviet economy. The increased administrative authority granted to economic managers at the regional and lower levels may make it somewhat more difficult for the top political leaders to direct all aspects of economic endeavor from the center, except as they are able to maintain this control through the regional organization of the Party, especially the regional Communist secretary. The regional councils (*sovnarkhozy*), which are much closer to the specific problems of their localities, may be more sensitive to local demands for consumer goods than were the industrial ministries in Moscow.

The program of economic reorganization has thus led to an improvement of interindustry and interfirm integration within given economic regions, at the expense of the integration of firms and industries in the national economy. The problem is further complicated because some industries remain under the old ministerial type of organization. Lack of integration will undoubtedly hamper the Soviet economy as a whole unless the regime is able to develop a basis for unifying the economies of the various regions.

The Soviet leaders have already experimented with several devices to provide this integration. One is the establishment directly under the Council of Ministers of a group of "industry" committees that parallel the old industrial ministries, but that have merely advisory rather than executive powers. Some *sovnarkhozy*, however, have tended to resist the advice of the committees when it runs counter to strong local interests.

The supervision of the republic councils of ministers (in those republics containing more than one regional council) as a way of effectively supervising intercouncil supply problems seems not to have succeeded, for in mid-1961 an intermediate supervisory level (councils for coordination and planning) was established in each of 17 newly created large economic regions to supervise and coordinate the work of the *sovnarkhozy* of their regions. Again, these are to be largely advisory and recommending bodies, whose recommendations, in turn, would go to the republic and all-Union planning and control agencies.

The most important technique for developing inter-regional integration is, of course, the central economic plan that is developed by staff agencies and put into force by the Council of Ministers. But if the plan is to be effective in securing the integration required, it must be so detailed and specific that it removes much of the discretionary power recently granted to the *sovnarkhozy*. Should this occur, the integration will have been achieved at the expense of interfirm and interindustry relations at the regional level, inviting the rise of problems that led to the economic reorganization in the first place.

An alternative to these moves to look for organizational solutions would be to develop a system of economic incentives that would induce *sovnarkhoz* officials and plant managers to make decisions that would be good not only for their local regions but for the national economy as well. The incentives would have to be devised in such a way as to limit the tendency toward local self-sufficiency where this interferes with national efficiency and to stimulate officials at all levels of the hierarchy to be more sensitive to the welfare of the economy as a whole.

IS THERE A SUBSTITUTE FOR THE MARKET?

The Soviet Union is certainly not going to adopt, in the foreseeable future, all the features of a market system. Economic priorities will still be set by the political leaders in Moscow. But if the maturing economy is to achieve the level of efficiency necessary to maintain growth rates in the seven to nine percent range, the regime may have to borrow some of the techniques of the market system to provide rapid, accurate information on the relative scarcity of the factors of production. In other words, some type of pricing system will have to be developed in which prices reflect relative scarcity and real costs of production.

The Communist rulers have already taken a few timid steps in this direction. The freeing of the collective farms from the compulsory delivery of produce is one example. The farm manager has the option of selling produce in a market, and thus prices in the market to some degree affect his planting and investment decisions—to the extent that he is permitted to exercise any discretion. The manipulation of market prices by the planners may thus to some degree replace "the plan" as the main directive over the farmers.

In many ways, a more interesting adaptation has been in the consumer goods sector of the economy. In the past, the typical manner in which the USSR planned the distribution of consumer goods was to estimate net disposable income in each republic and to provide the amount of consumer goods and/or to set the prices in such a way as to absorb this income. There was only the crudest concern for product mix and none at all for individual differences in tastes and styles. This method proved effective in an austere economy, in which consumer goods were so short in supply that the consumers had little alternative to accepting what was available. As incomes rose and as larger quantities of goods became available, however, consumers could afford to be more discriminating. A woman with enough clothes to meet her basic needs might save her money and wait until the dress style she wanted became available. A man could afford to be more particular about the quality and style of a suit. The result was that although most types of consumer goods remained scarce, some embarrassing surpluses began to appear. Indeed, certain products scarcely moved off the shelves.

In order to correct this situation, the system was modified. Now retail trade officials in the several republics are beginning to *order* the consumer goods they want from the producers or wholesalers, rather than merely distributing the goods sent to them on the basis of the economic plan. At this point, however, the retail-trade officials begin to encounter some of the fundamentals of a freshman course in the economics of the market. Since demand depends on price, the suit that will barely sell for 100 rubles may sell very well at 50. The retail-trade officials, to make the new approach an improvement, must have some device for measuring consumer demand and determining its elasticity for a wide range of products. The best and most efficient way (perhaps the only adequate way) of obtaining measures of these factors is through a market in which the consumer can use his "ruble ballot," and in which the prices are permitted to respond to supply and demand.

By 1961 surpluses in certain capital goods were also beginning to appear. The obvious solution to this problem would also be to allow factory management and *sovnarkhoz* officials to bid for their own capital goods. Here again certain elements of a market would have to be introduced to facilitate the making of a rational choice. But a decision on which capital goods should be purchased involves a consideration that is rarely present in a consumer-goods transaction; there is a range of alternative choices that would involve a different mix of capital and manpower, according to the production process in which the capital goods are to be used. The manager will want to choose the most efficient mix, but what criteria does he have to guide him?

A simple case will illustrate the problem. Suppose the *sovnarkhoz* in a region having an iron and steel complex decides to open a new iron mine and must provide for transporting the ore to the furnaces. The alternatives might be an electrified railway, a steam railway, or a road to accommodate heavy-duty trucks. Let us assume that the initial cost for the electric railway is 12,500,000 rubles; for the steam railway, 5,000,000 rubles; and for the truck highway (including the trucks), 2,000,000 rubles. The annual operating costs (including depreciation) of the electric railway are 250,000 rubles; of the steam railway, 750,000 rubles; and of the truck highway, 1,000,000 rubles. Which alternative is the most rational and efficient? One can answer this question if he knows the marginal costs of capital in the economy. In a market economy, interest rates provide a good measure of such costs.

Not only is there nothing really comparable in the Soviet economy, but Soviet rulers have steadfastly refused to accept the idea of interest rates, regarding them as a feature of the exploitative capitalistic system. One of the fundamental themes of classical Marxist doctrine, to which lip service is still being paid, is the labor theory of value. The official ideology, in other words, denies that there can be anything like a cost of capital. If capital "costs nothing" in investment decisions, capital costs tend in fact to become enormous. This is one of the reasons for the "gigantomania" that is so characteristic of many Soviet productive enterprises. If the economy is to reach optimal efficiency, capital costs will have to be calculated as a part of investment decisions. If they are to be calculated, they must be measured. If they are to be measured, there is no really good substitute for introducing the concept of interest rates, which, in turn, must be sensitive to supplies of and demands for capital if they are to be reliable guides in decision-making.

In short, we are arguing that if the Soviet economy, rapidly increasing in complexity, is to achieve the efficiency necessary for continuing rapid economic growth, certain characteristics of the market will have to be introduced to provide reliable guides for rational economic decisions. The market, however, is not an "automatic" decision-making system. Knowing how to use the information derived from market operations requires the professional skills of the economist or of the western type businessman more than it does the talents of the successful bureaucrat or politician. For the intricate economic machine to operate efficiently, economic decision-making will probably have to become the job of economic managers rather than of politicians. The price the political elite may have to pay for economic efficiency is the diminution of some of their control over the economy.

Khrushchev has shown a strong pragmatic bent. To him the critical question is, Will it work? This has led him to steer the whole Soviet system, and particularly its economic system, in directions far from those indicated by Marx and Lenin.

The strength of the income incentive in persuading men to work effectively seems to have so impressed him that he told the Twenty-second Party Congress in 1961 that the present "socialist" rule (Article 12 of the Soviet Constitution)—"Work in the USSR is a duty and a matter of honor for every able-bodied citizen in accordance with the principle: 'He who does not work, neither shall he eat' "—would continue as a supreme principle under Communism as well.

Given this strong practical approach, the current Soviet regime may well permit or even encourage moves in the direction of a decentralized and partly market-controlled economy that will be heretical to the ideological Communists.

THE OUTCOME OF THE ECONOMIC RACE

Given the apparent military stalemate created by mutual atomic deterrence, Khrushchev and his associates have challenged the United States to an economic race. Their industrial resources and manpower seem sufficient to permit them to realize their objective; only in agriculture is the paucity of resources likely to handicap their efforts.

The western observer must not underestimate the effectiveness of a directed economy as a means of maintaining rapid growth. The ability of its rulers to force heavy investment of resources into physical and human capital at the expense of current living standards may be the critical advantage of the USSR over the consumer-directed economy of the United States and may enable the USSR to win eventually any straight contest for industrial or economic output.

The programs that the Soviet regime may have to adopt in order to win such a race, however, may in time have great impact upon the structure of Communist control over the society. We have suggested that the problems of maintaining and measuring economic efficiency in a mature economy may ultimately call for the adoption of a decentralized and, to a significant degree, market-controlled economic organization. The discussion of "synthetic" or "shadow" prices in the context of mathematical-economic analysis of economic problems by Soviet economists themselves; the use of prices rather than the plan to control and direct agricultural production; the struggle to find some "true measure" of economic costs of production; and the continued emphasis on the further decentralization of economic decision-making in the Party Program for the Twenty-second Party Congress—all these give some indication that modifications in the economic machinery may be in process. The state will undoubtedly retain ownership of the basic resources and monopoly over all economic enterprises; what is suggested here is that the *means* of control may move toward a modified market system.

If this development occurs to any significant extent, it will lead to a further strengthening of the use of economic incentives for the workers and a consequent further rise in the influence of the consumer in the system. It will also tend to attach greater importance to successful decentralized "managers" rather than to the central "planners" as key personnel in the economic system. Shifts in the locus of decision-making away from the center in the economic sphere may even be accompanied by changes in the pattern of control in other areas of Soviet life. Whether in fact such developments take place depends upon the way in which the Party moves to maintain its power. Khrushchev may discover, however, that the type of people upon whom he must depend in the economic race have a different political and psychological outlook from those of the ordinary Communist functionary. If this is true, and if such personnel begin to gain a bigger voice in decision-making, the structure of the dictatorship itself may undergo some modification over time.

If the Soviet desire to catch up with the United States in economic production is given a high enough priority, the USSR, by mobilizing its resources efficiently, may achieve this objective over a period of years. But the very *means* required for the Soviet Union to make a good showing in the race may eventually lead to alterations in the traditional structure of Communist power—changes in a direction that would be welcomed in the United States, regardless of who is declared winner in the contest for greater production.

The partial transfer of the international struggle to the economic arena may thus have some hopeful aspects. We should not overlook the fact, however, that one reason that the Soviets are pushing so hard in this economic race is that they are convinced that by "winning" they will have created a nonmilitary means of achieving their objective of world domination that cannot be countered effectively by the United States and its allies.

4

THE FARM PROBLEM
À LA RUSSE

Philip M. Raup

Professor of Agricultural Economics at the University of Minnesota, Philip M. Raup has for many years devoted himself to land economics and economic problems of world agriculture. He served in the agricultural branch of our military government in Germany until 1949, and has been a consultant to the UN and its agencies. His study trips abroad in 1955, 1958, and 1961 included a research sojourn in the USSR.

Agriculture must baffle Soviet planners, for it is almost the only sector of their economic life in which a persistent element of private enterprise continues. Tied as it is to the land, agricultural production has eluded efforts of central planners to concentrate decision-making and control in a few key places and planning offices. Given its biological base, it is perversely unresponsive to many of the shock-brigade tactics that figure so prominently in Soviet campaigns to "overfulfill the plan."

Where these tactics can be applied, the USSR has scored some notable results. The collectivization drive of the late 1920s and early 1930s was one of the boldest (and bloodiest) efforts ever attempted to alter the structure of a primitive agricultural economy. In a twisted sense it succeeded, but at a terrible cost, for which the final reckoning has yet to be made.

A parallel effort, begun in the early 1950s and accelerated after Stalin's death, involved opening up the vast frontiers of the virgin-land areas south of the Urals, across northern Kazakhstan and into Siberia. This, too, succeeded. Between 1953 and 1960 113 million acres were added to the crop-land area of the USSR. This increase, greater than the total crop-land area of Canada and almost twice as large as the acreage of crop land in Australia, was largely achieved in the three years from 1953 to 1956. As an exercise in sod-breaking, it has no equal. As a sample of Soviet agrarian planning, it typifies both the strengths and the weaknesses of a policy constructed out of large and crude blocks of land, people, and ideas.

In spite of heroic efforts to expand crop land and raise farm output, the USSR has today what must surely be the dullest diet of any industrial state. Soviet data for 1958 indicate that 62 percent of the total calorie value of all food came from bread products and potatoes. In no country of western Europe do bread and potatoes figure so prominently in the diet. Only in Greece, Italy, and Portugal did they account for more than half of total calories in 1959.

Even more revealing is the fact that dietary goals for the conclusion of the seven-year plan in 1965 would reduce the share of bread and potato calories to only 46 percent, and it is highly unlikely that this can be achieved. This target figure is higher than that prevailing in the US from 1909 to 1913, when 42 percent of our calories came from cereals and potatoes. It is almost twice as large as the 24 percent contributed to the average American daily food intake by bread and potatoes in 1960.

The most likely prospect thus facing the Soviet consumer in 1965 is a dietary composition no better than that of the poorest-fed nations of Mediterranean Europe in the 1950s and appreciably below that prevailing in the United States 50 years ago.

The contrast between Soviet achievements in agriculture and those in industry is striking. The lead in heavy industry and lag in agriculture reflects a systematic exploitation of the rural population stretching back over more than three decades. The neglect of agriculture can be traced in part to the origins of the Communist movement and the attitude of early Communist leaders toward the peasant. Marxian philosophy was conceived in the heavily industrialized sectors of western Europe, tailored for an urban society, and given its first application in Russia, a backward, agrarian country. Marx himself was a city boy who never fully understood the problems of peasant life. Although Lenin and other Russian leaders shared Marx's distrust of the peasant, they saw that he could be used as a tool in the Bolshevik drive for power, and they fashioned revolutionary slogans to appeal to the peasant's age-old desire for land. The exploitation of the peasantry that began with the regime's ride to power on rural land hunger has continued to the present.

Following the consolidation of Communist power, the mid-1920s were characterized by a bitter internal Party struggle over what policies should be followed to achieve the maximum rate of economic growth. The policy that emerged was compounded of fear and hope. The fear was that the peasants, by withholding food from the cities, could exercise a veto on Soviet industrialization plans. The hope was that agriculture could yield the major contributions of capital and new wealth required in the forced-draft creation of an industrial state. The major instrument of this policy was the collectivization drive in 1929, inaugurating a quarter century of effort to extract the maximum "tribute" from agriculture at the lowest possible price.

By confiscating individual farmsteads and forcing the peasants into collective and state farms, the Bolsheviks set up machinery for the compulsory requisition of agricultural products and for curbing anti-Party opposition among the agrarian population. The result was near disaster. When peasants resisted collectivization, the regime resorted to coercive measures, and literally millions of people lost their lives. Production fell rapidly, as farmers left their crops untended or unsown and killed their livestock. In later years Stalin reportedly observed that the struggles of World War II did not pose as grave a threat to the Soviet regime as did the collectivization drive that convulsed the country in the early 1930s.

Although the program of collectivization eventually succeeded in eliminating nearly all of the individual farmers, Soviet agriculture emerged from the decade of the 1930s in a greatly weakened condition. By 1939 total grain output had returned to the precollectivization levels of 1928, but the proportion of animal products in the diet had fallen sharply. Total cattle numbers in 1939 were 20 percent below the 1928 figure, while dairy cows were 28 percent below. Milk availability in 1939 was only 73 percent and meat availability only 70 percent of the precollectivization levels.

World War II brought new crises in agriculture, draining the industry of manpower and devastating rich farm areas of European Russia. After the war rural exploitation continued through the policy of compulsory deliveries of farm produce to the state at low prices, paralleled by a policy of systematic underinvestment in the maintenance of the agricultural plant. Stalin resisted efforts to improve agriculture, showing little awareness that the initial capital creating potential had been exhausted and that low agricultural productivity was becoming a major barrier to further industrial growth. Policy under Stalin was antagonistic and exploitative toward agriculture, and the results of this policy are clearly visible today.

POST-STALIN REFORMS IN AGRICULTURE

The men who came to power after Stalin's death soon recognized that agriculture was a serious handicap to the growth of the Soviet economy, and they introduced policies to improve farm productivity. In both short- and long-run consequences, perhaps the most significant reform was the abolition of compulsory deliveries of farm products at artifically low prices. Between 1953 and 1956, prices for major farm products were increased, in some cases by more than five times their previous levels. Subsequent increases lifted prices in 1959 and 1960 to an overall level that averaged three times as high as that prevailing in 1953.

This policy of price increases was continued into 1962 when on June 1, prices paid for livestock products and poultry were increased 35 percent. The implications of the most recent increases are of particular interest because they are the only ones unmistakably associated with accompanying increases in consumer prices, averaging 30 percent for meat and meat products and 25 percent for butter. This shift in policy has had an important effect. In the past, the delivery of farm products to the state was achieved primarily through coercive methods. Farm managers who failed to make their deliveries were threatened with penal action, and the regime exerted additional controls by allocating tractors, farm machinery, and supplies through centrally directed machine and tractor stations. Since Stalin's death these measures have been partially replaced by price incentives. Mandatory deliveries remain, but higher prices have introduced this generation of farm managers to monetary incentives to an extent unknown in the past. Their response will be decisive for the course of agricultural productivity in the years ahead.

From the beginning of the collective farm system, the basic unit for reckoning labor wages on the farms has been the workday unit (*trudoden*). In its original conception, the collective farm, or *kolkhoz*, was based on the principle that the collective farmers as a group are owners of the land and inventory. Their income represents their share of the net profits of the farm, after operating costs and taxes and allocations to financial reserve funds have been paid. The workday unit is the device by which the net return is divided among the labor force in accordance with the amount and importance of the work done.

In contrast, the state farm, or *sovkhoz*, is based on the principle that the state is the full owner of the land, livestock, and equipment. The farm workers are regarded as an industrial labor force and are paid a a wage expressed in money terms (although part of it may be paid in kind), without making use of the workday unit.

On the collective farm, each task was classified and rated in terms of a fraction or multiple of the workday unit. A milkmaid, for example, might receive 1.4 workday units for every 100 liters of milk from the cows in her care; at the height of the season, a tractor driver might receive six or eight workday units for land plowed in one work day; and a pigmaid might receive eight workday units for each 100 kilograms of gain on the pigs under her supervision. The farm laborer's accumulated entitlement for the month (or the year) was the sum of these workday units credited to his account. Each unit carried a right to payment in kind, commonly in terms of bread grain, potatoes, and fodder grain, plus a small monetary equivalent, typically ranging from a few kopecks to one or two rubles. The cash settlement was usually made at the end of the year. As a result of the higher prices for farm products, it has been possible to increase the monetary value of the workday unit. In some cases it was raised to three or four times the previous levels, and a higher proportion of the income has been distributed in cash and at monthly intervals. The peasant has thus enjoyed a substantial increase in money wages.

An equally radical innovation in the traditional organization of the collective farms was begun in January 1958, when Khrushchev announced that the machine and tractor stations were to be eliminated. Since their organization early in the collectivization drive, these stations had remained under the direct control of the central government and had played a key role in the structure of political and economic power in the countryside. The original shortages of agricultural machinery and trained agricultural specialists made it impossible to provide every collective farm with the necessary equipment and technical personnel. By concentrating resources in the machine and tractor stations, the needs of several collectives could more readily be serviced from a central point. Government control of the stations also reflected the regime's distrust of the peasant's political loyalty and of his mechanical ability to care for farm machinery and operate it efficiently.

Following Khrushchev's announcement in January 1958, a formal decree in June outlined the procedures for the dissolution of the machine and tractor stations. Individual collective farms were permitted to buy the farm equipment and to spread their payments over several crop years. Tractor drivers and service personnel, who had been assigned to the stations since 1953, were incorporated into the labor force of the collective farms. Specialists in animal production, soils, and field crops were attached to government committees in the local districts, which work closely with the regional economic councils established under Khrushchev's program of industrial reorganization.

The aim of this reform was to consolidate responsibility for production under a single manager at the collective farm level. The division of responsibility between the collective farm and the machine and tractor station had become one of the weakest links in the agricultural chain, leading, in Khrushchev's phrase, to two masters in the same field. The remedy was drastic. There were 7,903 machine tractor stations in 1957; on January 1, 1961 there were 23.

One of the most dramatic phases of agricultural development in the Soviet Union has been the program for bringing the "virgin lands" under cultivation. This program started under Stalin but it was greatly accelerated after his death in 1953. Although 27 million acres were added to the sown area between 1950 and 1953, a part of this increase represented the resumption of cultivation that had been disrupted by the war. The major virgin-land effort came in the period from 1954 to 1957, when 90 million acres were placed under cultivation. An additional 23 million acres were added between 1957 and 1960. Thus in ten years Soviet crop lands were increased by 140 million acres, or more than 38 percent. Many of these lands, however, are in semiarid regions of Kazakhstan and Siberia, which are characterized by drought, early frost, low yields, and high year-to-year fluctuations. Variation in spring wheat yields in Kazakhstan, for example, is similar to that of the highest risk counties of North Dakota and Montana, and the level of yields is much lower.

The decade of the 1950s has also seen the consolidation of the collective farms into much larger units, with a resulting sharp decline in the number of farms. The number of collectives shot up in the early 1930s, rose more slowly to 1939, and declined during the war years. After the war the number increased, and by 1950 there were 252,000 collectives. In that year a drastic program of consolidation was undertaken, reducing the number of units to 123,700 in 12 months. As the policy of "super-collectivization" continued, the number of collective farms was further reduced to 85,600 in 1955, 67,700 in 1958, and 44,000 by January 1, 1961.

Along with the policy of fewer and bigger collective farms, the Soviet regime has increased the number of state farms, chiefly by establishing them in the virgin-lands areas and partly by converting collective farms to state farms in the older, more stable agricultural sections. From 4,988 in 1950, the number of state farms increased to 7,375 at the beginning of 1961, when they embraced one-third of the sown area of the USSR.

The resulting farms are truly huge. The average collective farm in 1960 included 15,600 acres, of which 7,350 acres, or over 11 square miles, represented cultivated land. The average size of state farms was 65,000 acres, with 22,000 acres, or 34 square miles, under cultivation.

The Soviet Union today has approximately 52,000 farm units, both collective and state, covering an estimated 502 million acres of crop land. In contrast, the United States in 1959 had 3.7 million farms and 329 million acres of cropped land. The USSR operates an acreage of crop land about 52 percent larger than that of the United States, with fewer farm units than there are in the state of North Dakota.

Simultaneously with consolidation of collective farms and expansion of state farms, there was a major shift in the balance among the various enterprises on Soviet farms. The tractor and the combine had traditionally been the symbols of an agriculture oriented around the production of grain crops. Foreign visitors and students of the Soviet economy had long observed that animal husbandry was one of the most neglected areas. Major fractions of the output of meat, milk, and poultry products were provided by the private sales of produce from the household plots of individual peasants. (These "private" tracts typically range from one-half to two and one-half acres in size.) Dairy production was especially disappointing. From 1948 to 1952, the number of milk cows had remained relatively constant at about 24 million head, well below the 33 million in 1928. Meat supplies were similarly low, never having returned to the per capita levels of prerevolutionary days.

It was in this setting that Khrushchev introduced his famous corn program, with subsequent emphasis on reduced acreages in oats and hay crops and increases in fodder crops and feed grains. After 1955, the planting of corn became a major criterion by which the regime judged the Party loyalty of farm managers. Other changes were also recommended to farm managers. After 1960, another test of Party regularity, if not of agronomic wisdom, included the shifting of land out of oats and grasses into continuous cropping. Price increases were also used to try to stimulate production. Prices received by producers for livestock products had been increased over fivefold between 1952 and 1960 and were increased an additional 35 percent in 1962. New emphasis was given to an increase in wage differentiation among collective farm workers, with piecework bonuses used liberally for the workers in animal enterprises. In the ten years from 1953 to 1962 the Soviet agricultural economy underwent a major transformation, from one dominated by a focus on extensive grain farming to an economy in which animal husbandry is playing the favored role.

CURRENT OBJECTIVES OF SOVIET AGRICULTURE

Shifts in agricultural policy after 1953 marked the beginning of a two-pronged drive: (1) to increase food supplies available to the cities

MAP I. THE MOSCOW METROPOLIS AND ITS ENVIRONS

The broad concentric zones of the city, as they are described in Chapter 2, are apparent on the map. There is the greatly improved and rebuilt area from the Kremlin outward to the Sadovaya (ring boulevard). Between the Sadovaya and the inner belt of railway lines and terminals lies the older, less redeveloped part of the city. Beyond that, massive new apartments, gardens, and enveloped, old villages spread to the limits of the built-up area. Between the present developed area and the city limits there is ample room for future growth. The environs outside the city limits are zoned as a greenbelt; future urban development there will be restricted.

MAP II. MAJOR URBAN CENTERS, AGRICULTURAL AND INDUSTRIAL REGIONS

The map shows that most of the great cities of the Soviet Union are in the so-called "Fertile Triangle" (Chapter 4, p. 100), which is also the agricultural heart of the USSR. Within the Triangle a number of major centers are clustered in four great industrial regions (Chapter 3, p. 55). Easily recognized are the central industrial region around Moscow; the eastern Ukraine industrial region centered roughly on Donetsk; the Urals region including Perm, Sverdlovsk, and Magnitogorsk; and the west Siberian industrial region, with its metropolis at Novosibirsk. Large cities outside the Triangle are in the valleys of the Causasus Mountains between the Black and Caspian Seas, in the cotton-growing irrigated oasis region of Soviet Middle Asia, or along the slender strand of the trans-Siberian railway between Krasnoyarsk and the Pacific Ocean at Vladivostok.

MAP III. THE NATURAL VEGETATION ZONES OF THE USSR

The tundra and desert regions are very sparsely settled and of little use. The vast taiga, while thinly settled and of very limited value for farming, contains a vast resource of timber. Comparison with Map II shows clearly that the agricultural land is developed mainly in clearings in the mixed forest (mainly birch, pine and oak) and on the treeless steppe (grassland). Note on Map II the location of the new lands of the post-Stalin era. Map III shows that location to be very near the edge of the desert.

(Maps drawn by Mark Anderson, Deparment of Geography, University of Minnesota)

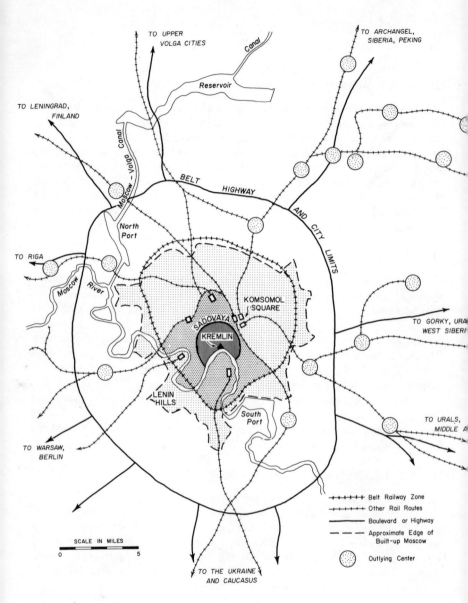

TO UPPER
VOLGA CITIES

Canal

TO ARCHANGEL,
SIBERIA, PEKING

Reservoir

TO LENINGRAD,
FINLAND

BELT   HIGHWAY

Moscow – Volga Canal

North
Port

AND CITY LIMITS

TO RIGA

Moscow River

Sadovaya

KOMSOMOL
SQUARE

KREMLIN

TO GORKY, URA
WEST SIBERI

LENIN
HILLS

South
Port

TO URALS,
MIDDLE A

TO WARSAW,
BERLIN

+++++++ Belt Railway Zone

+++++ Other Rail Routes

Boulevard or Highway

Approximate Edge of
Built-up Moscow

Outlying Center

SCALE IN MILES
0   5

TO THE UKRAINE
AND CAUCASUS

MAP I

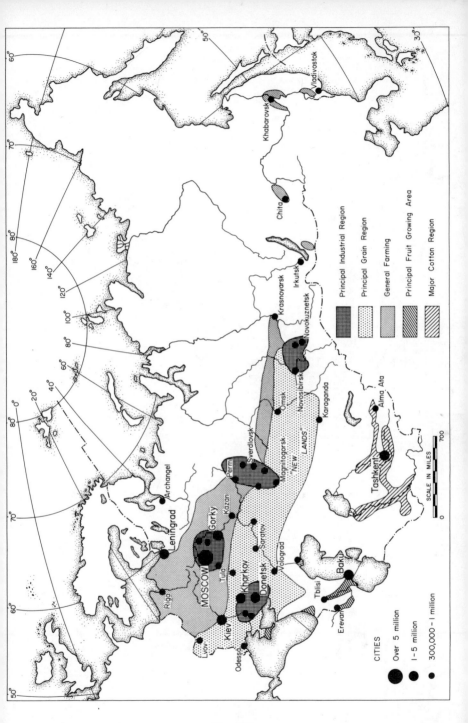

Principal Industrial Region
Principal Grain Region
General Farming
Principal Fruit Growing Area
Major Cotton Region

SCALE IN MILES

0   700

CITIES

Over 5 million

1 – 5 million

300,000 – 1 million

Vladivostok

Khabarovsk

Chita

Irkutsk

Krasnoyarsk

Novokuznetsk

Novosibirsk

Omsk

Karaganda

Alma Ata

Tashkent

"NEW LANDS"

Magnitogorsk

Sverdlovsk

Perm

Kazan

Gorky

Baku

Erevan

Tbilisi

Volograd

Saratov

Donetsk

Kharkov

Tula

MOSCOW

Kiev

Odessa

Lvov

Riga

Leningrad

Archangel

MAP II

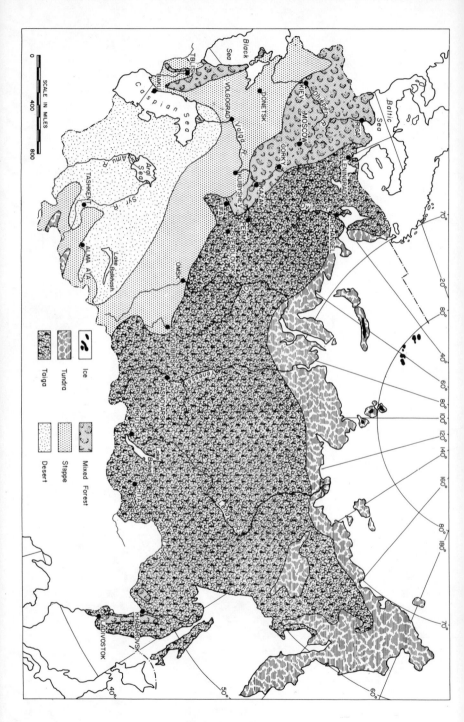

MAP III

and (2) to improve rural standards of living. These goals are to be realized by raising the critically low levels of physical output and labor productivity that have long impeded the development of Soviet agriculture. In dramatizing the task, Khrushchev outlined a program that was designed to make the USSR reach and surpass the United States in the per capita production of meat, milk, and butter.

The agricultural goals that have been set for the immediate future are hardly modest. In broad terms Khrushchev called for a 70 percent increase in total farm output between 1958 and 1965. While the key slogans of the propaganda campaigns have been built around the production of meat, milk, and butter, the grains and fodder crops still play a central role in the total planned output of foods and feeding stuffs.

For food grains, the 1965 target figure is set at a minimum of 164 million metric tons—about 31 percent higher than the 125 million metric tons harvested on the average during the three years from 1956 to 1958. With a currently adequate bread-grain supply, the 1965 target figures for grain emphasize fodder and feed grain output. While corn for fodder and ensilage continues to receive primary emphasis, it is significant that the targets for grain output apparently contemplate an increase in the production of corn for grain.

Projected increases in other important agricultural products are summarized in Table 4-1.

Since Khrushchev has chosen meat, milk, and butter as the symbols

TABLE 4-1

Product	Planned Output for 1965 as a Percentage of the Base Year	
	Base Year	1965 Target
Raw cotton	1957	135-145%
Sugar beets	1957	180-200
Oil seeds	1957	170
Flax fiber	1957	132
Potatoes	1957	167
Meat (slaughter weight)	1958	200
Milk	1958	170-180
Wool	1958	170
Eggs	1958	160

for his campaign to overtake the United States, it is instructive to compare the per capita availability of these items in the United States and the USSR as of 1956, before the current seven-year plan went into effect (Table 4-2).

TABLE 4-2

| | Per Capita Production, 1956 (Soviet Data) | |
Item	US	USSR
	in Kilograms	
Meat	102.3	32.3
Milk	343.0	245.0
Factory butter	3.8	2.8

For the Soviet Union to have matched the American levels of production in 1956 would have required 3.2 times *more* meat per capita, 40 percent more milk, and 36 percent more butter.

The butter figure provides a good illustration of the misleading inferences that can be drawn from comparisons of this kind. The trend in the per capita consumption of butter in the United States is downward and is augmented by a per capita consumption of margarine that exceeds that of butter. Only one third of total United States consumption of fats and oils is in the form of butter and margarine, with over half of total consumption in the form of shortening, salad oils, and the like. The Soviet consumption of margarine, on the other hand, is reportedly 30 percent below the butter consumption level, per capita. Thus, in comparing American and Soviet production, total fat availabilities are much more divergent than is indicated by the figures on butter alone.

The planned increase in Soviet meat availability to 16 million metric tons by 1965 is more than double the 1958 level and still below the amount needed to match current per capita consumption in the United States. While the USSR may conceivably be able to reach its goal in dairy products, the problem of increasing meat production is much more difficult.

Soviet technicians in 1958 clearly had doubts about their chances of reaching the 1965 targets for meat. In the meantime these chances have virtually disappeared. Official data report meat production of 8.8 million metric tons (slaughter weight) in 1961, only about 14 percent above 1958 and below the 8.9 million tons reported for 1959. The seven-year plan called for a doubling of meat production by 1965. Since 1959, meat production has failed to keep abreast of population growth. This helps explain why 1980 has replaced 1965 as the target date for the revised agricultural planning incorporated into the program adopted by the Twenty-second Party Congress in 1961.

Despite the enormity of the task, Soviet rulers are engaging in an impressive effort to realize their agricultural objectives. Their efficient propaganda machine has been carefully geared to arouse the rural population to increased productivity. Posters and billboards on farms and in the villages exhort the peasants to "overtake and surpass" the United States. Technical journals are full of articles of self-criticism that examine the barriers that must be removed if the 1965 goals are to be achieved. The curriculum in agricultural academies includes a seminar topic entitled "We Must in the Shortest Possible Time Exceed the United States of America in the Production of Meat, Milk, and Butter Per Capita." Matchbox covers are adorned with the picture of an ear of corn and the slogan, "Corn, the Wellspring of Abundance."

What are the prospects for achieving these goals? To answer this question we must examine key factors that affect the relative efficiency of agriculture. First, a look at the "physical plant"—the quality and degree of mechanization, the productivity of the land, the availability of fertilizers, and so forth. Second, we must analyze the organization of Soviet agriculture, since the institutional arrangement of an industry has an important effect upon productivity. And third, we must study some of the political factors, which in the Soviet Union play a significant role in determining economic policies.

THE "PHYSICAL PLANT" OF SOVIET AGRICULTURE

Although the Soviet Union is the largest country in the world, it is not endowed with rich agricultural land. The vast land mass is virtually split down the middle by the Yenisey River. To the east of the Yenisey the land is rough, hilly, or mountainous. To the west lies the world's largest plain, which, interrupted only by the Urals, spreads beyond the western boundary of the USSR to the Atlantic Ocean. The land itself is divided into five general regions. In the far north is the open wasteland of the tundra, frozen ten or eleven months of the year. South of the tundra is located the forest wilderness of the taiga—an area larger than the United States—blessed by half the world's reserve of softwood saw lumber, but handicapped by a growing season that is too short and too cool for farming. The third region, which lies east of the Caspian Sea, is the desert wasteland of middle Asia (one third as large as the United States), with narrow ribbons of irrigated land on its southern edge. Another region embraces the mountain wasteland and settled valleys that follow the southern boundary of the USSR (along the frontiers of Turkey, Iran, Afghanistan, and China) and spread northward over eastern Siberia. Wedged between the taiga on the north and the desert on the south is the section of the country known as the Fertile Triangle, narrowing eastward from the Baltic and Black Seas to an apex on the Yenisey River beyond Novosibirsk (see Maps II and III between pp. 96 and 97).

The Fertile Triangle is the best farming area in the Soviet Union, though it is fertile and productive only in relation to other regions of the USSR, not in comparison with good agricultural land in the rest of the world. The northern half of the Triangle is forest land, with many lakes, swamps, and large farm clearings; the rest is open, rolling, treeless steppe and grain land, sweeping 2,500 miles from the mouth of the Danube to Novosibirsk. Climatically this area is roughly comparable to the triangle on the North American continent whose corners lie in western Nebraska, Duluth, Minnesota, and Edmonton, Alberta— the "dry-farming" area of North America. The Soviet Union has no rich farm lands comparable to our corn belt or Mississippi delta.

In the use and management of land, the Soviet Union has made some notable progress. Climatic and topographic characteristics reduce the problem of water erosion to a manageable level if good tillage and rotation practice are followed. The chief difficulty stems from wind erosion. The frequency with which this subject is raised by agricultural experts in the USSR suggests that officials responsible for land management are deeply concerned with it. The virgin-lands development program is too recent to have permitted the accumulation of much experience in dealing with problems of land management and soil conservation during years of crop failure. The question of how to deal with such disasters seems to haunt some of the officials who will be held responsible for action when emergencies arise.

In the field of soil classification. Russian scientists have long played a leading role. This is evidenced by the fact that Western nomenclature for major soil types includes a sizable proportion of Russian terms: *chernozem, podsol, solonetz, sierozem,* and other designations.

At present a nation-wide effort at soil classification and mapping is underway. The aim is to provide each farm with a large-scale soil map in sufficient detail to indicate the management practices that should be followed. The classification endeavor parallels a modest program to develop crop-rotation practices. Soviet research in the agricultural sciences today can be understood as an attempt to discover the crop-rotation systems that are best adapted to the country's "natural zones." This preoccupation with natural zones is in itself a reflection of the Darwinian background and current status of Soviet knowledge in the earth sciences. Present research is heavily focused upon the task of determining what "natural" ecologic system originally characterized each region. Once the natural patterns are understood, the next task is to devise land-management and crop-rotation principles adapted to these fundamental patterns of nature.

This approach, though outmoded in western eyes, should not be condemned without reservation. It invites a parallel with older European and American theories of forest management, which held that the research task was to determine the balance that had prevailed among species in virgin forests and the management task was to restore this balance. Management of farm or forest lands on this principle fails to apply modern research findings concerning seeds, soils, and fertilizers. It is better than no management at all, however, and the Russians have applied these principles over a vast area with some success.

While we can commend Soviet land use and management, with some reservations, the same cannot be said concerning the development of knowledge of plant nutrition and fertilizer use in the USSR. The country has excellent resources for the production of phosphoric fertilizers. Its potassium deposits in the western Ukraine and Byelorussia are claimed to be several times larger than total world potassium deposits outside the Soviet Union. The development of these deposits and of nitrogen production in its several forms is far below the levels of Soviet mechanization and land management—a deficiency for which central planning authorities must be held responsible.

The USSR undoubtedly possesses the industrial capacity for a much larger output of chemical fertilizers than is currently being used. While some farms seem to be fairly well supplied, most suffer from severe shortages. Chemical fertilizer is confined largely to use on the "technical crops"—cotton in the central Asiatic republics, sugar beets in the Ukraine, oil seeds and horticultural crops in the regions of intensive agriculture in European Russia. Typical is the complaint of the Party secretary for Orenburgskaya Oblast (region), southeast of Kuibyshev, that the five million hectares of land in farms in his area had received only 5,000 tons of mineral fertilizers in 1958, or one ton for each 2,500 acres. That this deficiency was not made up by the use of natural manures was indicated by his further complaint that it was impossible to use animal manures because "they must all go for fuel."

In general, natural fertilizers are inefficiently used in the USSR. Manure spreaders are rare sights on Soviet farms. Although the collection of manure from the large dairy barns may be mechanized by the use of overhead rail cars, the fertilizing process itself is often poorly handled, with spreading frequently being done by hand.

In the development of tractor power and field equipment, the record is equally spotty. One generalization can safely be made: grain farming is substantially ahead of animal agriculture, both in level of mechanization and efficiency of resource use. The machinery for grain farming is reasonably well adapted to the tasks at hand, and recently it has become more widely available. From 1950 to 1960 the number of tractors on farms increased by 89 percent, and in recent years there have been significant though belated improvements in tractor design. As of January 1, 1962, the Soviet Union reported 1,168,000 tractors on farms, and approximately half of these had been delivered within the last four years.

The current output is predominantly of diesel type tractors, more efficient in fuel consumption than the older gasoline-burning and kerosene-burning units that comprised over half of the Soviet tractor inventory in 1953. According to Soviet reports, in 1953 diesel-burning units accounted for 45 percent of total horsepower in the agricultural tractor fleet; this figure had increased to 84 percent by January 1, 1960. By way of comparison, there were an estimated 4,770,000 tractors on farms in the United States on January 1, 1960, of which approximately one third were diesel-burning units, and two thirds were six years old or older.

Significant advances have been made in harvesting practices and in the quality of harvesting equipment. The standard Russian combine of the 1930s was a copy of the Holt-Caterpillar combine—a model produced in the United States in the late 1920s. Although these machines are still to be seen on Soviet farms, the design has been superseded by several models of self-propelled units, incorporating Soviet variations of more recent advances in combine design in the United States. Of the 497,000 grain combines on Soviet farms at the beginning of 1961, 47 percent are reported to be self-propelled units of postwar design. The early emphasis on the combining of standing grain has shifted to an almost total preoccupation with the system of "two-stage" harvesting, involving the development of equipment to windrow the grain in a hard-dough stage of ripeness, with subsequent combining from the windrows.

The Russian moldboard plow is heavy and cumbersome, failing by a wide margin to meet western standards in ease of draft and handling.

Similar observations are valid for other major types of crop-harvesting and tillage equipment. Machine cotton pickers are available in several models and observers report them to be reasonably comparable to American machines under similar conditions of use. Production has recently been stepped up for a variety of corn-harvesting machines, primarily for the production of chopped green fodder rather than for the harvest of ripe ear corn. In 1954, for example, there were 2,400 ensilage harvesters and choppers; by 1961 there were 121,000.

Among the major machinery items, one of the most serious Russian deficiencies involves the "all-purpose," or "row-crop" type, wheel tractor. Although available, Russian models, by current American standards, are underpowered and clumsy in design. Soviet technical journals and the transcripts of Party meetings contain repeated complaints about the inadequacies, as well as the short supply, of small tractors. The Russian proclivity for hugeness is nowhere more apparent than in tractor design; only in recent years have the authorities paid substantial attention to the development of smaller, more manueverable wheel-type tractors.

The large tractors, tillage equipment, and grain-harvesting equipment intended for use in extensive agriculture are reasonably well designed. While not plentiful, the supply does not constitute a major deficiency under existing conditions. The opposite situation exists for hand tools and the smaller items of equipment, particularly those used for forage and hay crops and in animal husbandry. It is a strange economy that produces a good tractor and a poor hoe.

Two other classes of farm equipment are notably lacking in Soviet agriculture—electric motors and materials-handling equipment. While electricity from local diesel-powered generators is available to many farms, there is an acute shortage of the small electric-powered farm equipment that constitutes a major part of the total stock of agricultural machinery in Europe and the United States. Equipment for handling bulk materials has played a major role in the technological revolution in American agriculture since 1940. This type of equipment is virtually absent in the Soviet Union. The lack of augurs, conveyors, hydraulic-powered and tractor-mounted scoops and forks, hay balers, blowers, baled hay loaders, silo unloaders, and so forth, produce strange contrasts in agricultural production. Grain that is combined by modern equipment and hauled from the field in huge motor trucks may be cleaned and winnowed by hand. The shortages of hay and forage-handling equipment and of equipment for grading, cleaning, and drying grain on the farms and at central assembly points are pronounced barriers to further advances in Soviet farming.

This deficiency in materials-handling equipment is one of the main reasons why labor in Soviet agriculture is inefficiently utilized. It is possible that Soviet labor efficiency in some phases of agricultural operation—plowing or seeding, for example—may compare favorably with that achieved on the average American farm in analogous type of farming areas. Any gain, however, is later lost because of labor-wasting methods of transporting, handling, and storing the product. The waste in manhours is great; the physical waste in terms of spoilage and deterioration is equally serious and has recently been severely criticized by Khrushchev.

Special emphasis must be given to the shortage of refrigeration capacity, which is apparent on the farms, at warehouses, on the railroads, throughout the distribution chain, and in the consumer's kitchen. A state farm near Irkutsk in Siberia will illustrate the cost-increasing consequences of this deficiency. This farm, with approximately 20,000 acres of cropped land, has contracts with six retail meat stores in Irkutsk for the sale of meat. During the frost-free season, the farm is able to slaughter only 24 to 36 hours ahead, due to the lack of refrigeration facilities at the slaughtering plant. This lack precludes economies of scale in the slaughtering operation and promotes loss through spoilage.

Another example of inefficiency resulting from inadequate refrigeration facilities may be seen in rail transport. A familiar sight on rail lines leading to Leningrad or Moscow is the slow moving livestock train, each with more than 40 cars of assorted animals. These trains have no slat-sided stockcars so familiar on American railroads, but only boxcars, with doors opened and the rumps and heads of cows, sheep, pigs, and goats visible. Hay for the trip is piled in the ends of the cars, with additional cars of hay interspersed throughout the length of the train. Attendants travel in the cars with the stock. Live animal transportation, necessitated by the shortage of refrigeration facilities, causes excessive shrinkage and wastes in stock, labor, and feed. Transport of this sort calls to mind the cattle boats that once plied the North Atlantic beween Canada and the northern United States and western Europe; by American standards, Soviet livestock transport is at least half a century out of date.

Technological levels in animal husbandry also reflect patterns of uneven progress. Milking machines are available and in use on the better farms. Artificial insemination is vigorously promoted in dairy herds, and visible success has been achieved in upgrading the quality of dairy cows. The American team of livestock specialists that toured the USSR in the fall of 1959 was told that artificial insemination was scheduled to be used in the breeding of almost one fourth of the total dairy and sheep herds in that year.

Many Soviet dairy herds are clearly in a transitional stage, with low-yielding cows intermixed with higher-yielding dairy breeds. Holstein types tend to predominate in the better herds, but there is a wide variety in size, color, and other features, indicating that artificial insemination has only partially succeeded in raising the level of breeding to accept-able dairy standards.

In common with much else in Soviet agriculture, the Russian hog is appropriately large. Sows that are shown to the foreign visitor average 400 to 500 pounds, reflecting feeding and breeding standards that are outmoded in northwestern Europe and the United States. An average of ten to twelve pigs per litter is considered normal. Although these large litters are impressive (typical well-managed American farms aver-age seven to nine pigs saved per litter), they have been achieved by breeding for large size and by holding sows in production to older ages than would be considered efficient on farms in the American corn belt. In terms of total labor use and feed consumption in the Soviet swine industry, the heavy sows and large litters should probably be entered on the debit side of the ledger.

The hogs are not only big, they are fat. Emphasis on fat is typical, of course, in food-short economies where butter and fats of all kinds are equated with the good life. A concentration upon fat, however, in an urban-industrial society, represents a waste of feed resources. The Soviet premium upon fat is reflected in the price structure for hogs. This is shown clearly in the price graduations for swine in two areas in the North Caucasus and the Ukraine (Table 4-3).

TABLE 4-3

RUBLES PER 100 KILO (live weight)

Krasnodar Area, Autumn, 1958		Kiev Area, Summer, 1960	
Bacon hogs	740	Lard hogs	1020
Fat hogs	640	Meat hogs	770
Meat hogs	600		

With meat hogs at the bottom of the scale, and a 25 to 33 percent premium for fat, the farm manager naturally concludes that fat is the appropriate goal in his hog raising program.

These price differentials are carried to the retail level. In 1958, lard at 22.50 rubles per kilogram was valued at approximately three times the live weight price of hogs per kilogram. It was the most expensive single pork item seen in state stores in the major cities, except for individual slices of overfat ham at 29 rubles per kilo. Fat bacon at 21 rubles was followed by pork loins or chops at 18 to 20.50 rubles per kilo, with the lower prices attached to the lean and meatier chops. Rib cuts of beef in the same stores were priced at 14 to 15 rubles per kilo and veal at 10 rubles.

In breeding and feeding standards and in price ratios, the Soviet swine industry closely parallels American hog production at about the time of World War I. The price of lard in the United States remained above the live-weight price of hogs until about 1937. In recent years, however, the price of American lard has fluctuated at levels approximately three-fourths the level of the live-weight price of hogs. In terms of the price premium for fat, the Soviet swine industry has seen little change from the standards of prerevolutionary days.

Although much of the land mass of the USSR is comprised of semi-arid grasslands that in similar areas of the world form the typical locale for beef and sheep production, the use of these grasslands for meat production is seriously retarded. The overwhelming proportion of beef comes from veal calves, dairy-type steers, and culled dairy cows. Beef types similar to Hereford, Angus, and Shorthorn are typically seen only on experimental breeding farms.

The unfamiliarity of Soviet farm officials with beef breeds of cattle is illustrated by an incident during an interview in the ministry of agriculture in Moscow. A foreign visitor was showing pictures of ranchland in the American Great Plains to an assembly of department heads, and several of the photographs featured white-faced Hereford steers on range pasture. "See!" exclaimed one of the officials, "they also have the *Kazakh* breed in America!"

In 1956, total meat production (slaughter weight) in the USSR came to 5.6 million metric tons. Of this total, 2.6 million tons, or 39 percent, were pork, 2.2 million tons were beef (primarily dairy beef), and an estimated 0.5 million tons were mutton. For 1958, meat production was reportedly 7.7 million metric tons, of which 3.3 million tons, or 43 percent, were pork. Pork was thus a larger proportion of total meat availability in 1958 than in previous years.

Official statistics show an increase in meat production to 8.9 million metric tons in 1959. This figure dropped to 8.7 million tons in 1960, and recovered slightly to 8.8 million metric tons in 1961. The decline in 1960 was apparently due to a sharp drop in the reported production of meat on the small "private plots" of farm workers. These statistics must be interpreted with care, in view of the pressure on farm managers and officials to overstate output, and on farm workers to understate the number of livestock kept on private plots.

Under current circumstances it is unlikely that the output from private plots is overstated in published reports. This fact lends added interest to the official statistics for 1960, which show that 41 percent of all meat, 47 percent of all milk, 80 percent of all eggs, and 63 percent of all potatoes were produced on private plots. Soviet reports indicate that these private plots account for only three percent of the total sown area, but for about one third of the total manhours worked in Soviet agriculture. The elaborate care given to household livestock is one of the explanations why this labor input figure is so high.

It is clear that whatever advances in the Soviet meat supply per capita are achieved in the immediate future, the primary share must come from the swine and dairy industries. The Soviet Union unquestionably possesses a large potential for the development of a beef-cattle industry, probably on a scale unmatched by any country except the United States. Under even the most favorable conditions the realization of this potential will require considerable time.

INCENTIVES FOR AGRICULTURAL PRODUCTION

From the beginning of collectivization, the classification and rating of all farm jobs in terms of workday units has placed collective farm labor under what may loosely be described as a piecework wage system. Until the price reforms of the post-Stalin era, however, the workers were largely paid in kind, receiving bread grain, potatoes, perhaps vegetables in season, and feed for household livestock. Higher prices for farm products have added a new dimension: it is now possible for the collective farm worker to earn a substantial cash reward for his labor.

By providing for monthly cash advances equivalent to 60 to 80 percent of the value of the workday units and by paying bonuses for production above the norm, Communist leaders seek to stimulate the peasant to improve his economic position through increased productivity. A dairymaid or a pigmaid may be able to double or triple her minimum labor wage by producing more than the norm. On one clearly superior Ukrainian farm in 1958, for example, the average cash income of peasants working on field crops varied between 400 and 700 rubles per month, while those working in the livestock enterprises averaged from 900 to 1,100 rubles per month. In contrast, the average industrial wage in mid-1958 in the Leningrad region was 1,030 rubles per month. On a better-than-average farm, these livestock workers in the Ukraine were receiving monetary rewards that equalled or surpassed the wage payments for industrial labor in one of the leading Soviet cities.

An example of the gradation that occurs under the piecework system can be seen in the dairy industry. At a collective farm in the Kiev region, for example, each milkmaid was credited with 1.4 workday units for every 100 liters of milk produced. A milkmaid had 14 cows under her care, with a total production during the summer months averaging from 160 to 180 liters a day. On this farm, in the summer, milkmaids were earning an average of 65 to 70 workday units per month. The pigmaids were credited with eight workday units for each 100 kilograms of gain on the pigs in their charge. With an average of about 80 head of swine per person, and with the rates of gain averaging one pound per animal per day, these pigmaids could earn from 75 to 80 workday units per month. These wages approach the remuneration level of tractor drivers, who have long been treated as an elite group in Soviet agricultural labor.

An interesting elaboration of this incentive pay system in state farms is provided by the example of pigmaids on a farm near Irkutsk. Tractor drivers on this farm could earn up to 2,500 or 3,000 rubles per month during the seasons of heavy work. These are variable wages, however, and they may drop sharply after the harvest is gathered. Workers in the swine enterprise were also earning 2,000 or more rubles per month, but their wages were relatively stable throughout the year. The swine maids at Irkutsk, for example, were caring for an average of 20 sows each. If the litters average at least ten pigs saved per sow, and the pigs each weigh a minimum of 16 kilo (approximately 35 pounds) at eight weeks of age, the swinemaid received a bonus that could bring her pay to more than 2,500 rubles per month. This rate of pay was approximately three times that paid for more routine types of farm work on this state enterprise. These illustrations show the degree to which the status of labor in livestock enterprises has been upgraded.

The significance of this upgrading acquires a new dimension if it is recalled that an estimated 59 percent of the entire farm labor force is female. Much of the recent improvement of wages has also involved an upgrading of female labor, since women on Soviet farms are largely engaged in the livestock enterprises.

The introduction of monetary incentives into the Soviet agricultural economy has widened the wage spread between higher- and lower-paid farm labor. These differences are now as great, or perhaps greater, than those prevailing in industry. In this respect, the contrast between the United States and the Soviet Union is particularly striking. There is almost no class of American farm labor in which the higher-paid workers earn three times the average wage available to the lower-paid workers in the same labor class. In the Soviet Union, spreads of this magnitude are commonplace.

There is a touch of irony in the fact that the Soviet Union today exhibits a wage structure resembling that of the United States a half century ago. Although the Communists denounce capitalism, they make greater use of "capitalistic" wage incentives to extract the maximum labor output than any of the leading industrial nations of the western world. While the USSR has employed these techniques for several decades in industry, an important new development is the use of prices and piecework wage rates in agriculture.

It would be a mistake to assume that the piecework method of wage payment is efficient. In order to determine the base upon which work-day units are calculated for each worker and each brigade, the entire output must be weighed, measured, and recorded. This means that products must be hauled to central scales, which are distant from the work site, so that an official tally can be made of the day's work. Hay, for example, may have to be transported from one farm unit to another for weighing and tallying at the central scales. In the dairy enterprise at least one accountant works full time at each barn tallying the amount of milk to be credited to the account of each milkmaid. These practices require additional timekeepers, tallyers, accountants, and similar nonproduction workers. More important, they preclude the bulk handling and comingling of products in the field or in the barn. A structural barrier thus prevents the full use of many types of bulk-handling equipment commonly found on American farms.

In an effort to encourage livestock production, a further money incentive was introduced in January 1961. For the remainder of the seven-year-plan period, to 1965, the tax on collective farm incomes derived from the sale of livestock or animal products is to be cut by 80 percent. The price increase of June 1962 on livestock products and poultry indicate additional reliance on money incentives to spur production.

The introduction of monetary incentives into agriculture will have profound effects on the industry. During the first 40 years of its existence, the Soviet Union was able to import from the West the technology of a market economy without adopting its price structure. The goal was maximum production in accordance with physical limits and political priorities. Collectivization after 1928, the war from 1939 to 1945, and postwar efforts at reconstruction combined to create a quarter century of continuous "crash programs." Considerations of costs and alternative opportunities played a minor role. The organizational and price reforms of the post-Stalin era have introduced money costs and rewards into this structure, requiring a fundamental readjustment in thinking on the part of planners, farm managers, and the rural labor force.

Nowhere is this new approach more apparent than in the standards by which collective farm chairmen and state farm managers measure their own performance. If one asks farm directors and other agricultural officials what they consider their principal goal to be, the reply is invariably, "To increase output per hundred hectares." This concept of the goal is symptomatic of the lag in thinking that will create one of the major barriers to the achievement of higher agricultural output. The goal of maximum output per hundred hectares reflects the siege economy that characterized Communist agriculture prior to the recent reforms. Such a goal is suited to agricultural units engaged in monoculture or in the production of a few major field crops, but not to an agricultural establishment that emphasizes the conversion of feed and fodder resources into animal products. In a complex animal conversion economy, the maximum-output approach provides little guidance to the farm director, who must ask himself, "Maximize the output of *what*, per hundred hectares?"

The manager's problem is to achieve the proper balance of enterprises on his farm. In the past, prices for the manager were merely bookkeeping entries. The key decisions were made for him in terms of quotas, norms, and delivery obligations. Now he has the added guidance provided by an administered price system, but the political goals are still presented to him in the old maximum-physical-output form.

The door is now open for the application of rational systems of cost accounting at the farm level—a new experience for the Soviet farm manager. Soviet technical literature is blossoming with articles concerning the proper calculation of depreciation rates on farms, possibilities for improving labor productivity through better cost accounting, and the need for more reliable statistical information to guide pricing authorities in their use of this unfamiliar instrument. In many sectors of Soviet agriculture a new generation of managerial talent will have to be trained before the full potential of a money economy can be realized.

POLITICS AND THE SOVIET FARM PROBLEM

Much inefficiency in Soviet agriculture derives from the fact that many decisions on economic matters are treated as political decisions, to be made by central authorities far from the producing units in a given region or type-of-farming area. Decisions as to the type of machinery to be produced, the kinds of buildings to be constructed, and the major crops to be planted are made by central government officers, who issue instructions to farm managers with the expectation that they will be carried out to the letter. After Khrushchev's campaign to plant corn, the visitor could see cornfields even near Leningrad, in the latitude of the middle of Hudson Bay, and near Irkutsk, only a few miles from the permafrost line. While growing corn may not be the most productive use for these lands, it nevertheless demonstrates the political loyalty of local farm directors.

Perhaps the most publicized illustration of political intervention in the area of agriculture was the forced acceptance of the genetic theories of Trofim Lysenko. Lysenko's theory of genetics holds that changes in environment can bring about fundamental changes in the characteristics of plants or animals and that these changes can then be transmitted by inheritance. This theory, with its stress on environment, is more compatible with Marxist-Leninist ideology than are the theories identified with Mendel, Morgan, and other geneticists in the West. Although Lysenko is more properly described as a selectionist than as a geneticist, his genetic theories received support from both Stalin and Khrushchev. It is possible that this mixture of politics and genetics may have delayed work on the development of hybrids in the USSR by as much as 20 years, or diverted it into unproductive channels. While Lysenko's fortunes continue to fluctuate, at present there appear to be no objections to developing hybrids, especially in corn. Collective farm chairmen, state farm managers, and agronomists attached to local government units express great interest in hybrid corn. Their only question is, "Where can we get more?"

Politics also inhibits research to determine the optimum size for Soviet farms. The question of how large operating units should be has been regarded as a political matter lying beyond the boundaries of technical research. Field size, on the other hand, is a technical question, and Soviet specialists have made detailed studies to discover how large fields should be for maximum efficiency. In shelter-belt areas, studies indicate the optimum width of fields to be 20 times the height of the highest trees at maturity, or about 400 to 450 meters (1,300 to 1,500 feet). The optimum length for fields to be has also been studied.

Table 4-4 shows some of the results of the research on this question.

TABLE 4-4

TIME LOST IN TURNING CORNERS IN PLOWING

Length of Field	Percentage of Total Time Lost in Turning Corners	
	Wheel Tractor	Crawler Tractor
Meters	Percent	Percent
200	46.9	52.4
300	34.2	38.6
400	23.7	24.0
500	17.5	19.0
1,000	9.3	14.8
1,500	6.8	10.7
2,000	4.4	9.4

As shown in the table, the percentage of time lost turning corners increases rapidly as field lengths become less than 1,000 meters, or one kilometer (0.62 miles). Some efficiency is gained with longer fields, although the rate of increase is small. Soviet experts have concluded that fields from one to two kilometers long are desirable in shelter-belt areas. When asked why the fields should not be longer in order to achieve maximum operating efficiency, one official replied that the tractor driver would be too far from service facilities in case of a breakdown and too far from home when it was time to go to lunch! The question of farm size, of course, is more important than the question of field size, but this matter is answered by political dogma and not by research.

The decisions of central authorities are also reflected in the huge new stanchion-type dairy barns on many of the collective and state farms, typically with facilities for 80 to 120 cows. "What do you think of our new barn?" one animal-husbandry technician asked an American visitor. But without waiting for an answer, he continued. "We wonder whether this is the type of barn we should be building, but these are the plans we received from the ministry of agriculture."

Khrushchev, at a February 1961 agricultural conference, asked where the designs for such "cow barns" were obtained. "Certain of our institutes seem to have been possessed by a kind of devil," he said.

"Their barn designs provide just about everything but a private mirror for each cow. This is nonsense."

These doubts underline the fact that a sizable capital investment is being made in a type of dairy barn that is today outmoded. Loose housing and loafing pens, replacing stanchion-type barns, characterize the more advanced dairy farms of northern Europe and the United States. Increasing reliance upon "milking parlors" and the efficient bulk handling of milk are eliminating the traditional milk can.

The virgin-lands program provides another curious and distinctive example of how political considerations influence decisions in Soviet agriculture. For the first three decades of Communist rule, agriculture played the role of an internal colony, exploited to the full for the benefit of urban industrial growth. By 1950 the wheel had turned full circle, and agriculture had become a drag on the further expansion of the Soviet industrial plant. Since crop yields were low in comparison with Europe and the better farming regions of North America, one might have expected the planners to step up investment and productive effort in areas where the agricultural plant was already moderately developed. Here was where the marginal ruble of effort could be expected to earn its highest return—yet this was not the path the politicians elected to follow.

Instead, a program was initiated to develop land in areas that had been marginal or submarginal, both in prerevolutionary times and under the Communist regime. A step-up in the agricultural effort in already established areas would have required a climb up the technological ladder to a more demanding level of applied agricultural science; thus the easier decision was made to expand at lower levels of technology into the dry, inhospitable lands of Trans-Volga, Kazakhstan, and Siberia. The virgin-lands program could utilize machinery and agricultural techniques that were already in existence. The USSR already had the capacity to produce the tractors, plows, and combines necessary for a vast new program of land development.

It is interesting to speculate on the reasons why Communist leaders, notably Khrushchev, are so enthusiastic about the virgin-lands program. For one thing, such a program lends itself to dramatization through the use of symbols that are familiar to men and women in all walks of life: the tractor, the combine, the motor truck. Moreover, the program can be easily adapted to the mass use of shock brigades of labor. Finally, it enables the regime to extend into new areas the state farm— a type of agricultural organization that is regarded as a step closer to true Communism than the collective farm and one that is well suited to manipulation and control by central authorities. It has already been mentioned that much of the recent increase in the number and size of state farms is due to the virgin-lands program. The foregoing arguments for the program are likely to be more appealing to Party officials in Moscow, however, than to the agricultural expert or informed farmer who may be primarily interested in maximum output for every ruble invested.

One important, far-reaching consequence of the expansion of sown areas has been to make the Soviet grain supply more dependent upon the weather. Although it has been estimated that 60 percent of the new crop lands lie at or below the 12-inch rainfall margin, the hazards of this move into marginal areas are modified somewhat by the improbability of severe crop failures in all wheat-growing regions in the same season. The impact of a severe drought in the Ukraine, for example, may be softened by moderate to average yields in Kazakhstan or in the Siberian portions of the new lands. This risk-spreading feature of the new lands program may have some long-run stabilizing effects. The fact remains, however, that a major percentage of the grain output of the USSR is now heavily dependent upon climate in regions that are periodically subject to drought. In sharp contrast, the expansion of agricultural technology in Europe and North America during the past quarter century has reduced the dependence of agricultural output upon climate.

The Soviet Union is thus faced with the prospect of alternating boom years of heavy demand and bust years of idle or underutilized agricultural resources. Over the past five years the USSR has entered export markets with surplus grain (largely spring wheat) in some years, only to face food stringency, if not actual shortage, in other years. A great burden is thus thrown upon the labor supply and upon transport and storage facilities.

Another intangible but important consequence of the virgin lands program is that the state farm is put to the test as an instrument of Communist policy. It will be important to observe how the reputation of the state farm holds up during drought years that are certain to come. At this time the program is widely hailed as an outstanding success of the current regime. In recent years the USSR has been the third largest wheat exporter in the world (after the United States and Canada). Indeed, the virgin lands program may permit the wheat lands of European Russia to be shifted to the production of feed grains and the support of animal agriculture, and these would be advances of major proportions.

The Soviet experience is strikingly similar to that of North America when the Great Plains were opened to the planting of wheat in the decades between 1870 and World War I. The Soviet Union today is enjoying the first flush of success of a gigantic pioneer effort redolent of the boom psychology that prevailed in the Dakotas, Montana, and the prairie provinces of Canada after the turn of the century and before the great drought in the 1930s. But one question that worries some Soviet farm experts is, What will happen when the drought comes? At the present time, agriculture in the virgin lands consists in working the fertility of an easily depleted topsoil. The expansion has already over-reached itself on some lands that will ultimately have to be cropped less frequently or returned to grass if they are to continue to be productive. One of the crucial tests of Soviet land management in the decade ahead will come when the dessicating winds of the southern steppes lift the dusts of Kazakhstan into clouds that may darken the sky of Moscow and beyond.

THE FUTURE OF SOVIET AGRICULTURE

One of the outstanding lessons to be learned from the history of European agricultural production and food management during World War II is that the rigid economics are the most fragile and easily upset by external shock. The agricultural economy of the USSR has been rigid because it has had to depend primarily upon basic inputs of the crude factors of production—land and labor. This rigidity in the organization of resources in Soviet agriculture is decreasing, but the evidence of this change is confined largely to the field of farm mechanization. Over the past quarter century the USSR has taken relatively rapid strides toward a higher level of mechanization, and if current programs are successful, the food industry will benefit greatly from technological progress. The farmers need more and better-designed machines as well as a full complement of smaller, supplementary equipment to increase the productivity of their labor. These needs are immediate and urgent and are repeatedly stressed by Soviet agricultural experts in their writings and interviews with foreigners.

Soviet leaders have recently exhibited a keen awareness of the need for something more than mechanization as a keystone of farm policy. In his interview with a group of American journalists in July 1962, Premier Khrushchev stressed the fact that the one great lesson the Soviet Union could learn from American agriculture concerned the way in which resources are organized and managed on American farms.

Improved materials-handling methods, better fertilizers, seeds, and agricultural chemicals, and better methods of animal breeding and feeding offer great potentials for progress, but they are still largely untapped in present-day Soviet agriculture. The keys to advances in these areas are managerial reform, agricultural education, experimental research, and the rapid diffusion of new knowledge on the farms. Here the Soviets still have the major steps ahead of them, and they may not be fully aware of the directions in which the path will lead.

The barriers to progress in the nonmechanical aspects of agricultural technology are formidable because they involve principles that are deeply rooted in Communist ideology. The team of soil scientists from the US Department of Agriculture that visited the Soviet Union in 1958 concluded that the Russians today are adhering to old theories and systems of soil classification, analysis, and management. The American experts, however, were impressed by the fact that these outmoded principles of soil science are well understood by agricultural technicians at the farm level in most sections of the country. This observation also holds true in other sectors of the economy, where Soviet officials cling to old economic theories and patterns of analysis, which they also understand very well. To some extent this lag reflects the indoctrinating power of the Soviet educational system. It is also an illustration of the uniformity of thought in the Soviet Union, a country that has been governed on the basis of averages calculated for huge blocks of land and people. The important point is that the crude and simple economic principles that sufficed for the early stages of agricultural development are no longer adequate.

An outstanding example of the restrictive effects that Soviet ideology has on agriculture is the Communist emphasis on the evils that allegedly flow from a system of private ownership of land. Since the USSR is limited in its supply of productive land, the most realistic hopes for achieving high levels of agricultural output rest in its ability to develop substitutes for land through technology and trade. A preoccupation with developing large farm units, together with the opening of new lands in marginal areas, has distracted attention from the more rewarding concern with increased output in existing farm areas. In line with this argument, a major obstruction to agricultural improvement stems from the rigidities of a policy based upon averages that embrace vastly different types of farming and production circumstances.

A major reform introduced after an exhaustive review at the January 1961 Plenum of the Communist Party involved removing most of the power of the ministry of agriculture to make key production decisions. A new farm machinery association was created in response to the many complaints about inadequate supply and defective design. More responsibility for research, plant and animal breeding and disease control, and related services has been given to the republics and to territorial and provincial offices. An effort at greater decentralization is being made, although price-setting functions and the analyses of farm financial performance and fulfillment of production plans are retained in the hands of the central government.

The efficiency of centralization can be seen in the speed with which the virgin lands program was executed and the machine and tractor stations dissolved. The overcentralization of agriculture, however, may inter- fere with the development and effective use of highly skilled technicians and managers capable of applying the new technologies so necessary for the achievement of Soviet goals. This hazard looms large in a system in which the organization of the industry and the training of its technical specialists are dictated by ideologically oriented leaders who seek to plan in minute detail an economy covering one eighth of the land surface of the globe.

Khrushchev has nailed the Communist flag to the mast of Soviet agriculture. The goal of "reaching and surpassing" the United States in per capita output may acquire such importance that the Communist leaders will be willing to tolerate major modifications in the Soviet economic structure. It will require major adjustments, both in ideology and in organization, if Khrushchev's goals are to be realized in this generation.

5

SOVIET SCIENCE
AND TECHNOLOGY

Victor Cohn

*A science reporter for the Minneapolis Tribune,
Victor Cohn began writing about Soviet science
in 1951, and in the summer of 1958 spent five
weeks in the Soviet Union. A series of articles,
done in October 1958, entitled "The Year of the
Sputnik," won the Westinghouse Award of the
American Association for the Advancement of
Science for the most distinguished science reporting of 1958 in an American newspaper.*

J. W. Buchta

*Associate Dean of the College of Science, Litera-
ture, and the Arts at the University of Minnesota,
J. W. Buchta was for many years chairman of
the University's Physics Department. He was editor of the* Reviews of Modern Physics, *has been
concerned with government-university relationships as a functionary of the National Science
Foundation, and has received recognition for his
outstanding contributions to the teaching of
physics.*

T he period from July 1, 1957 through
December 31, 1958, will be deeply engraved in the history of man's
scientific achievements. That period is known as the International Geophysical Year. Sixty-four nations, including the United States and the
Soviet Union, participated in the largest internationally coordinated

assault upon the scientific unknown that the world has ever seen. One of America's special contributions to geophysical exploration was to be the launching of a space satellite that was to give man his first direct physical contact with outer space.

Suddenly, on October 5, 1957, TASS, the official Soviet news agency, issued a momentous announcement: "As a result of the intensive work by research institutes and designing bureaus, the first artificial earth satellite in the world has now been created. This first satellite was successfully launched in the USSR on October 4 [1957]."

An American could hardly doubt the authenticity of the claim, for he had only to tune a shortwave radio to 40 megacycles to hear the steady "beep-beep" of Sputnik I; or he could gaze upward with a simple pair of field glasses on a clear evening in the last week of October and see the Soviet moon moving quietly through "American" skies. Nor could he deprecate the magnitude of this achievement by Soviet scientists and engineers, for in the months that followed, one Vanguard rocket after another either fizzled on the launching pad at Cape Canaveral or was blown up over the Atlantic. Every American failure was a poignant, and painful, testimony to the skill of Soviet science.

In the years following Sputnik I, the Soviet Union's rockets, sputniks, and spectacular shots into space—all of them technological achievements requiring a strong scientific base—have been much in the news. The space progress of the USSR, however, is only one part of the Soviet scientific and technological story. In the past decade Soviet scientists and engineers have assumed the world lead in the investigation of the Arctic. They built the first nuclear power plant, a small one to be sure, but a scientific "first." They developed the first long-range ballistic missiles and the world's largest hydroelectric plant. They put a jet airliner into regular and continuing operation two years before the United States did. They built giant atom smashers and nuclear reactors and the "first atomic ship for peaceful use," the powerful ice-breaker *Lenin*.

To those who have watched Soviet science through the years, its most impressive characteristic is its rapid pace of development. In 1946, a scientific visitor assessed Soviet science and found it "mediocre." In 1951, an American authority rated the Soviet Union as the world's "number three" scientific power, behind the United States and Great Britain. By 1957, he was assessing the Soviet Union as "number two," well ahead of Great Britain. An appraisal and comparison of science in the Soviet Union with that in other countries including our own can best be made by a field-by-field review. And even then experts disagree. Value judgments are involved. How does one equate one outstanding scientist with a dozen good ones? However, there is agreement that the Soviet Union is progressing rapidly and many American scientists believe that in x number of years—"five years," "ten years," the estimates vary—the Soviet Union may surpass the United States in many fields.

THE SECRET OF RAPID DEVELOPMENT

The growth of Soviet science and technology since the revolution, and more particularly in the last 15 years, has been truly phenomenal. But one should not make the mistake of assuming that the Communists started from nothing when they began building their scientific establishment. Tsarist Russia in the nineteenth century produced some brilliant scientists. Any high school student in a chemistry class has seen the name of Mendeleev on the periodic table of elements, but probably few realize that he was a Russian chemist. Pavlov is one of the outstanding names in the history of physiology and psychology. Less well known but of great significance in the development of modern mathematics is Lobachevski, one of the original developers of non-Euclidean geometry. Although there were not many scientists in Tsarist Russia, Mendeleev, Pavlov, and Lobachevski were great men even measured by the highest of international scientific standards. They and some of their less illustrious colleagues provided a base from which the Communists could build a modern scientific establishment.

From the beginning of the new regime, the Communists placed a high priority on scientific and technological development. Lenin preached that without science there could be no Communism. Speaking at the third All-Russian Congress of Soviets, just two months after the October revolution, he outlined a plan for scientific and technological research. Research could no longer be left to individual scientists. The Communists therefore directed the Soviet Academy of Sciences to serve as the top planning and supervisory body, and Lenin focused its attention on the development of industry, electrification, and the harnessing of wind and water.

In the difficult days after 1917, he also ordered scientists and technologists to help rebuild Russia and her military defenses. Lenin wrote in the spring of 1918 that "the development of natural resources by methods of modern technology will lay the basis for the unprecedented progress of productive forces." Industrialization and modern technology, he emphasized, were essential to "socialist construction."

Stalin was even more blunt. "We are 50 to 100 years behind the advanced countries," he asserted in 1931. "We must make good the distance in 10 years, or they will crush us. We must turn to science." More than ever, in the words of Julian Huxley, Soviet science was considered "an organ of the developing socialist society," and "one of that society's weapons against the rest of the world." In the period of Stalin's rule Soviet science and technology were given a mighty push. "Catch up and surpass western science" became a rallying cry.

But sheer determination to advance and the endless repetition of slogans were not in themselves sufficient to develop a modern, full-sized scientific establishment. Rapid scientific development required the mobilization of human and material resources, efficiently organized so that particular goals could be realized.

What the Bolsheviks needed was an organization to direct and carry on scientific endeavors and to gear these endeavors to the needs of the state. The central organization for this purpose had existed long before the revolution. As early as 1725, Peter the Great had created the Imperial Academy of Sciences as a directing and unifying force in scientific development. Lenin and his colleagues did not destroy this organization, but reorganized it as the Soviet Academy of Sciences.

Today the Academy of Sciences of the USSR is a very large and complex institution that initiates, directs, and coordinates research. There are more than 50 distinct research institutes under its direction, as well as dozens of laboratories, observatories, and museums. Its work covers all of the academic disciplines from physics and chemistry to history and linguistics.

The Academy has a number of important functions. First, it is the agency, subordinate to the Council of Ministers through an intermediate state committee on the coordination of research and development, that translates the general scientific and technological goals of the top political elite into specific research plans and projects. Second, the Academy continually surveys the various fields of knowledge in order to identify the fundamental problems that must be solved in order to further development. Third, it expedites the application of scientific and technological discoveries to the production process. Fourth, it trains many of the top candidates for advanced degrees.

Professor John Turkevich of Princeton University, one of America's foremost authorities on Soviet science, has likened the Presidium (the governing body) of the Academy to a "general staff." In the Academy, he points out, the scientists in the Soviet Union "have an organized program to take advantage of new discoveries, and to make sure there is research going on in every major field. They are planning in pure science."

An efficient organization for a crash program of scientific development would be of little use if funds to support the projects were not available. Recognizing this fact, the leaders of the Soviet Union have poured billions of rubles into high priority scientific development. The expensive research facilities, observed by western scientists visiting the Soviet Union in the 1950s, are indication of the huge amounts of money that have been spent. One of the most striking reports about scientific facilities has come from Professor Edgar L. Piret of the University of Minnesota, who in 1957 was among the first five Americans to tour new Russian chemical laboratories: "I was interested in seeing whether they were still a little backward in chemical engineering, like most of Europe, or modern. I found that they are either modern or getting there very fast." He visited Moscow University and three chemical engineering institutes, including the Mendeleev Institute in Moscow and the Lensoviet of Leningrad. He returned to the United States to show photographs of chemical engineering teaching equipment—equipment to handle and process gases and chemicals by what he called "the modern unit-operations method."

"Tell me," Professor Piret asks, "where in the United States have you seen equipment and instrumentation of this kind in undergraduate laboratories? We don't have it here, and we don't have the manpower to maintain it. Shell or Esso has, our big industries have, but we in the universities don't. In other words, the teaching laboratories I saw were much better equipped than those here. They make ours at the University of Minnesota look extremely limited, and we have one of the best unit-operations setups in the country."

Another technique employed by the USSR to speed up scientific progress has been the extensive borrowing of scientific information from the more advanced countries. Some information, primarily on projects of military significance, was gained through espionage. But the vast amount of scientific information accumulating throughout the world need not be obtained through espionage. This information is gathered in the USSR by diligent combing of all publications that might contain material of scientific and technical importance.

In 1952, an Institute of Scientific and Technical Information was established in the Academy of Sciences. In this Institute more than 15,000 publications are received, read, chopped apart, sorted, often translated, and then distributed to the Soviet scientists. The *Physical Review* is translated at the Institute, as are parts of *Life* magazine. In short, anything that might have new information about foreign scientific advances is systematically reviewed. Some journals, such as *Reviews of Modern Physics*, are not translated, but are reproduced by photo-offset processes and distributed to libraries. Many Soviet scientists read English and keep themselves abreast of American developments. As impressive as the facilities for collecting and disseminating information about foreign developments already are, they are rapidly being improved. "Now," says David Voskoboinik, head of the department of nuclear physics in the Institute, "we are working on machines, electronic brains, to help review information."

The knowledge that Soviet scientists and engineers have about American facilities and developments is indeed impressive. An American steel executive testified in 1954 about the knowledge a group of Soviet visitors to America had of our facilities: "They don't know just the location of our mines and smelters, they come with pinpoint knowledge of the location of every major piece of equipment in our plants. A group of Russians visited one of our mills, saw a ball mill we had shifted, compared notes with each other, then asked when we had moved the equipment."

Warren B. Walsh, Professor of Russian history at Syracuse University reported in *The Russian Review* (July, 1960):

The Soviets appear in some cases to be deliberately and skillfully using a sort of division of labor by waiting for the scientists and technicians of other nations to achieve certain results. Meanwhile, Soviet scientists concentrate on something else. One evidence of this tactic is in high polymer chemistry. The Soviets have exerted a large research effort in this subject, but they are trying to translate their findings into production by obtaining plants and equipment from the West. This does not mean that they are incompetent to develop such plants and equipment. It merely means that they see no point in repeating what someone else also has already done. They propose to do in the field of synthetic fibers what they have already successfully done elsewhere, namely, to use Western equipment and processes as prototypes for further development.

When one sees what a systematic program of borrowing from the West has been established, he can appreciate a joke that was heard in the Soviet Union during the 1930s and 1940s: "The most outstanding Russian inventor is REGUSPATOFF" (for "Registered, U.S. Patent Office").

Many Soviet scientists admit their indebtedness to American science. In 1957, Professor Turkevich reported: "At the Geneva atomic conference of 1955, I gave a paper on the use of isotopes in studying chemical reactions. A minister of the Soviet Union, their minister for cultural affairs, personally congratulated me. In return I said, 'I'm very happy competition between our countries in this case is not military or economic, but scientific'; I used the Russian word for competition—*concurensia.*

"He turned to me and said, 'Professor Turkevich, don't use that word.

It has a bad connotation—it means getting ahead by crushing the other fellow to the ground. We have a better way, and a better word— *sorevnovanya*—it's getting ahead by building on the other man's shoulders.' This to me is the thing. They're not out to crush us. They want to build on top of us. They have the most extensive program for collecting information ever conceived by man."

An extensive, centrally controlled organizational structure, ample funds, and systematic efforts to build on western developments are three reasons why Soviet scientific advance has been so spectacular. In addition, Soviet leaders have sought to attract talented people into scientific fields by endowing the role of the scientist with tremendous prestige. There are a number of indications of the high prestige enjoyed by leading scientists in the USSR. They receive handsome financial remuneration; a top physicist, for example, earns a higher income than a factory manager—he is in the same class with the most influential business executives and renowned ballerinas. He also receives other perquisites that are important in a scarce economy. While in Moscow, the foreign visitor passes a group of large individual homes on a fine residential street—a rare sight in any Soviet city. In answer to the question, "Who lives there?" the interpreter replies: "I do not know for sure, but they must be government officials or physics professors."

Some of the Soviet scientists who visit the United States subtly betray by their words and actions the deference they are accorded at home. In October 1957, Academician A. A. Blagonravov was in Washington, D. C. when the first Sputnik went up. An American reporter jokingly told him that the Russians were stealing the play from the world series. Blagonravov replied sternly without a touch of humor, "In Russia scientists are not compared with football [sic] players."

The prestige of the scientist is matched by his devotion to his tasks and to his country. This sense of dedication is manifested by many of the established scientists. Some observers liken the spirit found in Soviet scientific establishments to that found among western scientists at Los Alamos during World War II. Others think they see a drive that is motivated by a vast inferiority complex that many Soviet scientists and citizens seem to feel when they compare themselves with their western counterparts.

Among Soviet young people training for a scientific profession, one can find this high dedication to the country's needs explicitly stated. Ask an American college student why he is studying, and if one gets an answer, it is likely to be, "to advance myself." Ask a young Soviet student the same question, and he is likely to say, "because my country needs what I am learning"; or "to advance myself and to advance my country. You see, our people's welfare will improve with our country's welfare." One must, of course, discount the chauvinism that is to be expected when a young Soviet citizen is talking to an American. Still, after considerable allowance is made, one cannot help but be impressed by their identification of self-welfare with national welfare.

At the University of Moscow in mid-1958 a twenty-two-year-old senior in chemistry opened a conversation by saying, half aggressively, half puzzled, "Why did you not have Sputnik first?"

We replied, "I guess we didn't start soon enough. We didn't work hard enough."

"But why did you not?"

"Well, we made a mistake. We put other things first."

"In my country," he replied, "when the prestige of the country is to benefit, nothing else must come first."

In Leningrad, on the quay along the river Neva, a recent aeronautical engineering graduate and his friend, a fifth-year student of economics, were asked, "Why do students in your country study so hard?" The aeronautical engineer replied, "We have to or we may not stay in school. We will be able to lead better lives. And we will enable our country to catch up with you!"

The first of a code of 20 duties that every school boy and girl learns is: "To acquire knowledge persistently in order to become an educated and cultured citizen and to be of the greatest possible service to his country." Not all young people live by this rule. As we shall see in a later chapter, some are cynical, others are lazy. But the theme, "Work for your country," is drummed into the heads of young people from the time they enter school. The idea has penetrated the minds of many, scientists among them, and helps to account for the growth of science.

REGIMENTATION OF SCIENCE— STALINIST STYLE

Despite the prestige bestowed upon the scientist, one must not get the impression that the Soviet Union is a paradise for those who engage in scientific endeavor. Thorns are to be found among the roses. Many of the difficulties confronting the Soviet scientist can be illustrated by a brief description of the restraints placed upon scientific research during the closing years of Stalin's rule.

After World War II, the late Andrei Zhdanov, high-ranking member of the Politburo, directed Soviet science and culture. He purged many rebels, branded "academic" research as unworthy, and warned that everything had to serve the proletariat. *Pravda* contained statements such as "Soviet science is permeated with a spirit of partisanship. It is developing most in directions indicated most urgent by the Communist Party and our great leader, Comrade Stalin." All were required to bow before "the greatest scientist of our era, Comrade Stalin." Western scientists were portrayed as "jackals" who were attacking the Soviet Union for gold. Indeed, Soviet scientists participated in hate-America campaigns.

Political orthodoxy became one of the main requisites for advancement to high-level positions in all branches of science. Sometimes it was the most important criterion, as indicated by the way in which Trofim Lysenko, with his unsupported (some might say, ludicrous) theories of the inheritance of acquired characteristics, dominated the field of genetics. With the support of Stalin, he almost killed scientifically respectable genetic research. Geneticists who did not agree with Lysenko were hounded and even liquidated. Geneticist A. N. Vavilov died in a slave labor camp. His younger brother, then president of the Academy of Sciences, signed the papers condemning his work.

Nearly all fields of scientific endeavor were influenced by the oppressive hand of dictatorship. The brilliant physicist Lev Landau was jailed. (After Stalin's death he was released and won recognition as one of the world's ten leading theoretical physicists.) Physiology and medicine were gripped and weakened by a "super-Pavlovism" at which Pavlov would have scoffed. Psychology nearly vanished. Attacks on physics, geology, astronomy, and statistics were turned unpredictably on and off.

Many western scientists during this period thought that the stifling environment of the police state would destroy any true scientific development. As events have shown, they were wrong; science was hampered, but not destroyed. There are several reasons why it survived.

The realities of world political conflict and the importance of scientific development to military power placed some limits on how far politicians could intervene in certain crucial areas of the scientific enterprise. Some scientists paid enough obeisance to the Party and its ideology to keep out of trouble, and perhaps even found refuge in their work. "For many," Professor Turkevich commented during the end of the Stalin era, "I am sure food is the spur. If they do not produce, they and their families do not eat."

Undoubtedly, however, some scientists were genuinely devoted to the Communist ideology and accepted as necessities many of the restraints under which they worked. This, too, is understandable, since some scientists owed their education and positions to the revolution and the Party in a very direct sense. One of these men is Alexander Mikhail

Samarin, Deputy Director of the important Institute of Metallurgy in Moscow. His story indicates how many of the older generation of scientists and engineers must feel about Communism.

"My father was a peasant," he said. "My father was a peasant who could not read or write. We lived in a village of 600 houses, and in each there were four or five children, but in the whole village school there were only 50 boys and ten girls. I was one, and I went for four years."

He leaned back and smiled, displaying crooked teeth. His English was imperfect in form, but perfect in meaning. He was friendly and plain, a scientist for Russia's steelmakers.

"I was a boy when I went to work in a heavy machine factory. I was fifteen when the Revolution came. In 1921, when I was nineteen, I was able to start going to a special high school for workers and peasants."

He paused to strike a match with one hard-nailed hand, and was asked, "Who sent you to school?"

"My trade union," he shot back with hard pride. "And we got a salary. Our salary was 15 pounds of beans a month. It was a big famine then. That's what we had to eat. That's all. But it was all right. We were young."

After a few years of high school, young Samarin studied engineering and then metallurgy, and he completed his education in 1928 at the age of 30.

"I was just one of many, many thousands of people who went through these workers' faculties," he recounted. "And many of our professors said to us, 'You'll only be foremen, never engineers. Your parents were not engineers, you'll never be engineers.' Today I have many friends who went to the same workers' schools who are professors. My wife and my sister also finished the workers' faculty. They are physicians." His leather face wrinkled in smiles as he continued. "You see, I think the revolution was the best thing for my country."

If one thinks for a moment about the kind of life Samarin might have lived if the Tsarist regime had continued, the implications of his story begin to make an impression. It was suggested that if it had not been for the revolution he would certainly never have been educated.

He smiled wryly. "I think I'd be in prison in Siberia."

Unfortunately, this was the fate of many of Samarin's fellow-scientists under the capricious rule of Joseph Stalin, but in one way or another, Soviet scientists and science survived. When Stalin passed from the Soviet scene, the political atmosphere cleared somewhat and science flourished.

STALIN'S DEATH, SPUTNIK'S SUCCESS

In recent years the forward pace of Soviet science has received tremendous boosts from two major events: the death of Stalin and the success of Sputnik.

The Soviet Union since Stalin's death is a changed place; one finds it not free or even nearly free, but different and improved. Scientists are profoundly and particularly affected. Freedom for them has increased markedly, and the Stalin era of purges and bowing to Communism in every breath is over. Many disgraced scientists have been restored to prominence. Scientific investigation is now free, with few taboo areas. More and more scientists are meeting western scientists, and many are seeing the West. A new self-confidence and optimism are reflected in recent Soviet scientific achievements, according to critics who are qualified to judge.

The sweeter air has even begun to give some scientists a measure of political courage. One famous scientist restored to favor is Peter Kapitsa. Russian-born, working in Britain, he visited Russia in 1934 and was forced to stay (and was given lavish personal and research quarters). Around 1946, he refused to work on atomic weapons and was put under long house arrest. After Stalin's death, he re-emerged as head of his own institute and as a space research planner. Kapitsa even had the courage to write in *Pravda* that Khrushchev's industrial decentralization might cripple industrial research. Kapitsa's influence on younger men, as a result of his challenging Stalin and getting away with it, has been great.

Since Stalin's death, leading scientists have also balked at what they considered to be "arbitrary and unconstituional" rule in the Academy of Sciences. In what an American expert called a "revolt," they almost voted out the president, Alexander Nesmeyanov, a Communist Party member (who was finally replaced in 1961). One of the challengers was the renowned senior physicist and recent Nobel prizewinner Igor Tamm, who was one of Russia's representatives at the Geneva atomic energy conferences in 1961.

It is obvious at international meetings that Russian scientists are still under pressure, especially in such important fields as space activity where security and secrecy measures outdo almost any of our own. Every research institute has its scientific secretary and political watchman. Politics is still mixed into science. One of the first Soviet ice research stations, for example, set up "the first Communist Party organization in the North Pole region." Nevertheless, in many areas in which politics and important scientific or technological goals clash, fulfillment of the goals apparently comes first.

SCIENCE-BY-SCIENCE

It is clear that the Soviet Union has made tremendous strides in the development of its scientific establishment. But how do individual branches of Soviet science and technology compare with their counterparts in the United States? Some areas hold an outstanding place in world science; some are only fair; others are poor. Many are spotty—brilliant in some aspects but still far behind the West in others. A high-level naval research advisory committee, headed by Dr. C. Guy Suits, vice president and research director of General Electric, in June, 1959 reported the following: (1) It appears that currently the United States leads the USSR in most areas of physics, mathematics, medicine and chemistry; (2) the Soviet Union seems to be "on a par" with the US in aviation-space medicine, metallurgy, combustion, theoretical physics, meteorology, and oceanography; (3) Russia leads in physical chemistry and many areas of geophysics.[1]

This committee drew on expert opinions. There is much disagreement, however, among the best observers. The Soviet Union is a huge country. It has the good and the bad, the new and the old, the outstanding and the abysmally backward alongside each other. And sometimes visitors are puzzled or fooled by the fact that the work they see is going on in unbelievable shabby and jerry-built surroundings. Some visitors look too long at the falling bricks and fail to pay enough attention to the results of scientific research.

In physics in general and in the key nuclear sciences, there seems to be clear-cut US superiority. In both high and low-energy nuclear physics, the West leads. There has been a marked resurgence, however, in Soviet theoretical physics, Walsh reports after consulting with a large number of observers, "and it now appears that the Soviets may outstrip the West in quantum field theory, quantum electrodynamics and the theories of strange particles." Another recent report on quantum field theory, the mathematical fundamentals of the atom's elementary particles, says: "If, as seems likely, the study of quantum field theory continues to attract relatively more physicists in Russia than in the West, the quantity of Russian efforts will outweigh those of the West in the near future."

In solid state physics (which underlies progress in electronics, com-

---

[1] *Basic Research in the Navy*, Naval Research Advisory Committee, Washington, D.C., June 1, 1959. The committee included the head of the National Aeronautics and Space Administration; the vice presidents or research directors of Douglas Aircraft, Union Carbide, American Telephone & Telegraph, and International Business Machines; the heads of Buffalo, Stanford, and Pennsylvania State Universities, and three members or recent members of the President's Science Advisory Committee.

puters, and materials for rockets or nuclear reactors), Turkevich concludes: "The only field of excellence of the Soviet Union is that of
the thermo-electric devices which convert heat into electricity and electricity into cold." But here, too, another report says: "It is difficult to
avoid the conclusion that in another five or ten years their basic research
output will exceed ours." The USSR is without question behind in the
study of molecules and solids, but in the field of extreme low temperatures, Turkevich concedes, there has been a tradition of Soviet strength,
largely because of the work of Peter Kapitsa and his collaborators.

In mathematics, Walsh reports, "One may fairly say that the Soviet
Union is currently second. This generalization, however, is seriously
misleading unless it is immediately qualified. The Soviets are at present
the world leaders in the mathematical subfields of analysis, non-linear
differential equations (the subfield closest to applications), the theory
of control circuits, that branch of geometry which deals with complex
figures, and perhaps also in topology. They lag somewhat behind the
United States in mathematical logic, modern algebra, algebraic geometry and geometry as a whole. The Soviets excel in analytical number
theory, but the United States leads in other aspects of number theory.
An outstanding American mathematician, a scholar with a world-wide
reputation and many international contacts, believes that the United
States is currently ahead of the Soviet Union in mathematics. He immediately adds, however, that the Soviets are closer to us today then
we were to Western Europe in 1910."

Again, Dr. A. J. Lohwater, Rice Institute mathematician, predicts
that "if things continue at the present pace, they will in less than a
generation far surpass us."

Turkevich finds the Russians strong in physical chemistry, but over-
shadowed by the West. In organic chemistry, he says, there are at least
a dozen prominent organic chemists in America for every comparable
Russian. Various other observers find the Russians "well ahead"
in the physical chemistry of fast reactions (the reactions inside rocket
or jet engines, military explosives, and some new fast industrial chemistry). Their applied industrial chemistry is well behind that of the
United States. In all chemical research, according to the number of
papers published by world chemists, the United States is twice as active
as Russia. However, merely since 1951, the Russians have risen from
fifth to second place.

Many observers point to highly sophisticated Russian work in
metallurgy. Dr. Herbert F. York, until recently director of Defense
Department research and engineering, says: "My belief is that this is
an area where the Russians have more first-class people than we and

are training more." In engineering mechanics—which is concerned with the behavior of matter under force—Dr. W. A. Nash of the University of Florida, after visiting several institutes in the USSR, wrote: "We did not find the highest level of basic research any better than in the United States." But its quantity, he said, is now two to three times ours, and Russia is training so many students that it is "almost certain" that "within five to ten years their efforts will perhaps be of the order of ten times" our present effort.

American visitors a few years ago began, to their surprise, to observe outstanding Russian work in electronics. A physicist from the Massachusetts Institute of Technology who worked on our DEW-line air-defense radar, says that compared to ours, the Russian air defense system seems "better." In precision instrumentation the Russians still often buy a single instrument or piece of equipment abroad, then produce multiple copies. They have developed a high-level precision instrument industry, however, and the quality of their own instrumentation is constantly improving.

"Biology and biochemistry are in a sad state in the Soviet Union," Turkevich finds. Lysenkoism and politics are responsible. Indeed, as the Khrushchev era advanced, Lysenko regained at least something of the position of influence he had seemed to lose with Stalin's death. It was not until 1962 that he apparently experienced another setback. The future here is uncertain.

Soviet medicine is a victim of inadequate research in biology. Lacking independent biological and physiological research findings to serve as a starting point, affected sometimes by politics and usually by low priorities for manpower and spending, Soviet medicine is highly uneven in quality.

Soviet astronomy, which had lagged badly, is moving ahead in all areas, especially in astrophysics, a branch which is important in the understanding of space and of the atom. Four American astrophysicists who toured Russia reported in April 1959 that Russia is now turning out twice as many astronomers as we and might overtake us in 15 years in this field.

Today's much-advertised space sciences are, to a large extent, part of geophysics, the science concerned with the earth, the sea, and the sky. The findings obtained during the International Geophysical Year indicated that in the next quarter century, say by 1985, man may have a large measure of influence over the atmosphere. Weather modification would be an early target. Until the last few years geophysics had been one of the most neglected areas of science in the United States—not so in the Soviet Union.

Several prominent American geophysicists have found the Russians ahead of the United States in polar meterology and Arctic research and in some aspects of oceanography and very possibly in geophysics as a whole.

Some reports indicate that Russian theoretical work in seismology, the science of earthquakes, is less advanced than ours. An American seismologist said, however, that the Russians "have many more earthquake detection stations than we have, with real coordination, which we have not. They have much more sensitive, high-frequency instruments." At the 1958 disarmament talks in Geneva scientists from the United States had to cull Soviet literature in order to obtain information on conversion of energy into wave motion in the earth, because of a sharp Soviet lead in this field.

In meteorology, Dr. Harry Wexler, US Weather Bureau research chief, has found advanced research in Russia to be "all right but not brilliant." However, he points out that "our best minds and best instruments are still superior to theirs, but they have more minds, more instruments and money, and more expansion planned for the future."

With regard to oceanography, the Soviet Union has not produced basic research equal to ours, but it has long had a fleet of 18 research ships, two of them above 10,000 tons, while the US struggled along with a few converted yachts. The Russians have compiled more data on depths of currents and water temperatures, with immediate practical application to navigation of submarines.

At Nizmir, the big institute of earth and atmospheric science 22 miles from Moscow, director Nikolas Pushkov has told foreign visitors of the earth-magnetism-measuring ship his institute operates, the world's only nonmagnetic ship. The comment of an American scientist was revealing: "Their geomagnetic facilities top anything we've got. In fact, the whole place tops anything we've got in space, money, people, and time."

In geophysics, again and again, as in all sciences, observing Americans find work behind ours—and then comment, "It's their upward slope everywhere that counts."

SOVIET SELF-CRITICISM

It is not necessary to rely entirely on the the estimates of American observers concerning the shortcomings and deficiencies in Soviet science. Publications in the Soviet Union itself contain critiques that indicate some of the major problem areas.

One self-appraised weakness is a divorce between research institutes and universities. Soviet universities stress teaching but do not emphasize research as much as do American universities. Conversely, at research institutes, teaching is secondary, although it is here that the young man or woman seeking a doctorate must generally do research. The institutes often have a few staff members associated with a university, and most of them spend full time on tasks completely unconnected with teaching. Attempts to make research institutes into centers of scientific education have come to little because directors regard teaching as a drag on research.

A second self-advertised deficiency has been the domination of the scientific establishment by scientists of advanced years, many of them encumbered by an overload of bureaucratic responsibilities. Apparently, however, steps are being taken to alleviate this situation. In a publication of the USSR Academy of Sciences in February 1962, A. V. Topchiev, vice president of the Academy, announced a new program to shift direction of research institutes under the supervision of the Academy to younger men in the 35 to 40 age bracket.

Another problem that has been pointed up in the Soviet press is the lack of quick translation of scientific discoveries into production-line technology. At a 1961 meeting of the Academy, speakers complained that cooperation between science and industry was still unsatisfactory, despite major efforts and some progress. In practice, the annual plan that enumerates research achievements recommended for application to industry was composed chiefly of items of "secondary importance." The best contributions were being made outside the plan, thus reflecting poor planning and organization within this program.

The major criticism in the past several years has been directed at the organization of Soviet scientific and industrial research. A particularly important debate began in mid-1955. At the Twentieth Party Congress in 1956, Khrushchev commented on some of the issues raised in that debate:

The separation of the research activity of the Academy of Sciences, departmental research institutes and higher education establishments can no longer be tolerated. This separation and lack of coordination prevent the concentration of research activity on the solution of major scientific and engineering problems, lead to duplication of effort and waste of resources, and retard the introduction of research and engineering achievements into production.

Since that time attempts have been made to correct the deficiencies. The latest decree—and the most encompassing and important to date—

was disclosed at a meeting of the Academy of Sciences on April 10, 1961, and published in *Pravda* on April 12, amid the excitement generated by the first Soviet cosmonaut.

This decree created a new, high-level state committee on the coordination of research and development headed by a deputy chairman of the Council of Ministers. This committee was given the major responsibility for supervising the work of all organizations engaged in research and development and guiding them toward the fulfillment of important objectives laid down by Party governmental directives. To accomplish this task, it works closely with the state economic council and with the state planning committee to develop plans for research and development throughout the USSR and to introduce the latest scientific and engineering techniques into productive facilities. It must also play an important role in coordinating the work of the Academy of Sciences of the USSR with the academies of sciences of the constituent republics and with the research and development work done under the auspices of state ministries and departments.

The members of the new committee indicate its significance in the governmental structure. In addition to its chairman, who is a deputy chairman of the Council of Ministers, the members include the president of the Academy of Sciences; the minister of higher and secondary specialized education; the chairman of the state committee on automation and machine building; the chairman of the state committee on chemistry; the chairman of the committee on inventions and discoveries; a deputy chairman of the state economic council; and a deputy chairman of the state planning committee. Many of these members (including the new president of the Academy of Sciences) are men with considerable experience in military, rocket, and space technology. Some are engineers formerly active in defense fields who have now become industrial managers and political leaders.

The new organization will, of course, affect the activities of the Academy of Sciences. Although the Academy will remain the largest research unit in the USSR, it should now be freed of some of its bureaucratic responsibilities and from some of its technological (as opposed to scientific) tasks and able to concentrate on basic research. Indeed, the decree establishing the new state committee prescribes that "the work of the Academy should be focused on the most important long-run problems of science undergoing rapid development." This is precisely the emphasis that the Academy's leadership has been seeking.

Nicholas DeWitt, in an article in *Science* (June 23, 1961), sums up the significance of the organizational change:

Perhaps these measures are a recognition of a turning point in Soviet technological development: the point of diminishing returns from adaptation of Western technology has been reached, and new and vigorous domestic technological development becomes a necessity. The Soviet political leadership appears to be convinced that the invigoration of technological research activities can be more profitably achieved by separating functions, and by freeing the Academy of Sciences of the USSR to concentrate its attention on basic research and the long-run problems of science. Reorganization of the Soviet research setup could provide an effective mechanism for channeling scientific manpower and material resources into strategic areas of the physical sciences and engineering toward the achievement of the most ambitious long-run goal of Soviet power—world leadership in science and technology.

THE FUTURE TREND

Science in the USSR has become a god, revered and looked upon as the salvation of the country. Posters depict Young Pioneers—the little Communists—studying chemistry and machinery; on the subway, a girl in pigtails reads a science book; children's science books are subsidized and many of them are much better and cheaper than our own. The storybooks glorify science. "To measure the solidity of water under icebergs at the North Pole, to divert the course of a river, to hunt for uranium—these are the adventures that fill the storybooks," observes one writer on Russia. "Even medicine is sissy by comparison and is becoming more and more regarded as a job for sister."

The splendid (even frightening) success of the Soviet Union in developing its scientific establishment and the prospect for future scientific advancements should sober any American. We once made the mistake of assuming that science cannot flourish under a repressive political elite. Perhaps the conditions under which the scientific advancements were initiated while Stalin was in power will not exist again. While the mystique of the revolution rode high in the land, when many scientists and engineers owed to the rulers their opportunity to do *any* work in scientific fields, they then accepted restrictions imposed upon them. But there is some evidence today that man will not continue to be a creative scientist and at the same time a "political slave."

A highly placed Russian professor made this point well in a private conversation at a meeting outside the Soviet Union: "My country has changed since the death of Stalin. I think it has changed for good. One thing about the last war, you see, was good for us. Many thousands of our people saw how things were somewhere else. And they wanted something better too. I think a country cannot go back. Once a people have tasted the sweet, they do not want the sour."

At the same time—although the USSR may not return to the harsh conditions it suffered under Stalin—we must not assume that it must evolve politically in the direction of the western democracies in order to continue its scientific advance.

The style of dictatorial rule that Khrushchev has developed and now applies seems to give the scientist much of the freedom he desires without weakening the system of oligarchical control of the society. Indeed, one of the great and, in the long run, most significant accomplishments of the Soviet political leaders has been the integration of science and the scientist into the fabric of a totalitarian society. Professor Turkevich has commented eloquently on this accomplishment and the challenge for America that it involves: "The role of science is dominant in the future of nations and social and economic systems. That form of society . . . will prevail that best integrates science into its structure, that makes science a vital part of its defensive might, economic productivity, social well being, intellectual activity and spiritual aspirations. We in the West have been slow in carrying out this integration. As a nation, we have not been sufficiently imaginative in realizing the possibilities that science offers. . . . The rival Soviet system is pressing us in competition on many sides and promises even more vigorous competition in the future. . . .

"More subtle than the political machinations in Africa, Cuba and Asia is the Soviet use of science and technology for advancing the Communist system. . . .

"The present situation calls for an overall survey of the place of science in American society. . . . The greatest achievement of Soviet science is, to my mind, its integration within the totalitarian socialistic society. The challenge that I fear faces the United States and the Western world is how to integrate modern science into our democratic capitalistic society."

The existence of a scientific establishment that is integrated into the society under the direction of a new organization geared to launch an effort to surpass the United States makes it possible that one day the United States will be the second-ranking power in the realm of science. It is not that Soviet scientists are more brilliant or better trained than their American counterparts. Their quality is impressive; but it is their number that threatens to become overwhelming.

In 1956, when W. H. K. Panofsky, designer of the new giant linear accelerator at Stanford University, was visiting in Moscow, he was asked to meet a few of his Soviet counterparts. He had expected to meet "three or four." He was confronted with some 30 eager young men and women. The pressure of superior numbers is likely to be even greater in the future. In every area of science important to a modern technological society the Soviet Union is turning out people—and good people—at a rate far greater than the United States. The latest report on this, a comprehensive analysis written by Nicholas DeWitt,[2] predicts that in the decade of the 1960s the Soviet Union will probably produce four million university graduates, of whom 2,500,000 will be scientists and engineers. This is twice the number of scientifically and technically trained personnel that the United States is likely to produce in the present decade. The report also indicates that the quality of Russian training is as good and sometimes better than that of America and western Europe.

The progress of Soviet science in the future, as well as in the past, is inextricably linked with the development of the educational system. Thus before one can assess the strengths and weaknesses in the scientific establishment or make any guesses as to the future course of Soviet science, one must review the Russian educational program. This aspect of contemporary Russia will be considered in Chapter 6.

[2] *Education and Professional Employment in the USSR*, National Science Foundation, 1962.

6

SOVIET EDUCATION AS "TRAINING FOR LIFE"

Robert H. Beck

Professor of the History and Philosophy of Education at the University of Minnesota, Robert H. Beck has engaged in research and lecturing abroad, including work in the USSR in 1958. As editor, he has published The Three R's Plus, *and, as coauthor,* Curriculum in the Modern Elementary School *(with Walter W. Cook and Nolan C. Kearney).*

W hen the initial shock of the first Russian Sputnik had worn off, many Americans began to wonder how it was possible for the Soviet Union to beat the United States into outer space. In the search for reasons (or scapegoats), attention was focused upon the American educational system. Is enough emphasis being given to the "tough courses," such as mathematics, science, and foreign language? Are the capable young men and women in our colleges and universities spending too much time in the sports arena and on the dance floor? Is the emphasis in the American school upon learning as such, or merely upon learning to be liked?

In the course of asking these questions, Americans inevitably compare their educational system with that of the Soviet Union, almost as if the latter should be the model for judging the American system. How many hours a week do Russian children study physics and chemistry? How much homework is required of the Russian schoolboy? What is his attitude toward learning? And, finally, how does the graduate of a Russian school compare with his American counterpart?

Ironically enough, American interest in the Soviet educational system

138

reached its peak at a time when Soviet leaders were criticizing their school system and were preparing to make major reforms in it. The Soviet educational system, which had been hailed by some westerners as the key to Russian success in outer space, was being subjected to criticism and change at what should have been the moment of its greatest triumph. What was the problem?

KHRUSHCHEV'S CRITIQUE OF SOVIET SCHOOLS

On April 18, 1958, Nikita Khrushchev rose to address the Thirteenth Congress of the Young Communist League (*Komsomols*). His audience was attentive, for this gathering represented the cream of the dedicated youth in the Soviet Union. Any daydreamers in the group who were not sufficiently inspired by the mere presence of the top Communist leader probably awoke with a start when Comrade Nikita launched an extensive attack upon the Soviet educational system. Few topics could generate more interest among the young Communists, for educational attainment has long been an important prerequisite for good jobs in a society that has continually been plagued by a lack of technical skill. Since any change in the educational system might affect a young man's chance of securing a managerial or professional position, a government official who was suggesting major reforms would naturally command the attention of the assembly. These reforms were of interest to the western world as well, for the educational system is extremely important in shaping the future of the USSR. As in all societies Soviet leaders rely heavily upon the schools to shape the values and develop the skills of each new generation of young people who must become obedient citizens, reliable leaders, and industrious workers.

On that spring afternoon, Premier Khrushchev voiced his dissatisfaction with the values and skills that the educational system was producing. Too many young people, he contended, were clamoring to get into the universities and institutes—twice as many as these higher educational establishments had room for—and those who were rejected were reluctant to take jobs in factories and farms. With typical bluntness he attacked this pressure to obtain higher education and the state of mind that lies behind it:

Some young men and women . . . after graduating from the secondary schools, go to work in factories, plants and collective and state farms unwillingly; they look upon this as though it were an insult to them. This haughty, contemptuous, incorrect attitude towards manual labor is also manifested in some families; if a child is doing badly in school, some parents will tell him, "If you don't do well in school, you won't be able to enter a higher educational institution and will end up at a factory as an everyday laborer. . . ." I shall not even talk about the fact that such reasoning is insulting to the toilers of a socialist society.

When the First Secretary of the Soviet Communist Party vehemently criticizes the practices of such an important institution as education, quick action can usually be predicted. Five months later, *Pravda* carried a memorandum from Khrushchev proposing fundamental changes in the educational system, and on December 24, 1958, the Supreme Soviet, without a dissenting voice, enacted the proposals into law.

It was not too surprising that some type of educational reform should be in the offing in 1958. Like agriculture and industry, Soviet education is designed to serve the state. When a new economic plan is announced, the educational system is often adjusted in order to produce the trained personnel required by the new plan. In 1958 the Soviet leaders had launched a new seven-year plan, which was hailed as a major drive to enable the USSR to catch up economically with the United States. Thus an educational system that, according to official criticism, was failing to prepare Soviet youth for "socially useful labor" was obviously incompatible with such an ambitious economic objective.

But the sharpness of Khrushchev's attack and the sweeping nature of the reforms he proposed caught even the Soviet educators off guard. The Soviet people had reason to be proud of their educational system. In less than four decades it had virtually stamped out illiteracy in a country where the illiteracy rate (despite impressive gains during the last decades of Tsarist rule) had been about 60 percent before the revolution. Despite occasional setbacks, the schools had trained enough personnel to build an advanced industrial society. They had produced such competent scientists that the Soviet Union, with the aid of a few German specialists, was able to enter the Age of Space ahead of her foremost competitors. In the light of those attainments, students of Soviet affairs began to look for the reasons for a drastic remodeling of the school system. What form will the educational system take? How successful is it likely to be in realizing the objectives set for it? Before examining the educational system as reorganized by Khrushchev, it will be instructive to glance briefly at the older types of Soviet schools.

Until 1958 the vast majority of Russian students were enrolled in three types of preparatory schools: (1) the four-year school, probably the most common type in the rural areas; (2) the seven-year school, roughly equivalent to a combination of elementary and junior high in the United States; and (3) the ten-year school. At the end of World War II, Soviet leaders sought to replace the other schools with the ten-year school and to make the course of study offered there virtually compulsory for every Russian youth. Although the ten-year school, which combined academic studies with training in industrial arts, was somewhat comparable to the twelve-year program of elementary and secondary education in the United States, the curriculum was more rigid and probably more difficult than that of American schools. Since electives were unknown, all students were required to take mathematics through trigonometry, a foreign language for several years, and other courses in science, literature, and the arts. The Communists proudly boasted that by 1960 all Soviet young people would be enrolled in a ten-year school. They would all move at the same pace and study the same subjects from the same textbooks.

Western educators were, of course, skeptical about such utopian notions of education. Do all students have the ability required by this difficult course of study? they asked. Are there not individual differences among students that suggest the need for flexibility in the curriculum, that is, the need to gear the program to the needs and aptitudes of a heterogeneous student population? To these objections the Soviet educator answered that "individual differences" among pupils can be ignored; all can succeed in the ten-year school. This is a standard reply, dictated by the Communist Party line since 1936. In that year the Central Committee denounced all forms of psychological testing. Testing for individual differences in learning ability was labelled "pedagogical perversion"; all Soviet citizens were considered capable of being reformed and set on the road to indefinite improvement. To think otherwise was fatalistic and "reactionary." The idea that some students might not be capable of becoming engineers or scientists was, in the Soviet view, a vestige of the old idea that some men are born to be "hewers of wood and drawers of water." Measuring individual abilities was a "reactionary, bourgeois, pseudo science . . . based on the assumption of a fatalistic predestination of the child's fate by biological and social factors, by the influence of inheritance and unchanging environment." The testing of differences in ability of students in western countries was explained as a function of a classridden, capitalist society.

After the widespread adoption of the ten-year course of study in the Soviet Union, educators were immediately beset by many problems. Some students experienced difficulty in mastering the "hard" subjects. Occasionally *Pravda* published letters complaining that from 30 to 50 percent of the students in upper grades were failing mathematics and the physical sciences. In the schools ordinarily visited by the foreign observer, however, the failure rate is very low. This situation apparently is typical, and the reason is not hard to find. If it is assumed that all students have the ability to pass the ten-year course, a high rate of failure must indicate a poor teacher, or one who has "reactionary-bourgeois tendencies." To avoid being criticized, teachers spend a good deal of time helping the poorer students and award low marks only in the most exceptional cases. "We pull them through the grades" is an assertion made by many teachers.

The ten-year school system presented another difficult problem. Presumably all graduates were prepared for higher education, yet the universities and technical institutes were unable to accommodate all the young people who came out of the ten-year schools. As a result, enormous pressures were built up for entrance into institutions that offered advanced study. There were reports of parents who bribed the teachers to give high marks to their children and of powerful government officials who used their influence to gain special treatment for their offspring.

THE REORGANIZED SCHOOL SYSTEM

The ten-year school bore the brunt of Khrushchev's attack, and it was abolished under the new scheme that was introduced in 1958, to be completed by 1965. Although the school system is presently in a transitional state and no one can be certain about how permanent the changes will be, the older courses of study have come under such sustained attack that Soviet leaders are unlikely to move back to the more traditional curriculum in the immediate future. Indeed, Khrushchev told the Twenty-second Party Congress (1961) that the reforms had been successful: "The experience of reorganization has confirmed the timelessness and validity of the Party's measures." Khrushchev, at any rate, felt that the proposals he had recommended had been proved sound. For this reason it will be profitable to examine, even though tentatively, the new system of education as it appears to be operating.

The Soviet student goes through two stages of schooling before he enters a higher educational institution, if he is so fortunate. The first phase of his education is in an eight-year school—the *Incomplete General Education, Polytechnical, Labor School*—which is compulsory for all young people. The eight-year school replaces the seven-year school of the old system and places greater emphasis upon technical study and practical work in shops and on farms as preparation for their careers.

After completing his work in the eight-year school, the student, who will be approaching the age of fifteen, may continue his secondary education in one of several ways. (1) He may go directly to work in a factory or on a farm, and he may take a short course of academic study, either by correspondence or by attending evening classes, in a *School for Working or Rural Youth.* In his report on education made to the Twenty-second Party Congress, ("Improvement of the People's Well Being: The Flowering of Science, Education, Literature, and the Arts"), Khrushchev noted his satisfaction with the increase in the number of schools for "working and rural youth." Young people who are trained under this program come close to being both workers and students, and, according to Khrushchev, the majority of Soviet youth will fall into this category.

(2) The student may embark upon a three-year course in a *Complete Secondary General Education, Polytechnical, Labor School with Production Training.* This school, comparable in some respects to the three-year high school in the United States, combines general education with vocational training, although it does not involve fulltime work on the job. Graduates of this school will have completed the preparatory work for higher education, and most of the young people who are admitted to the universities and institutes are selected from this group.

(3) Secondary education may be continued by taking a one- to three-year vocational course in an *urban* (or *rural*) Technical school, which is closely attached to a factory or farm and which specializes in teaching one or two technical skills. (4) The student may also enroll in a two- to four-year course in a *Technikum,* a school that trains young people for skilled and semiskilled jobs in all branches of the economy.

The Soviet aim is to make education "training for life." All fifteen-year-old students, upon completing their work in the eight-year school, are given practical experience in productive labor. Khrushchev has said:

In my opinion, after they have finished seven or eight years of school, all school children, without exception, should take part in socially useful labor at enterprises, collective farms, and other places of work. Both in town and in the countryside, as well as at worker settlements, all children finishing school should go to work in production. No one must evade this stage. . . . I repeat, there must be no exceptions.

In admitting students to higher education, special preference is given to young people who have recently completed their military service or who have worked for two years in some type of labor. The insistence that all students, including the academically most able, have at least two years of "socially useful work" before entering the university has provoked outspoken criticism on the part of Soviet scientists. When, after the Twenty-second Party Congress, Khrushchev made it plain that a measure of criticism would be tolerated, scientists renewed and strengthened their protests of 1959 and 1960 against this program which postpones university studies for promising young scientists.

Little information is available on how students will be chosen to enter the various programs of secondary education. Selection may be made by teachers in the eight-year school on the basis of grades and a comprehensive examination at the end of the elementary course. The students with the poorest academic records will probably be chosen first for the fulltime work program, and then those who will enter the precollege program will be selected. Since Soviet educators have been discouraged from experimenting with testing programs, the methods of evaluating student performance at the end of the eighth year are apt to be crude and unreliable by American standards. In any event, the young people themselves will have little personal choice in selecting their training courses.

In addition to the schools already mentioned, the regime has established "schools for the gifted," which offer a two-year course to students who display an aptitude for music or the dance. Young people who are accepted into this program are not required to work while carrying on their studies. Although no action has been taken yet, Soviet leaders suggest the possibility that these special schools will be expanded to accommodate students of high ability in mathematics and science. As a result of Khrushchev's proposal at the Twentieth Party Congress (1956), restricted boarding schools have also been set up to provide an eight- to eleven-year training program for selected Soviet youths. Although fees are charged, the poor students are exempt from paying them, and special consideration is given to children from large and poor families. These schools are located in pleasant surroundings, and the students live on the premises, isolated from the "antisocialist" influences of the outside world. The curriculum emphasizes polytechnical subjects and is designed to turn out its quota of building technicians, machinists, operators of farm implements, clerical workers, and so forth. Five years after his proposal to establish boarding schools, Khrushchev was able to announce to the Twenty-second Party Congress that by 1965 there would be 2,500,000 pupils in these schools. In that same year there are expected to be 43 million youths in schools of less than university grade, with one twentieth of them in boarding schools.

A log cabin apartment illustrating the type of housing occupied by two million Muscovites

An apartment house for professors, located in a housing development for 300,000 people near the University of Moscow

New apartment housing development, Leningrad: a good example of the scale of housing projects on the fringes of major cities

A collective farm village south of Podolsk; note TV antennas

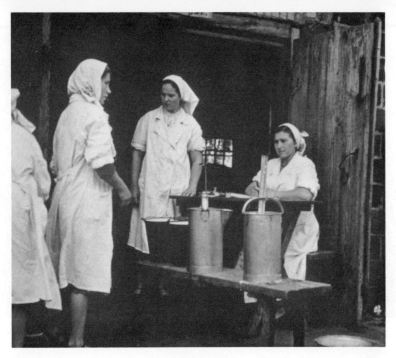

Milkmaids and production record keeping, collective farm near Kiev

Farm machinery display at the Soviet equivalent of a county farm near Rostov-on-Don

Recitation period in English class, Kiev school

Gymnasium class, Kiev school

Lunch room in a Kiev school

The Children's World, department store in Moscow devoted exclusively to children's goods

Window display of fabrics, store in Kiev. The dresses on the mannequins indicate the beginning of concern with style

Street scene, Rostov-on-Don. The man had just rescued his son from a near traffic accident

Street scene, Rostov-on-Don

Street scene, melon sale, Kiev

Workers in agricultural machinery plant at Rostov-on-Don relax after work playing dominoes

Street scene, Rostov-on-Don

THE NEW CURRICULUM

Although the subject matter of the new eight- and eleven-year programs continues to be rich, the curriculum differs in important respects from that of the old ten-year schools. In the field of language, for example, parents who live in republics where Russian is not the native tongue (in places like Uzbekistan and Kazakhstan) are now permitted somewhat more freedom to encourage their children to study the language and literature of their minority group, although the Russian language continues to receive a great deal of emphasis because of the role it plays in cultural and social intergration. Tacitly acknowledging that the language program in the past did not live up to expectations, the Soviet leaders have modified the arrangement for teaching foreign languages. Since 1959 some schools have begun to specialize in the teaching of a single language. Thus parents in urban centers may elect to enroll their children in an "English," a "French," a "German," or a "Ukrainian" school, and the students can begin instruction in the language as early as the first grade. Soviet educators hope that by the time the student reaches the eighth grade he will be advanced enough to study such subjects as literature, geography, and history in the language he has been studying.

The new curriculum in elementary and secondary education places a great deal of emphasis upon mathematics and science. The eight-year school concentrates upon basic mathematics, while the additional three-year program gives the student the mathematical training required for higher education. In both the elementary and the secondary schools, mathematics classes are offered at each grade level and they meet every day.

While the offerings in science are to be gradually increased under Khrushchev's reform program, they were extensive even in the pre-1958 system. The study of physics, for example, began in the sixth grade, and classes were held twice a week. Instruction in chemistry, also given two periods per week, began in the seventh grade. The Russian student who was trained under the ten-year program was getting much more science than secondary school students in the United States. For example, of graduates from American high schools in 1956, less than one-third had had a year (five periods per week) of chemistry, while only one-third had taken a year of physics.

Although the graduate of a Soviet secondary school (under either the old or the new system) will have been exposed to much more science than almost all American youngsters, it is nevertheless incorrect to assert that the Russian student has had six years of biology, five years of physics, four years of chemistry, and a year of astronomy before he completes the eleventh grade. As in most European countries, the Russian course of study distributes its subjects over more years, with fewer class meetings per week than is the case in the United States. In the ten-year schools, classes in mathematics and in Russian language and literature were the only ones that met daily. Biology met twice a week in grades four through six, three times a week in grade seven, twice a week in grades eight and nine, and not at all in grade ten. While the total amount of time devoted to the study of biology is greater than in American schools, it is thinly spread throughout the grades in the Soviet system. The Russians attempt to resolve this problem and to provide continuous, systematic study by having the same science instructor teach the students during all the years that they take a given subject. In the absence of reliable studies of the American and Soviet methods of teaching science to the young student, it is difficult to evaluate the finished product on a comparative basis.

While the time allotted to social studies was decreased by seven percent in 1955, no further cuts have been proposed since that time. Indeed, Khrushchev and the political writers who elaborated on his educational "theses" have underlined the importance of such studies. Such subjects as history, economic theory, geography, and other social sciences are employed to reinforce the ideological appeals of the Communist regime rather than as the means to objectively analyze social phenomena. In his history classes, the student is told of the age-old exploitation of workers and peasants by the ruling classes and of the liberation of the Russian proletariat by the Bolsheviks in the "glorious revolution" of 1917. In his study of Marxist-Leninist theory he learns the meaning of Soviet discipline and the attributes of the "new Soviet man." His geography teacher contrasts the welfare schemes of the Soviet community with the poverty of capitalist states. Textbooks and classroom instruction emphasize the grand design on which the homeland has presumably been formed, the vast natural resources of the fifteen republics, the impressive construction in the far north, the development of the virgin lands, and the opportunities on the Siberian frontier that await the ambitious youth. He is told of the dangers of "capitalist encirclement" and of the need for more warm water ports. Social studies are thus an important ingredient in the Communist propaganda effort.

The new curriculum lays heavier stress upon vocational education, reflecting Khrushchev's policy of preparing youth for "socially useful labor" in factories and fields. As we have seen, the postprimary stage of the student's education takes place in a school that specializes in polytechnical training or in a trade school of some type. The majority of students, who are also fulltime workers, secure this training through correspondence or by attending classes after working hours, while those who take courses during the regular days spend a portion of their time in "practical work" and on-the-job experience. Khrushchev's educational reform establishes new types of vocational and technical schools to take care of the hordes of students enrolled in the new program. Greater use is also made of the *technikums*, which combine elements of both the technical institute and the vocational secondary school to be found in the United States. These institutions exist for virtually every speciality, ranging from auto mechanics and mining to building construction and nursing school administration. In 1958, more than two million students were enrolled in the *technikums*, and the number is expected to increase sharply as the new program is gradually implemented.

Although Khrushchev has expressed his general satisfaction with the new emphasis educators are giving to preparing young people for later work, it is clear that not all Soviet schoolmen have been cooperating. In his glowing report to the Twenty-second Party Congress, Khrushchev said with obvious pleasure that "hundreds of thousands of young people are pursuing their studies without leaving their jobs," but added, as the one note of dissatisfaction in his report, "not all workers in education have as yet understood the tasks in the field of polytechnical education." Khrushchev was referring to the criticisms that were appearing in Soviet journals on education as early as 1959 protesting against taking so much of the school's time for work in factories and on farms. Any number of practical schoolmen feared that the raid on the school week would seriously weaken the academic program. But Khrushchev did not heed the criticism.

An important component of the new vocational program is the work-study plan under which most graduates of the eight-year schools continue their academic training after working a six-hour day. This is merely an extension of the part-time school program that has been in force for a number of years. In 1943, for example, youths between the ages of 14 and 25 were given the opportunity to complete their secondary education in special classes held after factory shifts. During the decade from 1946 to 1956, the number of these schools increased from 2,210 to 6,637. Under the recent reorganization, enrollments in such institutions are expected to increase by 400 percent. One aim of the work-study program is to provide additional education for workers who are forced to drop out of school before completing the elementary course, and who desire further training while holding regular jobs.

This educational alternative is likely to improve the quality of work in the schools that prepare students for higher education, since many of those who are unable or unwilling to handle advanced studies are dropped.

Nearly every factory that the westerner visits has a school for working youth attached to it, and the factory manager, outwardly at least, takes pride in the number of his workers who are enrolled in the work-study program. In Moscow, for example, school number 143 is a school for working youth connected with an automobile plant. The director of the school pointed out that by eliminating such "frills" as drawing, singing, and physical education, students could complete their part-time secondary education in three or four years. Not all workers, he pointed out, avail themselves of this opportunity, but those who do enroll have the maturity and motivation often lacking in students who are compelled to attend school.

Technical study and practical work are an essential part of the curriculum in the elementary school. For at least two hours a week the girls are given instruction in the domestic arts, while the boys receive training in such skills as woodworking and metalworking. In the schools that were open to foreign visitors in 1958, however, the shop work neither challenged the ingenuity nor enlisted the interest of the youngsters. All worked at the same task, and the hammering and sawing rarely led to the manufacture of anything interesting or useful to the student. The most practical exercise observed by the author was that of seventh-grade boys making bolts and screws for use in a nearby automotive plant. These items were being produced in quantity, and the students must have learned early in the course the simple skills required for making them.

Vocational training for pupils in the secondary grades is more realistic and generates more interest. The students spend several hours a week receiving practical training in agricultural work, carpentry, automotive mechanics, needlework, or electrotechnics (largely the study of simple circuits, culminating in the study of radio sets). In these schools there is usually enough equipment for the carpenters, needleworkers, and electrotechnicians, and the rural youth who are being trained on state and collective farms are able to keep themselves occupied. The obvious shortage of motors, however, greatly handicaps the study of automotive mechanics.

"Polytechnical training," according to an official source, "acquaints the children with the most important branches of modern industrial and agricultural production, imparts to them skills in handling the most widespread material and tools and develops in them the required labor knacks and endurance." Such statements are difficult to accept as one watches a young lad fashion a small bolt—the highest accomplishment of his workshop experience. Soviet schools are simply not equipped with the machines and the machine tools that are needed if the student is to develop the skills envisaged by the regime.

According to official claim, polytechnical instruction in the Soviet Union provides children "with the fundamental skills which will help direct them to the vocation of their choice." This statement must also be discounted. The entire program is directed toward the development of elementary skills in only four areas of work: carpentry, radio repair, automotive mechanics, and dressmaking. If a student chooses one of the four, he will have been "directed" to the vocation of his "choice." Any encouragement he receives in enrolling for a given training program is likely to be related to the technical needs of the economy, not to his own aptitudes and predispositions. Vocational counseling does not exist in the USSR, and the Soviet philosophy of education does not permit free selection of careers.

The real justification for the increasingly heavy emphasis upon vocational training is to be found in the Soviet need for trained technicians to operate the complex industrial economy. An estimated 20 million Russians were killed during World War II—more people than the United States had mobilized in that crisis. The population curves were further distorted by a drastic decline in the birthrate during the wartime period. In the post-Stalin era these demographic trends have been reflected by a marked decrease in the number of workers who would ordinarily have entered the job market. A diminished supply of skilled labor, of course, raised the threat of declining production. This problem could be partially resolved if more young people could be brought into productive labor, even though only part-time, at an earlier age, and if larger proportions of people in certain age brackets could be persuaded to enter the labor force directly. The educational reform is an attempt at such a solution, for young people still in school are expected to take their turn on the production line, while many fifteen-year-olds who have completed the eight-year course go directly to the workbench or plow.

A nation with ambitious economic goals and serious manpower needs cannot permit the gulf between manual and mental effort to become too wide. This is especially true of Communist Russia, which has always exalted the proletariat and glorified ordinary labor. Both Marx and Lenin warned that students must not isolate themselves in the classroom, but should engage at least part-time in productive labor. But many Soviet young people, according to Khrushchev, were beginning to look down upon hard work and to dream only of entering the university in order to secure a "soft" desk job. The ten-year schools, whose graduates had come to expect advanced training, were turning out more students than the higher educational institutions could absorb. The educational reform is designed to divert a large segment of the student population into the labor force on a full- or part-time basis, as well as to upgrade factory and farm work in the public eye. According to the official pronouncement on the reorganization of the schools,

the harmonious development of man is unthinkable without physical labor, creative and joyous, which strengthens the organism and heightens the vital functions. . . . The new generations of builders of communist society, as they participate in socially useful activity, must engage in physical labor within their powers and of the most diverse forms.

OLD VODKA IN NEW BOTTLES

Khrushchev's reforms have brought about major changes in the organization of the primary and secondary schools, but certain ingredients of an educational system—the habits of students, the classroom methods of instruction, popular attitudes toward learning, and so forth—are much more difficult to modify by government decree. Fortunately for the Communist rulers, education is highly regarded in the Soviet Union. Since advanced training usually means better jobs, most students are eager to learn. Competition in classrooms is intense and discipline problems are held at a minimum. Although the Russian student does not relish having his education interrupted by a compulsory work program, competition for advanced education is likely to make him even more highly motivated under the reform. In seeking to bolster the sagging labor force, the regime will probably benefit from such intangible factors as the prestige value of education and the intensified competition that comes with stiffened entrance requirements—heady spirits indeed for the new bottles.

Motivation and Discipline

While the American visitor is impressed by much of what he sees in the Russian classroom, a feature that particularly excites him is the motivation and discipline of the students. The intense desire of the students to learn permeates the atmosphere of the entire school system. Indeed, the students' willingness to work and the teachers' desire to keep them busy presumably led in 1952 to intervention by the Com-

munist Party, which decreed that homework must henceforth be limited
in order to protect the health of the young people. Homework for the
first grade was restricted to one hour a day and was progressively
increased to three or four hours for pupils who were continuing
beyond the seventh grade. If American high school students were
confronted with more than 20 hours of homework per week, doubtlessly
many would openly rebel. The industry of the Soviet scholar may be
due in part to the attitude of his parents, who recognize that education
is a ladder to success and continually impress this idea upon their
children. Indeed, the role of education in the progressive development
of the nation is an important theme in the official propaganda effort,
so that the student who malingers may begin to feel awkwardly un-
patriotic.

The responsibility for keeping students motivated and well disciplined
falls primarily upon the youth organizations of the Communist Party—
the Young Pioneers, which enlists youngsters between the ages of 9
and 15, and the *Komsomols,* which recruits young people in the 14 to
27 age bracket. Both of these organizations enroll more than 90 percent
of the student population; the few young people who do not join feel
left out of things and are often designated as "discipline problems."
In carrying out their educational responsibilities, the Pioneers and
Komsomols strive to reward the good behavior of their members and to
punish the bad. As a member of a small unit into which the youth
organizations are subdivided, each individual is made to feel that he is
a vital part of the group and that his leaders and colleagues have
confidence in him. Strong group pressures prompt him to work hard
in school so that he can justify the faith that other members of the
"collective" have placed in him. In a schoolroom situation, where the
class is the collective and the teacher is the leader, the student who fails
to cooperate is described as a "comrade who has betrayed himself
and his group." Representatives of the youth organizations help the
teachers by conducting special classes and review sessions for delinquent
students. Students who persistently shirk their duties may be severely
censured by their Pioneer or *Komsomol* units. Group disapproval, evidenced in censure by one's peers, is a powerful weapon for enforcing conformity; the threat of ostracism is difficult even for people of strong
character to resist.

The Soviet school has not always been the scene of such disciplined
harmony. The early years of the Bolshevik regime represented an
experimental period in Soviet education. Since the militancy of youth
was regarded as part of the impulse of the new order, discipline was
lax, and the teachers were virtually stripped of their authority. Indeed,

one of the tasks of the youth organizations was to keep a watchful eye on the teachers and to report ideological errors and bourgeois transgressions. When the regime began to introduce its gigantic programs of industrialization, however, there was a need for stability and discipline in the society at large, and these virtues were soon carried into the schoolroom. By the mid-1930s, Soviet education had fallen back into the more traditional pattern, and the authority of the teacher was restored. *The Rules for Pupils*, published in 1943, ordered the students to follow the instructions of the teacher and to treat him with respect. Before long the Young Pioneers and the *Komsomols* were restricted in their authority to criticize teachers and were converted into allies of the school administration. Since World War II, the youth organizations have been extremely useful in enforcing discipline, in urging their members on to greater achievement, and in underwriting the authority of the teacher.

Classroom Procedures

The basic classroom procedures, which are not likely to change much under the new program, are distinguished from the classroom regimen of American schools in two respects: the pace is faster and there is considerably more emphasis on formal recitation. The teacher usually conducts the class by calling on pupils to answer questions about the previous day's assignment. If a youngster gives an incorrect answer when he stands to recite, he must remain standing until someone in the class has answered the question properly. When the correct response has been given, the teacher turns again to each delinquent student, who must then repeat the right answer before he is permitted to sit down.

Though the pace is fast and a certain degree of tension is maintained, the question and answer procedure on the homework occupies the entire period, and no time is left for the student to work during the class hour under the teacher's supervision. The pupils must therefore study at home daily and be prepared to recite in each class. At the end of the week they are given a "report card," which enables their parents to evaluate their children's progress. The best grade is "5," "4" is good, "3" is average, "2" is unsatisfactory, and "1" is a failure.

Oral examinations are also characteristics of Soviet schools. Regular oral quizzes are administered quarterly, and the student is expected to take major state examinations when he completes his elementary schooling and again when he finishes the secondary course. To prepare for the state examinations, the pupils stop all schoolwork for at least a month and begin an intensive review, or "cram," period. This is a time of excitement and tension, especially for the parents, who realize that the future careers of their children are at stake. A few weeks before the examination is to take place, the education authorities in Moscow issue a pamphlet outlining the general subject matter areas on which specific questions will be asked. The questions themselves are drawn up by the teachers of each school, who write them on cards, three to a card. On the specified day the students enter the examination room one by one and draw a card from the bowl on the examiners' desk. After about ten minutes of preparation, each student delivers his answers before a panel composed of the school director or his assistant, the teacher of the particular subject being examined, and a teacher of the same subject from another school.

What can be said about an examination system of this type? To begin with, it forces the student to undertake a thorough review of his work at two important stages in the educational process. The price paid for his review, however, is great inflexibility, for no Soviet school dares to spend time on material that is is not listed in the state syllabus, from which the examination topics are taken.

Perhaps an even more serious drawback is the nature of the examination itself. Although the general topics are centrally prepared and state inspectors check upon the administration and grading of the examination, the tests are not standardized in the American or British sense. Since the specific questions are prepared by the individual teachers, the actual content of the examination varies from one school to another. Similarly, the standards of grading may differ from place to place; the student who receives a grade of "5" in one school may have acquired considerably less knowledge than the superior student at another institution. University professors frequently complain in Soviet newspapers and pedagogical journals that they cannot tell from the examination marks whether a given student is adequately prepared for advanced study.

Another weakness of the Soviet system stems from the enormous pressures that work to prevent many students from failing (even though they may deserve such a grade) and to have a reasonable percentage receive the top grades. As we have already noted, a high rate of failures does not testify to the high standards of the school, but rather to the inability of the teachers to teach effectively. In accordance with the underlying assumptions of Soviet ideology, psychologists and educators in the USSR believe that environment is a more significant factor in a child's development than heredity. Since it is taken for granted that the educational environment must stimulate the student, it follows that the classroom is the first place to look in assigning blame for the student's academic failure. Did the teacher provide the proper type of atmosphere? Was there a true invitation to learning? The teacher who wishes to avoid criticism will naturally be tempted to keep the failure rate as low as possible. To be sure, the visiting teacher on the examination panel provides some check. But even this precaution is of limited value, since the visitor realizes that teachers from other schools will soon sit on his panel and that it may be unwise for him to develop a reputation for being hard on the students of his professional colleagues. The school administrator who sits on the examination panel is likewise not interested in having a great many failures recorded for the school he heads.

THE GRADUATE OF THE SECONDARY SCHOOL

Although in many respects a rigorous comparison between the Soviet and American systems of education is impossible at the present time, the observer often wonders how the Russian graduate of a secondary school compares even in a general way with the American high school graduate. In all probability the Russian student will have been exposed to more mathematics and more science, both physical and biological. He will have had more classwork in geography, and, without question, he will have taken more shop work—several years of it. While the training in metalworking and woodworking, automotive mechanics, and electrotechnics may be somewhat specialized and taught with the use of antiquated machinery, the Russian boy *and* girl do become familiar with the operation of simple hand tools and machines. Only the American youngsters who have had a full year of industrial arts will have had comparable experience. The emphasis in the United States on general education has placed the badge of disdain upon training in industrial arts, since it involves work with the hands and seems tainted with vocationalism. Soviet educators have been somewhat more successful in combining within the same curriculum the training of the mind and the training of the hands. The latter, they feel, develops skills that may be as useful to the scientist in a laboratory as they are to the lathe operator in a factory. Most western observers agree that the Soviet school system provides excellent training in the more difficult subjects and that it is efficiently geared to the needs and values of Soviet society.

Perhaps the Soviet youth is to be distinguished from his American counterpart not so much in academic matters as in his sense of direction. He has been taught since early childhood that all Soviet citizens must work together and even sacrifice for the advancement of the entire society. But quite apart from patriotic sentiments that dramatize collective goals, the Soviet youngster soon comes to realize that his own career will depend in large measure upon his success in school. The knowledge that a silver medal at graduation will help to open the way to a lucrative and prestigious job tends to give concrete meaning and purpose to his schooldays.

Few American young people are systematically exposed to a philosophy of intense dedication to national progress. Although most Americans do not question the propriety of such earnestness, their relative prosperity and their desire for comfort have fostered a climate of frivolity that overshadows a sense of serious purpose, and these attitudes have naturally been carried into the classroom. It must be admitted, however, that despite the defects of American education, high school graduates in the United States are probably better prepared than their opposite numbers in Russia to assume individual responsibility for finding their way in the world. Independence and individuality—important themes in American culture—are not prized in the Soviet Union.

HIGHER EDUCATION IN THE SOVIET UNION

The Soviet youth who has completed the three-year course in secondary general education or who has performed well in one of the technical schools may apply for admission to a higher educational institution. These higher schools include universities, pedagogical institutes, advanced special schools for those gifted in the arts, and institutes for advanced specialization in such fields as technology, agriculture, medicine, railway communications, and physical culture. Varying considerably in prestige, there are 45 universities in the USSR—at least one in each of the 15 republics. The dream of most Soviet young people is to become a student at the University of Moscow, a huge "cathedral of learning."

Soviet officials in 1958 reported that two million students were enrolled in higher education, although some of these young people were probably engaged in correspondence study. Of the two million, 770,000 were attending teacher-training institutes, 750,000 were studying in a variety of technical institutes, 178,000 were listed as students of medicine, and 184,000 were specializing in political economy (economics with a heavy mixture of Marxist economic theory and Leninist political philosophy). In his report to the Twenty-second Party Congress,

Khrushchev claimed that in the Soviet Union there were 4,000 scientific institutions and some 350,000 active scientific workers. But it is difficult to tell what constitutes a "scientific institution" and who qualifies as a "scientific worker." Equally puzzling in meaning is Khrushchev's boast that "the total number of persons engaged in mental work in our country is more than 20,000,000." In 1958 the number of Soviet students in higher education was only two-thirds the comparable figure in the United States. The enrollment in Soviet universities and institutes is strictly limited, and entrance is based on stiff competitive examinations. From all reports, there are many more applicants than openings to be filled.

The barriers to higher education have been raised even higher under the new educational program. After surveying the economic and political needs of the regime, the central planning agency determines the number of openings that are available in the universities and institutes. Under the old system, high-ranking students of the ten-year schools were virtually assured of admission to an institution of advanced learning. Now the gold and silver medal winners in the secondary schools are required to sit for entrance examinations along with the other applicants, although they are given priority over students from technical schools who may have scored as high on the tests.

Perhaps more important, however, is the requirement that most graduates of the general education program in the secondary schools must have completed at least two years of employment in production work prior to admission. (Of these graduates 20 percent—presumably the better students—are permitted to begin advanced study immediately upon graduation.) As already indicated, this aspect of the reform, protested by scientists, is designed to increase the supply of skilled technicians and to break down the distinction between manual and mental effort. There has been an increase in the number of university students who have worked a year or two before entering the university. Khrushchev told the Twenty-second Party Congress, "More than half the students admitted this year to the day-time branches of the higher schools have had practical work experience." Nevertheless, half did not. The universities and institutes were becoming overcrowded, and, according to Khrushchev's hints, too many of the students were from families of the intelligentsia. The two-year stint on the assembly line would not only serve to discourage many young people from applying for admission, but would make the sons and daughters of the elite associate more closely with the ordinary citizens. The justification for the two-year work requirement, which is advanced by many educators, would in the United States be termed "guidance." These educators argue that the seventeen-year-old graduate of the old ten-year school was too immature to make a wise vocational choice, and they are hopeful that two or more years of practical experience in a factory or on a farm will better prepare him to select his area specialization. Such an argument would be more convincing, however, if the teachers and school administrators had requested this work experience *before* the Khrushchev reform. Coming as it did after Khrushchev's attack, the justification advanced by the educators creates the impression that they were merely "falling in line."

In addition to the work requirement, the new law imposes certain standards for the political beliefs of candidates for admission to higher schools. To attest to his political reliability, each candidate is expected to present his *kharakteristika*, which is issued by his *Komsomol* unit, his trade union, or the local Party committee. The assumption is that the leaders of these organizations will have had an opportunity to judge the student's ability, his willingness to sacrifice, and his capacity for obedience. When the youth receives his *kharakteristika*, he has in effect passed a political test—an important step along the road to higher education.

The academic programs of students in the universities and institutes are, on the whole, inflexible. The collegians may be assigned to one of about 60 study programs, each of which is highly specialized. The Soviet curriculum lacks courses that the westerner would regard as part of a "general" or "liberal" education. It is assumed that all educated Soviet citizens will have had courses in the history of the Communist Party, Marxist-Leninist philosophy, and related studies, all of which are designed to give young people the "proper" ideological outlook. In addition to the courses that provide political indoctrination, students in higher education are required to take military training, physical training, and two years of a foreign language. The young Soviet scholar has little time left for elective courses. During the five years of university study leading to his "undergraduate diploma," he will have electives only during the third and fourth years—electives that permit him to specialize even further. The student of science however, has no room in his program for electives of any kind.

While the university student in France or Germany looks upon term examinations as a violation of his academic freedom, the Soviet student (like his American counterpart) is faced with a battery of examinations. In addition to his semester tests, he is evaluated on his assignments and ordinary quizzes. If his marks are satisfactory, the student is permitted to enroll in courses the next semester. But if he does not measure up in the semester examination or in some undetermined fraction of the assignments or quizzes, he is reported as failing and is forced to drop out of school. As in the lower schools, however, the failure rate is very low, perhaps no more than four or five percent in a given class.

Unlike many American colleges, higher educational institutions in the Soviet Union apparently do not provide counseling services for individual students. Recognizing the need for more intimate knowledge of students than can be supplied by a grade transcript, however, the authorities in each institution assign groups of approximately 25 students to each of the various departments. Three faculty members, usually a professor, an assistant professor, and an assistant, have primary responsibility for the group, and they come to "know" the individual students in much the same way that an elementary school teacher can "know" his pupils when there are only 25 in the class.

This cursory view of higher education in the USSR will enable us now to set up an imaginary model of the collegiate career of a Soviet student. Perhaps he is a member of a group of 25 in a department of "radio chemistry," a field of specialization that he selected (or that was selected for him) as late as during his fourth year at the university. Once he has enrolled in this specialty, the department assigns him to an adviser and allots him a place to work in the laboratory. He is now ready to begin a "diploma project," which must be completed by the end of the fifth year. The fact that much emphasis is placed upon the "project" has led some observers to regard it as a distinctively Soviet requirement. In many respects, however, the project resembles the research papers that some American universities require of undergraduates who seek an honors diploma. The difference perhaps lies in the generality of the Soviet requirement, for all Soviet students must complete their "diploma project" before they are graduated. In other words, every candidate for the diploma is expected to engage in independent and original research, under the supervision of his adviser. There is little information on how original this research is or what "originality" means within the context of Soviet higher education.

Much more information is available concerning the manner in which the "diploma project" is defended by the student. This procedure resembles the European and American ceremonies attending the examination of a candidate for a doctoral degree. The Soviet student is examined orally and publicly, "defending" his work against an "opponent" who is appointed by the examining committee to raise objections against the project. An outside observer is naturally impressed by the seriousness with which the diploma project is taken, although he may wonder whether the examination justifies the amount of professional time that it occupies.

The candidate who passes his diploma examination can look back upon five years of serious, intensive study. Not all of this work, of course, has been in the classroom. Even before the recent school reforms, the chemistry student was expected to spend two months during the fourth year of his program in "practical work" in the commercial laboratory of some chemical enterprise. Under Khrushchev's program, the student spends part of his time during *each* of the five years away from the university working in industry or agriculture. So that this practical experience will not impede the progress of his academic study, the student will be transferred from daytime to evening classes (if he works near a university) or to the correspondence division. Indeed, in 1960 slightly more than half the students enrolled for advanced work were taking courses in the evening or by correspondence.

Soviet educators thus rely heavily upon correspondence study. Two universities carry on all of their instruction through this method. The programs of correspondence study, as well as night school classes, enable the educational system to reach students who do not have access to a regular university campus. The more ambitious and able students who have full time jobs can thus earn their diplomas by diligent work on their correspondence lessons. If their field of specialization involves laboratory work, the factories or farms that employ them are expected to grant special leaves so that they can attend a university or institute that offers the necessary laboratory experience. Students who are granted such leaves are entitled to pay on the basis of their average wage during the previous year (up to 1,000 rubles per month), as well as a travel allowance.

Since the Soviet regime is interested in training qualified students in areas that are deemed essential by the policy makers, it is willing to support the candidate for a diploma during his years of study. How much the young collegian is subsidized depends upon the type of institution he attends, the number of years he has completed, his academic standing, and his political loyalty. Apparently the lowest stipend is 220 rubles per month—80 rubles less than an old woman who sweeps the street in order to supplement her social security allowance receives. In 1958 the minimum payment to students ranged from 220 to 300 rubles per month. Although these stipends seem small, the living costs for students are not high. Tuition fees were abolished a few years ago, and, if the student does not live at home, he is usually able to secure cheap living quarters in the city where the educational institute is located. A would-be teacher studying at a pedagogical institute in Kiev paid only 15 rubles a month for accommodations in the student hostel. Living expenses are even lower at the University of Moscow, where student apartments (each with two rooms and bath) are assigned to the residents without charge.

The student's stipend increases as he advances in his training program. By the time he is ready to begin his diploma project in the fifth year, he may receive 750 rubles per month, almost as much as the beginning wage for a factory worker and about half the salary of an assistant at the university and one sixth of the base pay for professors. It is only during the early stages of his collegiate career that the Soviet student probably needs to supplement his small stipend by finding summer employment.

The ordinary Soviet student in higher education has a great deal to lose if he does not apply himself to his studies. Low grades are likely to cost him his stipend just as surely as bad conduct or ideological weakness, and if he is not awarded a diploma, he will not be able to command the type of job desired by most young people. Although comparison with American students is very difficult, the Soviet collegian probably studies as intensively as his American counterpart; indeed, because he faces severe competition for admission to higher education and, once accepted, is confronted with the possibility of losing his stipend, the Soviet student may be pressured into working harder than many American students. Some Soviet professors complain, however, that Russian students are somewhat lazy in comparison with the highly motivated and industrious students from China.

The most likely path for the Soviet student who has earned his undergraduate diploma leads to work. Although a few will be singled out for graduate study, most will be assigned to posts that the regime needs to fill. In contrast with the American system, no student simply graduates and then spends his time seeking employment. About three months before the graduation date, the university authorities post a list of job openings, for which the Soviet student may file an application. This list is a compilation of needed skills, drawn up on the basis of estimates submitted by a variety of planning and administrative agencies. Graduates of institutions of higher education are assigned to specific jobs for a period of three years by a state commission on which the universities and the ministry of higher and specialized secondary education are represented. There is evidence to suggest that a student's marital status, his training and ability, and his job preference are taken into account. In the "distribution of teachers," according to some Soviet informants, the students with the poorest academic records are likely candidates for assignment to posts north of the Arctic Circle or in remote rural areas. Ordinarily the student is required to accept the position assigned to him, although for reasons of health (and sometimes because of personal influence) the commission might reconsider certain assignments.

The most promising college graduates may be encouraged to apply for postgraduate study and work toward an advanced degree. The first of these degrees, the *kandidat nauk*, requires three years of graduate study, at the conclusion of which the student submits and defends his thesis. The second degree is the *doctor of sciences*, which is awarded infrequently and carries great prestige. Resembling the French *doctorat d'état*, it is granted only after the scholar has completed several years of professional work and has made a highly regarded contribution to original thinking. In their design for graduate training, Soviet educators have followed a pattern that is more familiar to continental Europeans than to Britons or Americans. The *kandidat* degree in a Soviet university is probably superior to the master's degree in an American institution, but less formidable than an American doctor of philosophy. On the other hand, the scholar who holds a doctor of sciences degree has hurdled higher barriers than the American PhD and is probably on a plane with the recipient of the most advanced French degree.

Soviet universities select their professors from among the *kandidats* and the doctors of sciences. Unlike higher educational institutions in other countries, the universities and institutes in the USSR do not grant tenure to their professors. Every five years the "chairs" are declared to be vacant, and any scholar may apply for the "vacated" positions. This practice creates the impression that professional posts are competitive. In reality, however, a professor is likely to continue in his position if he is politically "reliable," and his competitors are not usually successful in their bid for the "open chair."

THE CHALLENGE TO AMERICAN EDUCATION

There have been both successes and failures in Soviet education during the past 40 years, but the achievements have been more frequent and significant than the failures. The rapid growth of the economy and the spectacular advancement in some areas of science are in part achievements of the educational system. As such, they present a challenge of the first magnitude to American education. Can we develop an educational system that will provide the skills necessary for a rapidly growing economy and at the same time serve as a major force that preserves and strengthens the basic values of a democratic society?

A number of problems in the American educational system will have to be solved if this country is to meet the challenge of Soviet education. Small rural schools in unconsolidated districts are not equipped to provide thorough courses of study, the necessary library and laboratory facilities, and competent teachers. Wide differences in educational facilities and opportunities between "poor" and "wealthy" states lead to a waste of needed talent. Courses of study are often the result of historical accident rather than careful planning, and the sequence of instruction tends to inhibit rather than enhance the learning process. All too often, for example, an American student takes only one year of a science or a language, with no further exposure to that subject. Frequently, the lack of adequate funds in many schools prevents the use of modern teaching aids, with the result that the student wastes a great deal of valuable time. These problems, while not easy to resolve, need to be dealt with if the American schools are to train young people to take their place in a modern industrial society.

It is not necessary for American education to adopt the extreme centralization and standardization so characteristic of the Soviet system. No national ministry of education is needed in the United States to enforce a single pattern of education. Although the process by which the American people evaluate and modify their school system is slow and often discouraging, the defects are uncovered by the citizens themselves, who then seek to work out a solution at the local level instead of relying upon a political oligarchy to reform the entire system from above. While it is more difficult to arrive at a decision by democratic processes, the result is easier to live with, for it represents the views of educators and parents alike and reflects the peculiar needs of the local community. And this process is far more compatible with the goals of American education—to aid the personal development and self-realization of the individual.

In the Soviet Union the aim of education is to indoctrinate the student with the values of a Communist society and to train him in the skills that the regime needs. The current reforms, issued from the center, will be carried out as far as possible in every remote locality and will probably increase the efficiency and effectiveness of the Soviet schools. An increasing supply of adequately trained laborers and professionals will most likely be produced during the coming decade.

The success of the program of indoctrination is more difficult to assess. That the Soviet educational system plays a major role in shaping the values and personalities of all who go through it is beyond question. But a look at the recent products of the school system—the youth of the Soviet Union today—suggests that the role of the school is not always that which was planned.

7

SOVIET YOUTH

Thomas F. Magner

At present Thomas F. Magner is professor of Slavic Languages and chairman of the department of Slavic Languages at Pennsylvania State University. Formerly the chairman of the department of Slavic and Oriental languages at the University of Minnesota, Dr. Magner is the author of several books and articles in the field of Slavic languages and linguistics.

The careful control exercised by Soviet rulers over the educational system reflects the importance they attach to the training of young people in the acceptable Communist values. In the words of an old Russian folk saying, "The colt needs the greatest care and discipline." Since the days of the revolution, the regime has recognized that from each new generation will be drawn an elite of future political leaders and administrators, as well as an army of future workers and citizens. If the system is to be perpetuated, the youth of the Soviet Union will have to be vigilant, industrious, loyal and obedient, and willing to sacrifice themselves for the welfare of the community. On frequent occasions, both Lenin and Stalin pointed out that the youth of the USSR represent the hope for the future. Some insight into the future can be gleaned, therefore, through an understanding of the young people—their hopes and fears, their aspirations and frustrations.

For centuries the state described in Plato's *Republic* has stood as a model for societies in which the youth are molded according to an official design. The Soviet Communists have sought to apply the philoso-

163

pher's model to a modern industrial society. They have established a network of institutions and organizations to nurture and indoctrinate the young child from the time he leaves the cradle until he is old enough to assume the responsibilities of adult life. When a mother goes to work, she can leave her infant in a state nursery, where the child spends a great deal of time until he is ready for kindergarten. When he reaches primary school age, he enters upon a long period of indoctrination that is designed to train him to be a productive worker and a politically reliable citizen. Supplementing the formal education and classroom work are organized hikes and tours conducted by teachers and youth leaders in each locality. The regime has also developed an elaborate summer camp program that combines ordinary recreation—swimming, hiking, and folkdancing—with moderate doses of propaganda in daily study sessions. Each year thousands of young people look forward to a vacation at a camp sponsored by a government agency or by the factory where their parents are employed. As the children grow older, many are attracted to such organizations as the Young Naturalist Stations or the Technical Stations, which bear some responsibility for cultivating a desire to be patriotic, zealous in surpassing work quotas, and obedient to official directives. There is also a mass program of sports and physical training sponsored by state or Party organizations.

THE PARTY'S YOUTH ORGANIZATIONS

In the task of shaping the minds and characters of the young, the Soviet rulers rely heavily upon a hierarchy of youth organizations that are closely linked with the Communist Party. These organizations recruit members at three different age levels. The *Little Octobrists* (named for the October revolution) enlists the youngest children of school age. When he is 9 and has entered the third grade, a youngster joins the *Young Pioneers;* by the time he is 14 he is ready to enter the *Young Communist League (Komsomols),* where he will ordinarily remain until he is 27. The Party recruits most of its members from the ranks of the *Komsomols,* and if a student's record in the organization is outstanding, he is likely to be among the favored few who are singled out for probationary membership in the Communist movement. Card-carrying Communists, of course, make up only about five percent of the total population, while the Young Pioneers enlist more than 90 percent of the eligible young people. Although the proportion of *Komsomol* members is not so high, more than 90 percent of the Soviet students belong to the organization.

As an illustration of the organizational blessings that flow to the Soviet youth, it will be useful to examine more closely the Young Pioneers, whose members number almost 20 million. To get an idea of the range of Pioneer activities, one must imagine a single organization that performs all of the function of the Boy Scouts, the Girl Scouts, the Future Farmers of America, the YMCA, the YWCA, church youth groups, and the extra-curricular program of the schools. In other words, activities which in the West are sponsored by a wide variety of organizations are in the Soviet Union the monopoly of the one youth organization that caters to a particular age group. The purpose and some of the activities of the Young Pioneers have been explained by one of the officials as follows (*Soviet Pedagogy*, March, 1959):

> The Pioneer organization nurtures in young Leninites the best human traits of communist society: unbounded love towards the fatherland, diligence, tenacity, and persistence in achieving goals, lofty benevolence, courage and cheerfulness. . . .
>
> The Pioneers take charge of the young animals on collective farms, raise poultry and rabbits, strive for high yields of corn on the Pioneer fields, plant greenery and beautify school grounds, workers' settlements, villages, plant park zones along the railways and motor highways, collect waste paper and scrap metal, participate jointly with senior class students in the construction of school buildings and dwellings. . . .
>
> Together with their older comrades, the Komsomols, the Pioneers celebrated the 40th anniversary of the Young Communist League with great gifts of labor. The Pioneers of Byelorussia sent to the virgin lands 100 tractors which were produced from scrap metal they had collected, and they created rabbit breeding farms at all seven-year and secondary schools. The Pioneers of Lithuania raised 33,000 rabbits. The Pioneers of the Stalingrad region . . . raised 10,000 rabbits and 25,000 chickens and ducks. . . .

The Young Pioneers have impressive facilities for carrying out their program of indoctrination and character development. A major building in every city has been converted into a Pioneer Palace, which serves as the headquarters for Pioneer activities. The Pioneer building in Rostov was formerly a Tsarist bank. In Leningrad it is the splendid Anichkov Palace. A day in this enormous Pioneer headquarters illustrates what the organization at its best can provide for Russian youngsters. One of three hundred rooms is devoted to recital of classic folk tales, and here little children, sitting on traditionally decorated chairs, listen to their favorite stories and view storybook pictures that are painted on the wall. A nearby room paneled in rich walnut provides a quiet atmosphere for older youngsters who desire instruction in chess. Other rooms are devoted to the language "circles," where the children receive expert instruction in the language of their interest. The Young Pioneers can also engage in such activities as woodworking, model-building, music, ballet, and the theater. The Pioneer Palaces provide recreational opportunities for many young people whose homes are overcrowded, and they offer a program of instruction that supplements that of the regular schools.

While the Pioneer Palaces in Leningrad and other large cities are indeed impressive, these massive buildings are able to accommodate only a fraction of the youngsters of the area. A large number of children are assigned to other Pioneer buildings dispersed throughout the city. The facilities available in these supplementary quarters, however, are not up to the standard of the more famous palaces to which the foreign visitor is ordinarily exposed.

The staffs of the Pioneer Palaces are carefully selected and well trained. Many of the teachers of English appear to have a better command of the language than some of their counterparts in the public schools. Judging from the exhibitions of model building and the performances of the young ballerinas, one must conclude that many of the instructors in these fields are also first-rate. In addition to their professional skill, of course, the officials in the Pioneer Palaces are prepared to instruct their young charges in the basic teachings of Marx and Lenin.

The organization of Young Pioneers is closely integrated with the school system; indeed, there is in each school a full-time staff member who is responsible for directing the activities of the Pioneers in that institution. Members of the Young Pioneers can readily be identified by the red neckerchief they wear to school. Prominent in each school building is the Pioneer room, elaborately decorated with red flags and a huge bust of Lenin, which houses the trophies won by the local Pioneer chapter. The pledge of allegiance that is inscribed on the wall in huge letters serves to remind the young people of their responsibility to the organization and the proletarian movement it represents.

The primary aim of the Young Pioneers is character development. The youngster is nurtured in collectivist values so that he will be willing to subordinate his personal interests to the welfare of the group. He is taught to obey his parents and teachers, to respect physical labor, and to encourage his fellows to study with diligence. It is anticipated that many of the Pioneers will eventually be graduated into *Komsomol* membership, where their political indoctrination begins in earnest.

The *Komsomols*, which grew from 9,300,000 members in 1949 to 18,500,000 in 1959, enroll a large proportion of the older students in the USSR. Although membership is voluntary, young people are drawn into the organization by social pressure and by the realization that affiliation will make it easier for them to secure an education, since *Komsomol* officials have an important voice in the distribution of scholarships and other awards. The *Komsomols* sponsor a thorough program of "political education," stimulate the youth to join special work brigades and harvest teams, help expose violations of Communist discipline, and exert pressure upon the members to be diligent in their studies and to serve as examples of civic loyalty. Subjected to careful training and supervision, the young *Komsomols* serve as an important reservoir of talent from which reliable Party members are recruited.

To execute their program of indoctrination, the youth organizations have at their disposal a vast network of mass communication facilities. The authorities publish, for example, 44 magazines for children and 30 for young people. In addition, the *Komsomols* publish 107 newspapers and the Pioneers, 25. Since the establishment of a children's literature publishing house in 1936, more than 500,000,000 children's books have been published. Each Pioneer Palace has a library for the use of the members, and many cities have special children's libraries. In addition, each public library usually has a separate section for young people. The education authorities in Moscow operate a children's book palace, which has a department that conducts research in the field of youth literature and in the methods of guiding youngsters' reading programs. An annual festival of children's books held during the spring recess is frequently attended by a number of Soviet writers, who meet with their young readers. In the realm of the drama, the Soviet Union has more than 100 theaters that specialize in producing works for young people. All of this literary effort is closely supervised by state and Party officials, and the editors are carefully chosen for their "ideological purity." Their function is to moralize and uplift, to denounce the wicked, and to praise those who work hard and obediently follow the Party's lead.

RESTLESSNESS AMONG REGIMENTED YOUTH

It is easy to assume that the programs of massive conditioning are successful—that young people, indoctrinated from early childhood, react to the auditory and visual stimuli in an acceptable manner. Undoubtedly a great many young people accept uncritically the official values and the sudden shifts in the Party line, and join the mass chorus that echoes the arguments of the Kremlin, even though perceptive observation would enable them to see the contrast between reality and "asserted truth." The regime, however, has not been entirely successful in molding the Soviet youth, as can be seen in the official condemnation of certain attitudes and behavior among the young people, in the unrest that has been reported in some universities, and in the conversations that foreign visitors have had with Soviet students.

Even in a society that seeks to convert the youngster into a "new Soviet man," human beings respond differently to the same pressures. Despite the uniform pattern of indoctrination, the Communist system has undoubtedly produced a generation of young people with many differing outlooks, attitudes, and aspirations. Although it is not possible to conduct a careful survey of Soviet youth, it will be useful to examine four "types" of young people observed in the USSR.

Vanya, the All-Soviet Boy

If Jack Armstrong were to stride manfully onto the Soviet scene, he would be wearing his *Komsomol* button and he might typically be on his way to preside over a highly organized "volunteer" meeting of his school's chapter of the Young Communist League. And he might be named "Vanya." At any rate, we may use Vanya to personify all the youthful virtues and ideals that reside, by official decree certainly, and perhaps even in reality, in Soviet youth.

Vanya lives with his father and mother and one brother in a one-room flat in a skyscraper apartment building in Moscow. The bath and kitchen are shared with several other families. Vanya does not mind the cramped space because he knows about the wonderful housing goals of the seven-year plan, and every day he can see for himself the miles of new apartment houses going up in the suburbs. Vanya does not have time to loiter around the apartment, for he is a journalism student at the huge Lomonosov University in Moscow, and his studies and *Komsomol* activities keep him occupied away from home.

During the summer Vanya works hard in a *Komsomol* detachment on a large state farm in Kazakhstan. In answer to Khrushchev's appeal for help in the "virgin lands," he and his classmates have volunteered as farm laborers. Only twenty-one years of age, Vanya has not as yet acquired a family of his own. He will probably not get married for six more years. When he does marry and settle down, his wife will continue to work, with time out for the typical two pregnancies.

Vanya has definite opinions—perhaps even strong convictions—on most subjects. Girls must be sweet and demure; they must dress moderately; and they must refrain from using lipstick and smoking. "To kiss a girl who smokes is like kissing an ashtray," is one of Vanya's favorite sayings. If you were to ask Vanya about the reaction of a girl to a young man who smokes, he would regard your question as unworthy of serious consideration.

Vanya and his contemporaries were the subjects of a revealing report in the *Young Communist* in January 1959. It had been suggested by some members of a department of culture and of a youth commission that public debates among the youth would enable them to bring their doubts into open discussion and to reach a mutual understanding of the things that disturb them. It was reported that even the question of open discussion precipitated disagreement among local officials:

Immediately there were enthusiastic supporters and violent opponents of debates as a form of upbringing. The former argued that debates were necessary, that they would awaken in young people a desire for greater knowledge and would inculcate in them a principled attitude and an ability to defend their opinions in discussions. The latter expressed their apprehensions: Suppose no one should speak up, or that the speakers should manage to confuse the straightforward issue? There might also be demagogues who would spoil everything. In general, they argued that this was something new, untested in practice—who could tell how it would turn out? In the end, however, the optimists won the day.

And so the officials sponsored a series of public debates, not, however, on controversial subjects such as "Capitalism or Communism—which is the Better System?" or "Soviet Foreign Policy in the Middle East," or "Stalin: Hero or Criminal?" These questions could hardly concern Soviet youth. Instead, officials selected such innocuous subjects as "What Does it Mean to be Cultured?" "What Should a Real Friend Be?" "My Calling," "What are Your Dreams?" "On Taste and Manners," and "On the Hard Way and the Easy Way."

The debates were declared to be a rousing success and were credited with developing maturity among the young people. The contributions of the young men and women, the *Young Communist* continued in its report, became more profound with each debate:

For instance, everyone recalls the speech made by the sailor Anatoly Lebedev. He had been abroad more than once, and in the debate "On Taste and Manners" he spoke convincingly about the superiority of the Soviet man's ideology over bourgeois ideology and sharply criticized those who blindly imitate foreign fashions and kowtow before the "American way of life" without knowing what it essentially is but seeing only its external and ostentatious side.

The debates help in the concrete, practical struggle for culture, a healthy mode of life and high moral standards on the part of YCL members and other young people.

The ideal Soviet young lady—Vanya's feminine counterpart—has recently been making vigorous appearances in the Soviet press in connection with the government's campaign to persuade young women to take up permanent residence in the virgin lands of Siberia and Kazakhstan. In *Komsomolskaya Pravda* (February 8, 1959), a group of feminine members of the Young Communist League made a ringing appeal:

On the Road, Girls!
Our dear friends, young women workers of Moscow, Leningrad, Kiev and other cities of our motherland! . . . The decisions of the 13th Young Communist League Congress call us to this; the Congress addressed an appeal to the girls of the country to go to work in the regions of the virgin and idle lands, to apply our dedicated, efficient hands there and to create comfort in these rich regions that have already been settled. This is the call of the Party, which has approved the decision of our YCL Congress. This is the call of our YCL duty.

That is why many of us—a group of 350 Ivanovo girls . . . have decided to take up permanent residence in the regions where the virgin lands are being developed . . . many of us have never worked in the fields or on livestock sectors. But is this an obstacle? What we don't know today we will learn tomorrow!

On the road, to the far places, girls!

A few weeks later, *Komsomolskaya Pravda* elected to print a letter that came from a construction site that had been abandoned by 25 out of 50 girls. This letter reflects the frustration experienced by some of these idealistic youth and would probably cause hesitation among other *Komsomol* girls who might be contemplating the attractions of the virgin lands.

Nobody is interested in our living conditions. Our leaders never visit our living quarters. We have formed the impression that there is an abyss between our present life and our former life. We have only met with indifference and carelessness. All our ideals have disappeared and our happy thoughts about our work have been eliminated. We feel as if our souls are being marred.

It is, of course, impossible to say what proportion of Soviet youth is represented by Vanya. Vanya himself is quite real; the foreign visitor encounters his type on more than one occasion in various Soviet cities. The majority of the Soviet young people are probably less zealous than

Vanya, but they nevertheless move along docilely in officially approved channels. But there are problem groups and these are a recurring theme in the Soviet press. They are discussed here not because they are large groups but because they represent social "trouble spots." The cloth, according to the proverb, unravels from the edge, and it is the periphery of Soviet society that now demands our attention.

The Golden Youth

The "golden youth" is the name given to the sons and daughters of high Soviet officials—administrators, Party functionaries, army officers, and others—who enjoy a relatively high living standard. Among these upper-income groups there has emerged the spectre of delinquency and decadence, motivated not by poverty and squalid surroundings but by satiety and boredom. These are the golden youth of the wild parties, of the villa weekends, of drunken driving in state cars. Ironically, it is difficult for an authoritarian society to cope with the derelictions of these young people, since their parents occupy powerful positions. Wealth and power extend a measure of protection in all societies, but much more so in the Soviet Union, where questions and criticism may be directed downward to the lower officials, but rarely upward to the new "barons."

A scandal reported by *Komsomolskaya Pravda* (August 15, 1956) involved the two sons of I.G. Kabanov, minister of foreign trade. The lads teamed up with a third youth to rob apartments and used the proceeds from the lootings to finance drunken orgies with three girls, whose fathers turned out to be a general, an aviation colonel, and a colonel in one of the police agencies. Although the Kabanov boys were later acquitted in court, the other four young people were sentenced to 12 months' imprisonment.

In a story entitled "The Slug," the Soviet army newspaper *Red Star* (April 14, 1959) recounted a scandalous incident centering around a student at the Dzerzhinsky Military Academy, Gennadii Tikhomirov. The boy had gathered together some women "of light behavior" and had used them to make pornographic movies that were later shown for entertainment purposes. The shocking fact revealed to the Soviet public was that the culprit was the son of an important government official, the vice chairman of the legislative assembly in Moscow. Why had the authorities at the academy not known about Gennadii's activities? Their answer was that they were reluctant to concern themselves with the lad's extracurricular behavior for fear of antagonizing his influential father.

The sensational cases of Gennadii and the Kabanov boys are probably not representative of the golden youth. A more typical incident, it would seem, involves a disoriented group of *Komsomol* members whose activities were recently described in the Moscow edition of a Young Communist newspaper. These youngsters from well-to-do homes violated Soviet morality by leading idle lives, drinking, and trading in foreign goods that they had procured from tourists. Young people of this type resist the call of the virgin lands so that they can continue to enjoy the luxuries of urban life. Frequently they take on foreign names and employ English slang—a fashion well known to foreign visitors, who are startled at first to hear Russian boys sporting such names as "Bill," "Les," and "Jimmy," usually in imitation of western jazz musicians.

When Soviet planners urge their citizens to work hard so that their country can "overtake and surpass the United States," they do not fully realize the implications of the slogan. In addition to being an industrial giant, the United States is noted for the high level of material goods and the physical comfort that its citizens enjoy. When Soviet youth learn more about western life through the Voice of America, from the western movies that now appear on the screen, and from contacts with foreign visitors and the foreign books and magazines that fall into their hands, the spirit of competition becomes more heady than their political leaders had bargained for. Imitation rarely stops at the machine, but extends to the objects and values that the Soviet youth regard as new and different—the things that add adventure and variety to their drab, austere, and boring existence. They begin to crave the luxuries that they see other people enjoying. The Soviet rulers have convinced their citizens that the United States must be imitated; and some of the young people tend to equate America with the Americans they come into contact with, carrying the imitation into realms of individual dress, language, gadgets, music, and so forth.

The Stilyaga

The least that can be said for the *stilyaga*—the "teddy boy" or "zoot-suiter" or "flaming youth" of the Soviet Union—is that he does have *stil'*: a *style* in dress, in actions, and in language. Although the word *stilyaga* is not new in Russian, it appeared for the first time in a dictionary only in 1961. To a foreigner, it seems as though the word is applied rather loosely to any Soviet youngster who affects eccentric clothing that sharply contrasts in style and color with the drab fashions of the cities.

If the victim of Lev Osanin's heavy-handed satirical song (*Krododil*,

February 20, 1955) may be considered typical of the *stilyaga*, one might picture a twenty-year-old youth attired in light-blue slacks, a multicolored tie, a yellow-spotted vest, and a green coat. This sartorial splendor would be accentuated by a flashing gold tooth and crowned by a carefully trained lock of hair. "Is it a passing parrot, or is it someone who, as a child, was dropped on the floor?" asks Osanin's popular song. "Or perhaps the poor fellow is only sick." "No, none of these," concludes the song; "that chap is simply a *stilyaga*."

In Osanin's song the *stilyaga* is further distinguished by his handsome forehead "without a trace of higher thoughts" and by his wild dancing, which threatens the stability of a dance floor. An affinity for jazz (which seems to signify most popular western music) is, next to colorful apparel, the most distinctive mark of a *stilyaga*. Press reports and conversations with Soviet citizens concerning this species add a host of negative characteristics, ranging from political apathy to a broadly-interpreted *khuliganstvo* (hooliganism). The *stilyaga* label seems to be attached to any youth who brazenly challenges the precepts of Soviet puritanism.

A study of *stilyaga* slang expressions reveals that the interests of the Soviet teenager are similar to those of his American counterpart. Fearlessly violating the language taboos that are observed by the conventional elements of the society, the *stilyaga* has special adjectives for various types of girls, an impressive number of words for drinking; and a variety of expressions for marginal social types—"blackmarketeer," "fixer," and the like. The unflattering epithet for police is *musor* ("garbage"), while Premier Khrushchev is referred to as *kukuruznik*, which can be translated as "cornball." In beatnik fashion, many slang terms have been devised for money, sex, and similar "vices" that are not to be mentioned in polite Communist circles. The emphasis of Soviet slang upon special words for clothing, expressions for securing clothes, and jargon to describe business transactions with foreigners seems novel to the western observer but reflects the unique experiences and aspirations of the Russian youth. Like their counterparts in western countries, the Soviet young people have their *brod* ("Broadway"); in Moscow it is the lower section of Gorky Street, while in Leningrad it is Nevsky Prospect.

Nearly all Soviet youth, whether upstanding or delinquent, are greatly attracted by modern music. "Music, USA," a program of the Voice of America, is not jammed, and its musical offerings are very popular. American musical selections are quickly transcribed on tape, disks, or even on used X-ray plates, and the transcriptions pass rapidly, and often profitably, from hand to hand among the younger set.

The "Spiv"

Besides the young men who seek out foreign visitors for acceptable reasons—to practice their English, to inquire about the outside world, or to exhibit their hospitality—there are hardy groups of "operators" who cluster around tourists in order to acquire western items for resale in the Soviet Union. For lack of a better designation, we may refer to such a speculator by the British term, "spiv." A "spiv" may dress like a *stilyaga* (indeed, he may even be one), but basically he is the fast-talking, eager manipulator who is officially earmarked as an "idler" or a "social parasite." He carefully spots a foreign visitor in a museum, on the street, or in a park and offers to buy souvenirs, clothing, books, contraceptives, or western currency (for an amount considerably in excess of the official rate). Such activities are officially frowned upon, although the post-Stalin rulers have found them difficult to control.

While they are probably exaggerated to underscore the moral lesson, frequent press accounts of "spiv" operations suggest that the problem is widespread and serious enough to disturb the authorities. *Komsomolskaya Pravda* (January 17, 1959), for example, presented case studies of four "spivs" in Moscow. In featuring the story, the newspaper was creating in lurid form a composite picture of the "depraved" youth who must be officially censured and "re-educated" to appreciate the dignity of manual labor.

One of these young men, twenty-year-old Yura Zakharov, listed as his occupation trumpet playing at "left" concerts. Yura, of course, did not play respectable Soviet music, but was addicted to "rock-'n'-roll and boogie-woogie." According to the account, the lad spent his daytime hours exchanging religious ikons for chewing gum, cigarette lighters, souvenirs, and "foreign junk." The article reports the following interview:

Knows the Criminal Code: Trading ikons for foreign junk is exchanging souvenirs, not speculation. Keeps some souvenirs and sells the rest. It's no crime to sell a gift or a souvenir. Property status? Doesn't own a wheelbarrow.

"What do you mean, wheelbarrow?" asks the floor attendant [of the large Moscow hotel].

"We call a privately-owned car a wheelbarrow," Yura explains patiently. "Who's the 'we'?"

"Well, we people—you know. The kids from the center, that is. The people who hang around the Metropole Hotel in the evenings."

A worthy companion of Yura was Sergei Sytov, a young man who lost one job after another through indolence and finally turned to the more exciting occupation of ikon selling. While protesting to the authorities that he was engaged in "intellectual work," he met with the other boys "from the center" each morning, and together they employed their talents in looking for foreigners with whom they could "do business." Lacking in "modesty and self-respect," they would presumably "do anything for a pack of foreign cigarettes or chewing gum."

The same article reported an even more bizarre case of a young playboy nicknamed "Broadway Booby." When he ran afoul of the law and was sent to prison, he became lonesome for the night life of Moscow, and he recorded his yearning in a letter to one of his friends:

Greetings, my young friend. This frost isn't for me. I'm an aristocrat. I was put in charge of some cultural work here, but they quickly "understood" me. They cut my hair and put me on a strict regime. And I had been counting on getting to the capital in time for the holidays and drinking a toast to the dear girls—to our kittens. You know my weakness. I love the sweet kittens, especially with make-up and, of course, a pedicure. Well, never mind; I'll be back in Moscow soon, and I'll make up for lost time and will overtake and surpass you.

The Soviet press, of course, oversimplifies and exaggerates, selecting extreme cases in order to drive home the point to the mass of readers. Regardless of journalistic distortion, however, the "boys from the center" do exist in real life. This is one of the reasons why the regime has resorted to such measures as the "antiparasite" law. The authorities are making a concerted effort to discover people like Yura, Sergei, and "Broadway Booby," and to convert them into "all-Soviet boys" like Vanya.

The Hooligan

Hooligan, that obstreperous Irishman whose rowdy tactics made his name an epithet to London police 70 years ago, has achieved a measure of fame by the latterday extension of his name to the "tough" elements of Soviet youth, the *khuligans*. A youngster becomes a *khuligan* when he commits *khuliganstvo*, or hooliganism. This term designates a broad area of antisocial behavior, ranging from "disturbing the public order" (rough language in public places, wild dancing, drunkenness, and roaming the streets) to more violent crimes (robbery and assault). This category of crimes is so ambiguous that even young people who allegedly nurture "rebellious attitudes" or who exhibit an unhealthy interest in foreign visitors can be brought to account. The *stilyaga* and "spivs" are, of course, often listed as *khuligans*. While the *khuligan* may in some respects be compared with the juvenile delinquent in western society, he is similar, in his lighter offenses (for example, kissing a female companion on the dance floor), to the exuberant teenager of America and Britain. As in most countries, even more serious forms of hooliganism can be explained as being generated by youthful frustrations.

Whatever its cause, the Soviet authorities take a dim view of the species *khuligan*, as seen from a report in *Pravda* (December 1, 1958):

Who are these gangsters? They are young fellows—the oldest is 24— but each has committed more than one act of hooliganism, has participated in more than one brawl, and has been in more than one knife fight. They refuse to engage in any kind of labor, and when they say the word "work" they sneer like true parasites. These young and healthy lads seek an easy life at someone else's expense. To them an easy life means stealing, murdering, getting drunk, and disturbing the peace.

To our great regret, we still meet such people on the streets, hear their coarse abuse in the streetcars, trolley busses and busses, and suffer from their savage attacks. They keep us from working and relaxing in peace and pollute our glorious city like foul-smelling garbage, like green mold.

"No mercy for hooligans, the wreckers of human society," writes Professor Nekhoroshev [ironically this means Professor No-Good]. "They must be destroyed like rats and bedbugs. Unfortunately, however, there are some people who appeal for humaneness, resembling those Tolstoyans who didn't dare to take the life of a flea or a cockroach."

Hardened criminals may be called hooligans, but in the younger set hooliganism typically takes the form of boisterous behavior, usually associated with drinking. A *Pravda* article (July 6, 1961) reports on hooligans in Krasnoyarsk.

. . . There are many drunks and rowdies in streets here. At the delicatessen next door to the House of Soviets, young people buy vodka and drink it right on the spot. When they are drunk, these insolent young people loiter on the sidewalks, push women and children out of their way and board streetcars and trolleybuses out of turn. The hooligans are completely out of hand in the Park of Culture and Rest: they create disturbances, molest passersby and start brawls. . . . There should be no indulgence of them at all. In every city, settlement and village, at every enterprise and state and collective farm, a situation must be created in which the ground under the loafers, pilferers and hooligans will crumble.

In recent years cadres from the Young Communist League have been organized as junior vigilantes to aid police in identifying and apprehending hooligans. The vigilantes must have had dramatic successes in their raids, if we accept the statement of a recent Soviet visitor to the United

States. Mrs. Nina Orlova, a specialist in civil and private international law, exhibited a keen interest in the Minneapolis juvenile court that she inspected. There are no such courts in the Soviet Union, she observed, since the low rate of juvenile delinquency makes special courts unnecessary. Hooligan the Irishman would probably have snorted at this slur on the hardy and active breed of *khuligans*.

LIFE COMES BUT ONCE—SO ENJOY IT!

Although there are undoubtedly other types of Soviet youth besides the golden youth, the *stilyaga,* the "spiv," and the *khuligan,* these are the categories that seem to disturb the regime the most. These groups, of course, overlap, and it is not unusual to find the *stilyaga* or the "spiv" becoming a hooligan, though only a member of the golden youth could theoretically function in all four designations. Recently a young man with some of the characteristics of three of the types wrote a letter to his friend Serge, urging him to come to Moscow to "discover life in its most subtle forms," in the company of a carefree group whose slogan was "live for the moment." This letter, which eventually reached the editors of *Komsomolskaya Pravda* (June 8, 1958), was printed along with doleful editorial comment. It read as follows:

Serge,
   Greetings!
As I already wrote you, I flunked in Aviation. Then I worked for four months, but now I'm neither working nor in school. I'm sitting home, getting ready for the exams. Think I'll try to get in again. I study only during the day. At night, though, Serge, . . .! I just don't have the words to describe it in a letter—if you come, you'll see for yourself. A group of us have gotten together—four *chuvaks* ("hepcats") and four *chuvikhas*; in our lingo that means "babes." We hold to freedom of morality. Our slogan is "Live for the moment [hurry to live]." We have no political goals, only moral ones. Here's how it works: each individual does whatever he wants to—if one wants to, he drowns himself in wine; another may want to go wild with rock-'n'-roll, while still another may go after the pleasures of love. If you'll be in Moscow, then together with me you'll get to know life in its most subtle forms.

Serge! It's difficult to describe everything in a letter, especially in the literary language, since I've become so accustomed to the wild lingo. . . . If you want to know, here's something about fashions. Now that it's hot, cowboy shirts, worn hanging out, and "advertising" shirts are all in style. Loud neckties have become a memory, and only the hicks wear them.

Wearing pointed shoes is popular. I have an English pair, suede and really sharp-toed, but I think that I'll sell them since things are tight with the folding stuff (money). Short coats and trench coats are fashionable. In jazz it's all "rocky" (rock-'n'-roll), and some people dance it, too. There are a lot of foreign things of nylon, from ladies' coats to jackets and shirts, but they're expensive. They say there'll be a Pan-American exhibition in August; then we'll do a colossal *bizness*. (Perhaps, you and I can do it together.) They're very many foreigners here and it's very easy to get things from them, since they need Russian money. All Moscow is drinking only Czech and German beer. . . . Well, Serge, I can't describe it all. Besides, the ink in the pen is all gone. So *gud bay*, dear pal; write, you rascal, more often. Since it's possible we'll get a new "shack," get yourself over to the information bureau. My *mama* will soon "take off" with pappy for a vacation resort. Then it'll be real deluxe here. . . .

Come on, Serge. We'll find a real babe for you, we'll teach you to "dig" rock, you'll become a person, so come on.

This letter may have been handed over to the newspaper by Serge, by his parents, by the police, or it may even have been composed by staff members of the paper. The source, however, becomes less important if one keeps in mind the didactic and minatory functions of the Soviet press. Such an item does not appear merely to titillate newspaper readers, nor is it printed in order to represent the lightheadedness of the writer. *Komsomol* officials publish the letter primarily to focus public attention on those young people whose behavior resembles that of the writer and whose nonconformist attitudes are repugnant to the authorities.

Though the regime is obviously troubled by their colorful dress and their antisocial antics, these deviant types do not appear to hold any political views as such or to nurture any thoughts of rebellion. To be sure, some of these young people, especially the *stilyaga* and the "operators," exhibit a mild weakness for western frills and may have acquired the capitalist urge to make a "quick ruble," but this can hardly be called prowestern orientation. Indeed, most of them appear to be naïve about the western world and uninterested in its politics. Seeking release from boredom, they are attracted by the gadgets, the lively music, the detective novels, and the thrill of meeting and talking with foreigners.

Although evidence of spirited and flamboyant behavior among the younger set is plentiful, the western observer has less to go on when he looks for concrete signs among youth of dissatisfaction with the political system. Occasionally a young student will ask the American visitor,

"Is it really true that you can criticize your government?" and he may express hope that one day he and his friends will be able to form discussion circles where they can freely exchange ideas on political questions. The rare young man who has enough courage to visit an American in a hotel room may betray his political attitudes by rustling paper to jam the microphone he assumes has been planted as he inquires about life in the United States.

Under the pseudonym "David Burg," a former student in a Russian university has reported on some of the political attitudes he observed. (*Harper's* May 1961.) He divides the opposition tendencies among the politically conscious young people into three general groups. (1) The "neo-Leninists," under the influence of the egalitarian ideals of the early Bolsheviks, believe that the Soviet regime has lost sight of the goals of the October revolution, and they urge a reduction in the power of the Party bureaucracy and the police and a greater measure of democracy in both the political and economic realms. The members of this group, however, give full support to the one-party system and favor the retention of a highly centralized economy. (2) The "liberal socialists," who have lost faith in the achievement of utopia, desire a political democracy and a collectivist economy, to be operated by democratically organized cooperatives rather than by the state. (3) The "antisocialists," whose limited contacts with foreign visitors and western literature have convinced them that the West has greater freedom and higher living standards, are "procapitalist" in outlook and desire to rebuild their society into a political democracy that permits some private ownership of property. The members of this group, according to Burg, are really technologically oriented and are not comfortable in ideological and intellectual discussions. Indeed, they tend to idealize western forms without really understanding them.

Even though their numbers may be small, it is exciting to learn that Soviet young people hold ideas like these, despite the rigorous program of indoctrination. In sharp contrast to the golden youth, the *stilyaga*, and so forth, the young people that Burg is discussing are not delinquent types, but are youthful intellectuals seriously thinking about alternative ways of organizing the social order. On the whole, however, these students are rather naïve about the workings of political institutions and the requirements of a modern industrial society. It is doubtful that these small groups of intellectuals pose a serious threat to the existing power structure. The "antisocialists," whose ideas are probably anathema to the Communist rulers, appear to be the most unsophisticated politically, while the students whose position has been more clearly thought out hold views that are closer to the Communist pattern.

In any event, the members of all three groups would be helpless against the power of the Soviet state if the regime decided to turn its terror upon them.

CYNICISM AND INDIFFERENCE AMONG SOVIET YOUTH

While the attacks upon stereotyped delinquents and intellectuals who succumb to "alien views" are dramatic and win headlines, Communist leaders are perhaps even more disturbed by the apathy and lack of ideological zeal that they detect among wide segments of the younger generation. As they undoubtedly recognize, such attitudes among young people can become serious problems for a regime that is concerned with perpetuating itself.

Occasionally even the foreign visitor encounters expressions of cynicism and indifference among the young people he meets. There is, for example, the young man who, after listening to a discussion of foreign policy between an American and several of his colleagues, whispers, "You know, I hate politics!" There is also the graduate student in a technical institute who, as he walks through the park with his new acquaintance from America, tells how some of his friends who love the bright lights of the city have managed to dodge the volunteer labor brigades in which every Soviet youth is expected to participate. He admits that he has grown cynical, although in his younger days, he says, he was driven by a spirit of selfless devotion to the cause. It was when he was graduated from the Young Pioneers into the *Komsomols* that he first encountered the young people who exploited ideology for personal advancement, he relates. The young science student frankly admits to the American visitor that he finds the *Komsomol* discussions of Communist ideology and "Soviet vistas" utterly boring. These discussions are as lifeless to him as are his classroom courses in Marxist-Leninist theory. A few of his friends, he points out, openly express similar sentiments.

Such cynicism is understandable. Some young people are visibly troubled by the gap that they detect between life as it is supposed to be and life as it really is. They have doubts about the system of privilege that has developed in the so-called "new society." While they are impressed by the personal sacrifice made by some loyal Soviet citizens, they hear of "fixers" being employed by factories to expedite the flow of raw materials; they read about fraud and embezzlement; and they learn that influential people have exerted pressure upon teachers in behalf of their children. They know that even Khrushchev has spoken of favoritism in the admission of students to higher education. When their associates are assigned to positions that, in their view, they do not deserve, some young people begin to suspect that not all of the youth have acquired the virtues of the "new Soviet man."

Although the regime does not admit that some of its young people have grown skeptical, it frequently launches campaigns in the press against the "apolitical" attitude found among the young people. The authorities complain about the youths who frown upon manual labor, who do not respond enthusiastically to appeals for increased production, and who do not accept their responsibilities in the *Komsomols*. Such behavior, according to Soviet officials, stems in part from the failure of many young people to become acquainted with life beyond the classroom—a defect that they anticipate will be remedied by the reorganization of the educational system.

As testimony to the official concern about the apathy of youth, *Komsomolskaya Pravda* recently printed a questionnaire in its columns, which it invited young people—and some prominent oldsters—to answer and return to the newspaper headquarters. Although it was described as a "poll," the sampling procedures left something to be desired, and the replies printed so far suggest that the experiment was part of a calculated campaign to turn popular censure upon both the delinquents and the apathetic. It is significant, however, that the editors saw fit to raise such questions as, Are you satisfied with the current crop of young people and their goals? What are the strong and the weak character traits of Soviet youth? Do you have a personal goal, and, if so, what is it?

As could be anticipated, the newspaper received many replies that expressed satisfaction with the younger generation. Others who replied, however, were critical, although they were extremely careful to point out that the censure was applicable to only a fragment of the youth. Some young people, the critics explained, are not eager to go to the virgin lands or to construction projects far from home; they worship western fashions and "shallow music," and they seem disposed to travel paths "strewn only with flowers." The most sensational letter was a "confession" from a young woman in Moscow, who soon became the main target in other letters to the editor (*Komsomolskaya Pravda*, January 26, 1961):

I am only 19, but there is so much apathy in me and indifference to all my surroundings that adults can only wonder, and I hear the same remark over and over again: "So young and already tired of it all. What will happen to you when you're 30?" But surprising as it may be, the fact is that life is not very interesting. And this is not only my opinion but the opinion of the people I go around with. . . .

Money is everything. Luxury and well-being, love and happiness. If you have money, you have friends and companions, you have everything at all you want. You condemn those who do not work, who do nothing. Why, they are only to be envied, because they are enjoying life. We live only once!

The Moscow poet M.V. Isakovsky had people like the young Muscovite in mind when he listed the negative traits of a minority of the youth (*Komsomolskaya Pravda*, March 16, 1961) :

. . . reluctance (partial or complete) of some to work: "Work is something only fools like," they say, "and we are not fools"; a craving for the easy life, the desire to take as much as possible from society and give as little as possible to it; fear of all difficulties (hence the reluctance to go to the countryside from the cities, especially from Moscow, and hence the determination of rural young people to get to the city) ; imitation by some young people of the behavior of the "gilded youth" of the West; worship of things foreign (not of the real values, material or spiritual, created abroad, but of all sorts of tinsel, all sorts of trash); a churlish attitude to girls and excessive lack of inhibition in the behavior of some girls; hooliganism in all its form and manifestations.

YOUTH: A PRODUCT OF THE SOVIET ERA

The sixteen-year-old Soviet youth today was born right after World War II, and he entered the first grade in 1953, the year of Stalin's death. The Bolshevik revolution took place 45 years ago—a span almost three times the lifetime of a sixteen-year-old. Although the Soviet propaganda machine pours out a continual stream of facts and legends glorifying the revolution and the exploits of acceptable Bolshevik heroes, the young people are less stirred by these events than were the earlier generations who experienced them. To them the revolution is now history, and the bogey-men of the Tsarist era seem less real. The Soviet youngster has been growing up in the postwar phase of the socialist society—a society that has already survived civil war, famine, purge, Nazi invasion, the heavy demands of postwar reconstruction, and the trauma of de-Stalinization. Having known nothing but this type of society, which, he is told, must inevitably progress to a higher stage of Communism, the youngster probably feels no close connection with the stock horrors conjured up by the Communist leaders: feudal aristocracy, capitalist exploitation, Tsarist police, and so forth. Now all the inescapable imperfections of his human society are likely to be associated in his mind with his present rulers. If all the triumphs of his land are to be labeled "Soviet," so also will be at least some of the failures.

8

THE SOVIET AIRWAVES

William S. Howell

Associate Chairman of the Department of Speech and Theater Arts at the University of Minnesota, William S. Howell has made a special study of Soviet radio techniques and programs. He has published several articles in this area and he is also coauthor of the textbooks Discussion *(with Donald K. Smith) and* Persuasion *(with Winston L. Brembeck).*

E. W. Ziebarth

Dean of the Summer Session at the University of Minnesota, E. W. Ziebarth was formerly educational director of the Central Division of the Columbia Broadcasting System, is coauthor of several books and numerous articles, and has twice been joint winner of the Peabody Award. He also holds the First Award for news interpretation of the National Institute for Education by Radio and Television, and has been given the American Federation of Radio and Television "Best Commentator" citation.

An American returning from the Soviet Union remarked, "In Russia you don't watch TV—TV watches you." At one time it may have been only technological limitations that prevented the Soviet leaders from making this 1984 nightmare a reality. The fact, however, that the comment has a certain grim humor suggests that there are important differences between radio and television in the Soviet Union and the United States. The most important difference, of course, lies in the objectives of the media.

FUNCTIONS OF THE MASS MEDIA

The Soviet regime can never assume that the indoctrination program in the schools and youth organizations has been completely successful. The ideal of the "new Soviet man" must be presented to the people day after day, in endless repetition. And what better way is there to do this than to use radio and television to preach the gospel of Lenin and Marx? What to Americans are normal functions of the mass media—providing information, news, and especially entertainment—are secondary in the Soviet Union. As is to be expected, political indoctrination is fundamental, and the extent to which it becomes an obtrusive part of virtually every segment of the broadcast day is startling to American viewers and listeners. It has been suggested that this indoctrination is a type of "national institutional commercial," substituted for the goods and services advertising that dominates a great portion of our own programming.

The Soviet leaders are perfectly frank about the functions of their mass media and make no apologies either at home or abroad. One widely quoted directive points out, for example, that radio must assist in circulating

political information . . . [and] must mobilize the masses for the fulfillment of the tasks of socialist construction . . . In order to become a genuine loudspeaker for the Party addressing the millions of workers, political information [on the radio] must be outstanding in its loyalty to the Party's interests . . . and activity. We reject all indifferent, "objective information."

Other instructions stress the belief that radio must carry to the masses "the inspired word of Bolshevik truth," that it must "spread the truth about the class struggle," and that it is "a powerful means of political development of the workers." Certainly, the objective would be more efficiently achieved if each television set were in fact an Orwellian eye peering into the corners of private homes, reporting popular response to the message.

ORGANIZATION OF THE BROADCASTING INDUSTRY

If the broadcasting system is to serve efficiently the objectives of the state, it must be exclusively controlled by the state. There can be no pattern of competing private networks and local stations such as exist in the United States. The entire domestic radio and television system operates under the state committee of television and radio broadcasting, which is appointed by and reports to the Council of Ministers of the USSR. This committee is granted an exclusive license to practice, and the question of competition simply does not arise. As its name implies, the responsibilities of the committee extend throughout the republics of the Soviet Union. Subordinate committees, which have been established in each of the republics, presumably maintain relations with the state committee in Moscow and help in determining policy. It is doubtful, however, that they influence significantly the pattern of the all-Union transmissions from the central source in Moscow.

A special unit of the Communist Party—*Agitprop* (department of propaganda and agitation)—works closely with the state committee of television and radio broadcasting in designing propaganda activities. Indeed, Agitprop takes the lead in developing and executing effective propaganda strategy that will support the policies laid down by Communist leaders in the Party Presidium.

TELEVISION PROGRAMMING

In a country where the major "advertiser" is promoting a way of life and owns and operates all radio and television outlets, one might expect political indoctrination from morning until night. But this kind of programming soon reaches the point of diminishing returns; people, even in the Soviet Union, eventually get to the point where they turn off their sets. There must be bait on the hook, and the authorities try to provide drama, music, and some nonpolitical commentary to attract an audience to the significant political broadcasts. To suggest, however, that the political message in the Soviet Union takes the place of the American commercial is only partially accurate, for it is often not separated in time from the substantive material of the programs themselves, so that the listener or viewer must make his own psychological separation.

What kind of program, then, does the Russian television viewer have to watch? First, there is straight, unadulterated political propaganda and indoctrination. Even these programs, however, take many different forms. A worker who has greatly overfulfilled his quota may appear before the cameras in his factory garb to tell how he achieved his success and call upon all other workers to follow his example. An editor of *Pravda* may give a speech discussing and interpreting a change in the Party line or a new production scheme. Following the Hungarian uprising, for example, a special film was prepared purporting to show how this "counter-revolution" was instigated by Americans and supported only by the fascists and other reactionary groups in Hungary. This film was shown several times a week until virtually every set owner had had a chance to see it, and most had every opportunity to memorize its not entirely memorable lines.

Many of the so-called "news programs" would fit into this category because their content is so different from that of newscasts in western nations. There is lengthy discussion of production quotas, ceremonious awarding of prizes for various accomplishments, and biting comments about western imperialism. Editorials taken from leading Soviet newspapers are read at tedious length, but the newscasts almost never include stories of human interest or of personal fortune, good or ill, or of robberies, murders, fires, and accidents. When this kind of material is included, it is used to demonstrate a point. An incident of juvenile delinquency, for example, is reported when there is a campaign to wipe out this social problem. An automobile accident may be reported if an effort is being made to reduce the number of accidents, but not because the accident itself constitutes news.

The live telecasting of a sporting event, a concert, or even a theatrical production is another regular part of the schedule. This is perhaps the most impressive television programming done in the Soviet Union. Unlike the American practice of emphasizing studio productions, Soviet television drama is often a straightforward presentation of a play from a Moscow theatre, and the televising of concerts or sports events is especially well handled. Although both audio and video quality may leave something to be desired (despite high theoretical standards), many of these programs are superb because the theatrical presentation or concert itself is superb. And since the Soviet producer does not feel compelled to use startling or unusual camera angles, one is frequently treated to a play or concert of high quality with a minimum of distraction.

Strictly informational or educational programs make up a third category. An official from the ministry of agriculture may bore his audience for an hour and a half on the best ways to plant and cultivate hybrid corn if, indeed, anyone leaves his set on that long. There may be a program on dressmaking, or a learned lecture on Tolstoy. This type of programming is usually unimaginative at best, and might be compared to American educational television at its worst.

A People's Television University provides educational programs of reasonably high quality to substantial numbers of students. It is difficult to arrive at meaningful estimates of the number of such telestudents, but if the term is loosely defined, they may well number in the hundreds of thousands. Although the educational films used on such programs are usually effective, live programming often lacks the life and color to which Americans are accustomed, even in educational television.

A fourth program category is the "regular feature," including a hodgepodge of materials in which music and relatively light drama predominate. Among the best and the most popular regular features are the children's programs. Animated cartoons *á la* Disney, fairy tale hours, and puppet shows frequently open the evening schedule. The Russian puppet theatre, from which many of these performances are borrowed, is among the most distinguished of its kind in the world, and these puppet shows are often superb, although even they include a surprising quota of political material.

The Russians have even ventured into the field of give-away programs with an enthusiastic but devastating result. Irving R. Levine, for example, tells of a program called "Evening of Funny Questions" that was organized to give boxes of candy and neckties to contestants who excelled in imitations or recitations. On one Saturday evening in the autumn, the master of ceremonies pointed out that it was now about time for Muscovites to begin digging out their winter clothes, and added that the first three people to get to the studio wearing winter garments would win prizes. He also invited others to come to the program origination point where they would find what he called a "hospitable welcome." Free prizes in a land where shortages of consumer goods are chronic brought Russians of all sizes, ages, and occupations dressed in their fur hats and heavy coats. They rushed on to the small stage in such numbers that they tripped over camera cables and blocked lenses as they gesticulated and argued about who was there first and therefore eligible for the prize. The chaos became uncontrollable, and the video portion of the program was cut off the air. Finally, an obviously harassed announcer uttered a phrase as meaningless in one language as in another: "The sponsors of this evening will take time in order to make out the situation." At that point, both video and audio were cut and nothing was seen on the screen for about 30 minutes. Following the break, another announcer, this time somewhat more composed, appeared to explain that the evening's programs were cancelled because of "organizational difficulties." That ended the programming for the evening, and for the time being ended the Soviet experiment with give-away programs.

Less dissonant variations on the theme were developed at a later date, however, and it is interesting to note that Major Yuri A. Gagarin, the first Russian cosmonaut, appeared on such a program only a few days after his triumph in space on April 12, 1961. His appearance was a part of the concerted effort to use all mass media to achieve maximal impact from the achievement. On that program the man who crossed the space frontier collected almost enough prizes to fill his space capsule. Included among them were such things as books, flowers, paintings, and even a statue representing his triumph.

Some mention should be made of that staple of television programming in every country—the old movie. They are used in the Soviet Union too, although they are happily supplemented with current films, including some foreign films, especially from the satellite countries. According to one Soviet official, feature films are shown on television almost as soon as they are released. "No 1935 cowboy movies for us!" he is reported as saying. This contrast with American practice reflects the different purposes of the mass media of communication. Movies, like radio, television, and the press, are primarily instruments of indoctrination. Instead of releasing movies to television at the time profits can be maximized, they are released at the time indoctrination can be maximized. This usually means early television showing.

In the Soviet Union there is little daytime television. The regime does not wish to distract the worker from his major tasks. This means particularly that there is no substantial programming for housewives, presumably on the assumption that they are out doing "socially useful labor" and cannot be bothered by anything as frivolous as television. This pattern is gradually changing, however, with weekday telecasts between noon and one o'clock and Sunday and holiday programming from ten in the morning until midnight. It is presumed that on Sundays and holidays there will be less interference with the work schedule of the daytime viewer.

Americans who are accustomed to absolute precision in program schedules are sometimes startled to find Russian programs beginning or ending substantially off schedule, with no one showing the least concern. A program may start five minutes early or five minutes late. An early evening program may run as much as half an hour overtime, which means, of course, that the next program will also be that much late. Although such practices probably annoy the viewer, they may account for the absence in Russia of the frantic activity and tension during a production that are found in broadcast studios in the United States.

TELEVISION EQUIPMENT

The Soviet Union* is obviously investing a great deal of money and creative energy in the development of television. But in this society which lacks consumer goods, are enough television sets produced, sold, and viewed to make the effort worthwhile? In the major cities of European Russia, television-set ownership is fairly widely distributed. A walk through even the poorer sections of the cities reveals forests of television aerials sprouting from virtually every kind of dwelling. The price of sets in department stores in 1958 ranged from 800 rubles to 3,000 rubles, with a 14-inch diagonal-screen model selling for about 2,000 rubles. This is not expensive when compared with the price of yardgoods, clothes, and washing machines. But to the Russian industrial workers with an income of 700 to 800 rubles a month it must seem "stratospheric." In talking with substantial numbers of Russians of varying income levels, however, the foreign visitor hears few complaints about cost; what seems to be more disturbing to the ordinary citizen is the shortage of sets at any price. As one young man of limited income expressed it, "We believe there is so much for the people to learn by means of radio and television that the state will not permit the prices to go too high. I have a television set that cost me only a little more than two months' salary." While this appears to be exorbitant by American standards, it did not seem so to this young man whose salary, it later developed, was about 800 rubles a month. He spoke of seeing ballet and opera performed by companies not normally playing in his city, of theatre and motion picture performances that he did not have time to attend in person but enjoyed and occasionally watched at home. Especially important in his case, he said, were the lectures on economics and politics, subjects outside his profession.

In 1958, the number of television sets in the USSR was estimated to be three million; by 1961 it had increased to slightly more than five million. While this rate of growth is not startling by American standards, it is nevertheless substantial, and the communications minister and other Soviet officials optimistically predict that the number will be sharply increased in the future, with a goal of 25 million sets to be reached by 1965.

The growth in the manufacture of television sets has been accompanied by a substantial increase in the number of television broad-casting centers. In late 1958 the Soviet Embassy reported the existence of more than 60 such centers, with the number increasing each month. Reflecting characteristic ·optimism, the embassy report not only listed a quota of 75 centers by 1960, but cheerfully predicted that the quota would be surpassed.

This optimism was apparently justified. A 1961 report of the office of research and analysis of the United States Information Agency indicated that 4 new television centers and 9 relay stations had been completed, giving the Soviet Union a total of 88 television centers and 84 relay stations in actual operation at the beginning of 1961. These figures were later confirmed by Henry Shapiro, the Moscow bureau manager of the United Press, in part as a result of an interview with the director of the state television and radio committee. Considerable progress has already been made in linking outlying stations with the television system in Moscow. By mid-1961, for example, 30 stations serving 22 different regions had been directly connected to the Moscow relay. Future plans include linking the capitals of the 15 republics with a unified country-wide television network. The authorities also plan to link Moscow with the Intervision network of eastern Europe and through Intervision with the west European Eurovision network. In June 1961, the Soviet television audience saw its first "live" broadcast originating from western Europe as they watched Queen Elizabeth "troop the line" on her birthday.

It will probably be some time before the USSR develops a pattern of interlocking transmitters comparable to that in the United States. Even if the Soviet Union had a single language and a relatively homo-geneous culture, a land mass of more than 8,500,000 square miles and a widely scattered population of more than 200 million would in them-selves create communication barriers not easy to overcome. When to these physical difficulties are added sharp differences in cultural back-ground, more than 80 languages, and a multiplicity of additional language variants, even the most ordinary "domestic" service becomes a problem in what amounts to international communication.

A particularly interesting development in this multilingual environ-ment is the simultaneous transmission of programs in more than one language. The Tashkent television station, for example, is reported to be simultaneously transmitting some programs in Russian and Uzbek. For this kind of television the receiver is equipped with a switch that enables viewers to choose the language they wish to hear.

Although the Soviet Union has, during the past few years, made impressive gains in the expansion of television facilities both in the number of stations and the distribution of sets, some of the claims must be subjected to careful scrutiny. An assertion made in 1961, for example, that all major cities were being served by television, and that TV was thus available to nearly one-half of the Soviet population, is somewhat misleading. What this statement means is that television service had reached major cities whose *total population* represents almost one-half of the population of the entire country. Since only a fraction of the residents of these cities have access to television sets, the assumption that about one-half of the population was being served seems unwarranted.

Although ordinary television receivers are not yet available to a great many Soviet families, Russian technicians are experimenting with color television. Interestingly enough there arose in the USSR a dispute concerning color television development that was not unlike one that occurred in the United States. Soviet experts first experimented with a sequential system involving a disc with three light filters—red, green, and blue—rotating before the transmitting tube with a similar disc synchronized to rotate before the television screen. They quickly discovered limitations in this procedure, as, for example, the lack of compatability with the black and white system. Clearly, it was undesirable to develop a system that would cause the rapid obsolescence of black and white sets while demand for any set so far outran supply. This disadvantage, plus the necessity to increase the size of the receiver in order to accommodate the disc, and the inevitable intricacy in synchronization and the low quality of the image, prompted them to abandon the sequential principle and utlimately to develop a compatible system similar to that used in the United States.

Regular transmission in color is limited to one hour a week and to the Moscow and Leningrad areas, but experimental telecasts are made three times a week by the state research institute of the ministry of communications. Orders have also gone out to manufacturers to begin to make small consignments of color sets. By the end of 1961, however, only a few hundred sets had been made available to the consumer. It is doubtful that there will be much investment in color television until more of the country is blanketed with black and white transmitters.

RADIO EQUIPMENT

The huge area and cultural diversity of the USSR, which make adequate television coverage difficult, also complicate the problem of providing radio coverage for the entire country from a central source. In order to handle the problem of transmitting a radio signal over vast distances, the Soviet radio industry employs short- and medium-wave bands for domestic as well as foreign broadcasts. This is a unique feature of Soviet radio, for the USSR is the only country to use shortwave extensively for domestic coverage.

Another unique characteristic of radio broadcasting in the Soviet Union is the use of the local radio-diffusion exchange, or the "wired radio." Subscribers to the radio-diffusion exchange have a loudspeaker in their homes that is connected by wire to the central exchange. A sensitive, high-powered radio receiver in the central exchange picks up signals from a distant transmitter and relays them to the private loudspeakers. In addition to the fact that it simplifies the problem of covering a wide geographic area, this system has many advantages from the Soviet point of view. In a country plagued by a chronic shortage of electronic equipment, the use of wired radio allows a much wider distribution of sets than would otherwise be possible. Moreover, the owner of a wired radio has no opportunity to select his own programs, including foreign broadcasts. The listener often has the alternative of, let us say, Radio Moscow, Radio Kiev, or radio off—hardly a wide range of choices.

The radio-diffusion system has grown rapidly since its origin in 1929. Today there are about 24 million speakers in the radio-diffusion exchanges, or about one speaker for every nine people in the country. These, of course, are in addition to the conventional radio sets.

According to the publication *USSR Speaking*, the Soviet Union in January 1935 had 2,300,000 regular radio sets. At that time there were 25,500,000 sets in North America and 23,500,000 in western Europe. These figures become more meaningful when they are related to population. Whereas there were 13 to 14 receivers for 1,000 people (or one set for every 75 persons) in the USSR, North America had 160 per 1,000 people (or one set for every 6 persons). By 1940 the Soviet figure had risen to only 24 to 27 per 1,000, while some western nations reported up to 200. According to the best estimates available, the Soviet Union had only about 10 to 12 million regular radio sets in 1961.

If we keep in mind the fact that until 1947 many of the collective farms were without receiving apparatus of any kind and that individual farmers rarely had an opportunity to listen except at a central location, we will have a more accurate picture of radio coverage during the post-war period. Rural areas, and even some of the more remote republics as a whole, were seriously underequipped.

RADIO PROGRAMMING

The prospective listener has a wider variety of radio programs available to him than does the television viewer. While there is only one TV channel in most cities, three different programs are offered on radio. The main service, presumably designed for the largest audience, is on the air from six a.m. until one a.m. and carries a program schedule of news commentary, drama, and music. The second and third programs are on for a shorter period of time and are a bit more highbrow, concentrating on music and drama or on readings from serious literature.

The radio-program schedule shows a high concentration of music and drama. The deputy director general of radio Moscow reported that 1,800 musical programs are broadcast each week and a minimum of 250 broadcasts each year in the series "Theater over the Air," which presents new plays or new productions of classic drama. While the figure for musical programs is difficult to interpret, it does reflect the heavy reliance upon musical fare. The largest of the Radio Moscow studios is open to the public much as are the concert halls in Moscow, and the broadcast concerts are attended by large numbers of studio guests.

The emphasis on music in the domestic broadcasting schedule is reflected in the titles of programs such as "Concert Quiz," "How to Understand Music," "Musical Lectures," "Musical Dictionary," "Musical ABC." "Musical ABC" is among the most interesting of these, since it deals with the fundamentals of music and tries to familiarize listeners with principles of melody, harmony, consonance, notations, types of musical expression, and other basic and relatively uncomplicated concepts. A step or two up the scale in complexity, "How to Understand Music" is more systematic and thorough, and the top level "Musical Lectures" brings to the microphone well-known musicologists, professors, and composers. Still another series, "Get Acquainted with . . ." is designed to give unknown composers, poets, singers, and others an opportunity to perform before a large radio audience.

A quick look at some of the 1,700 literary and dramatic broadcasts presented during a typical year reflects an obviously political as well as aesthetic pattern: among the new works introduced were those of Dacroub (Lebanon), Mohammed Diba (Algeria), and Boren Bochu (India). The works of composers from nations that Russia wishes to influence appear to be presented with more than normal frequency.

Children's broadcasts, which are of special importance in the Soviet system, average at least four hours a day. For example, in 1955, according to data quoted by Viatcheslav Tchernychev, then deputy director general of Radio Moscow, about 2000 broadcasts for children were presented. These were devoted largely to music and to what are called "educational" materials. These programs, however, are not designed for in-school listening, as is the case in Britain and in many sections of the United States.

Lectures and talks are, of course, a basic part of the fare provided for the Soviet listener. Soviet sources list up to 430 talks a year dealing with scientific and economic matters. Medicine, agriculture, and the biological sciences are also included in the schedule of "talks," and in the case of medicine an effort is made to cover practical public health instruction under the title "Advice from the Doctor." Talks dealing with "economic matters" are often Party-line indoctrination, as are some of those that deal with the biological sciences, although most observers appear to accept talks on medicine and the physical sciences as informative and objective, if not sparkling.

EFFECTIVENESS OF SOVIET BROADCASTING

Little is known about audience response to Soviet radio and television. There is no equivalent of Hooper or Nielson to tell us which programs are popular and which attract no significant audience. The general desire to buy radio and television receivers and the remarks made by Russians to foreign visitors suggest a reasonably favorable reception of the radio and television fare.

That neither television nor radio programming is wholly acceptable to the entire population, however, is made abundantly clear by letters published in the Soviet press. Complaints have become so general that the television center has set up a special committee and staff to answer questions and to study critical reactions in order to determine what new programs to introduce, or what old ones to revise.

The writing of letters is encouraged for a variety of reasons. Programmers want to know what is popular and what is not popular with the listeners or the viewers. In addition, however, the foreign observer gets a distinct impression that criticism is encouraged because it is a safe area in which citizens can be given the feeling that they are participating in decision-making and policy formulation.

The self-criticism columns of the newspapers frequently contain letters from irate listeners who complain about programs and the quality of reception. It is difficult, of course, to interpret such criticism. Sometimes, quite obviously, the critical letters have been officially inspired and lead to a fully documented criticism that culminates in the dismissal of a director, producer, or even a top executive.

Broadcasting, both radio and television, is openly viewed as an instrument of national policy. No official with whom one speaks makes any effort to suggest anything else. It is true that in many cases these officials speak of the educational impact of these media, the cultural opportunities provided, and even occasionally refer to the recreational aspects of some programs. But questions about the central objective are usually met with looks of astonishment, since clearly the system has always been viewed by the people who work in the industry as an instrument of the state and the Party. The Party, however, is not always happy with their performance. For example, the July 5, 1962 issue of *Pravda* criticized Soviet radio and television because of their failure to carry enough Communist propaganda. That organ of the Party complained that radio and television failed to attract to their microphones enough Communist Party leaders. The article then restated the function of radio and television: "The direct duty of radio and TV is to acquaint the working people of the Soviet Union with questions of the international situation, with the foreign policy of the Soviet Union, to propagandize the achievements of the world socialist system, to tell of the struggle of the peoples for peace, democracy, and socialism, and to expose the antipeople policies of the imperial states."

Whether or not these media do their job effectively is difficult, if not impossible, for a westerner to judge. Indeed, such a judgment is probably almost as difficult for the Russians. Some of the broadcasting is, by American standards, excellent; much of it is unimaginative, dry, and almost incredibly "talky." In making his appraisal, however, the American must bear in mind that he is inevitably making comparisons within the framework of a free and competitive system of broadcasting, whereas the Russian is making his comparison largely with his own past experience with his own system. Exceptions are those occasional BBC, Radio Liberation, or Voice of America programs that get by the jamming system. All in all, Russian broadcasting probably serves its limited objective effectively, and to us it may be one of the very best reflections of what the current Soviet regime considers to be important.

RADIO AS AN INSTRUMENT OF FOREIGN POLICY

Since broadcasting is an instrument of control in the hands of the Communist leaders, it is natural that they would employ the medium to gain support for their foreign policy and to increase Soviet influence throughout the world. In fact, the Russian Communists were among the first leaders of a state to recognize the potential propaganda value of the foreign broadcast. According to the files of Radio Moscow, the Communists began to send radio signals beyond their frontiers in the autumn of 1920, when Lenin and Trotsky initiated propaganda broadcasts to Germany in the hope of igniting revolution in that country. When the revolution ended in failure, however, foreign broadcasting was stopped for a number of years.

Efforts to reach the outside world by radio were made again in 1927, on the tenth anniversary of the Bolshevik revolution. At that time radio facilities were provided for the foreign delegations so that they could broadcast their impressions of the Soviet Union to the people in their homelands. Two years later, the regime initiated a regular schedule of broadcasting in foreign languages over domestic facilities, primarily for the benefit of western specialists who had come to the USSR to assist in the program of industrialization.

The development of these domestic foreign language broadcasts soon led to the programming of regular broadcasts to other countries. In October 1929, the department of foreign service broadcasts was organized in Radio Moscow, and regular programs were transmitted, first in German and then in French and English. This service was greatly expanded during the 1930s, and by 1941 programs in 11 different languages were being broadcast regularly, while several other languages were being used intermittently.

Today programs are broadcast daily in approximately 39 languages. Several "services," however, are beamed in a single language, depending upon the audience that the regime desires to reach. In English, for example, there are the North American Service and the Pacific Coast Service (each of which uses the speaking style of the American Midwest), and the British Service and the Far Eastern Service (in standard British dialect). Radio Moscow attempts a comprehensive coverage of regional, political, and language groupings. The use of high wattage and several different frequencies is fairly successful in overcoming distortion, interference, and other irregularities in long distance shortwave listening. Frequencies are changed at intervals throughout the year to take advantage of atmospheric conditions associated with particular seasons.

THE "VOICE OF RUSSIA" BEAMED TO AMERICA

Many of the significant characteristics of Soviet broadcasts to other lands may be illustrated by an examination of the North American

Service of Radio Moscow—the "Voice of America" in reverse.

Soviet broadcasting to North America became a vital operation in 1940 or 1941, when Joe Adamov joined the staff. After more than two decades, he is still a moving force in the North American Service. Evidence accumulated through many years of listening and from conversations with the personnel of Radio Moscow indicate that his ideas have largely determined programming and broadcasting practices.

According to Adamov and Alexander Alexandrov, the director of English language broadcasting for Radio Moscow in 1958, the extensive and expensive shortwave broadcasting to North America is designed to accomplish two objectives: (1) to communicate a cross-section of *true* information about the Soviet people to residents of the United States and Canada; and (2) to build a favorable attitude toward the Soviet Union. These goals are hardly surprising, for they are the asserted objectives of every world power that engages in international propaganda.

The personnel of Radio Moscow prepare from two to three hours of original programming each day for the Pacific Coast and North American Services. Items are repeated selectively, depending upon international events and the propaganda themes that are to be stressed at a particular time. The original programs and the repeat broadcasts ordinarily total about 12 hours a day. The North American Service can be heard on nine or ten different frequencies, while four frequencies are used for the Pacific Coast Service.

Much of the radio time is devoted to news and commentary. The style of news broadcasts suggests that the staff has studied and copied American practices. Except for the alternation of male and female voices —a common European practice—news presentation (but not content) is much like that of a radio station in the United States. News is broadcast "every hour on the hour." Fairly recently "Headlines of the News," a forty-five second to one-minute digest of the major news items to be expanded later, has begun each broadcast. Less recently "commentary" has been separated from "news," and the typical newscast of ten minutes is routinely followed by five minutes of Soviet opinion on a currently controversial issue. An illusion of objectivity is probably the reason for this separation, although the listener would find it difficult to decide which had the greater proportion of opinion, the news or the commentary.

Next in prominence in broadcast time is music. Apparently the management of the North American Service has decided that music has propaganda value. Increasing emphasis upon music has produced quarter- and half-hour periods of well-planned Soviet classical or folk music and, most recently, of American popular music, much of which has been recorded in the United States. Music periods were formerly interrupted by short features carrying political messages, but now music programs tend to consist only of music and a commentary of strictly musical concern.

Another series of programs is designed to give the North American listener a glimpse of "Life in the Soviet Union." Typical programs in this category include "Science and Engineering." "Meet the People," "What is Communism?" "Youth Parade," and "Soviet Musicians."

The top program in the North American Service—the offering that carries a major portion of the propaganda message—is called "Moscow Mailbag." This program is a chatty, informal round-table of three performers who answer questions sent in by American listeners. According to Joe Adamov, the questions are selected on the principle that the questions which are most likely to embarrass the Soviet Union will be of greatest interest to the American audience. The picture Radio Moscow would create is that of three artless panelists informally and frankly answering the "hottest" questions that American listeners can throw at them. A look at the program in preparation, however, reveals that a great deal of planning and study are behind this informal and "spontaneous" program.

The basic strategy of the program calls for a careful balance of three contrasting but complementary personalities. The regular moderator is a highly genial, friendly, middle-of-the-roader who frequently softens the somewhat extreme contentions of the other participants. Victor Kruprianov played this role in 1958. Joe Adamov plays the part of political and philosophical theorist. He handles difficult questions on such matters as religion in the USSR and Communist authoritarianism. He provides glib and persuasive "common sense" explanations of Communist doctrine, demonstrating the rhetoric of the demagogue in the apparent confrontation of difficult questions. His techniques of evasion are so skilled as to be artistic. In short, he makes the present policies of the Soviet government seem to be invariably wise and just, under the current unusual circumstances!

Sergei Rudin is a typical third panelist on "Moscow Mailbag," playing the role of the "academician." He supplies an informative approach whenever it is appropriate, filling in statistical information and details of historical background, new developments in science, and activities of the Academy of Sciences and of the universities. The other panelists josh him mildly from time to time for his tendency to appear erudite. Because he appears bookish, his occasional definite conclusions on political issues have the illusion of being factually supported.

The sequence of topics on "Moscow Mailbag" is not a random arrangement. The early questions deal with noncontroversial matters and those that permit the injection of humor. As the program progresses and after the listener has been disarmed by the friendly tone of the initial questions and answers, the issues become more fundamental. These warm, attractive radio personalities soon attempt to transfer a favorable response on inconsequential topics to issues on which the Soviet Union and the United States disagree. The informality and the congeniality of manner persist throughout the program, but, in the latter part, the language changes to a hard-hitting condemnation of American actions or policy and all-out support of the Soviet version of the issue being discussed.

Although the "Mailbag" discussion conveys an illusion of casual spontaneity, it is very carefully prepared. A week or so before the program is produced, Adamov selects the questions and distributes them among the participants. With the help of the research people and facilities at Radio Moscow and the Lenin Library, each panelist assembles the information that will be useful in answering the questions for which he is responsible.

At the time the program is to be recorded the only script is a one-page list of the questions to be answered, with the names and addresses of the questioners; the names of the panelists who are to answer the questions; and a notation of any music or special audio effects to be used. Each participant brings whatever notes he needs to help in answering the questions assigned to him.

The moderator opens the program, proceeding directly to the first question and designating the participant who is to answer. Although one person has primary responsibility for supplying a particular answer, all the panelists manage to "chime in" so that everyone appears to be helping to supply the requested information. The conversational flavor is maintained, speech is colloquial and sometimes slangy, and personal references are frequent. In production, however, the effect is choppy and erratic, due to the use of a "make-remake" technique. As soon as something is not adequate, someone calls "stop." After discussing what should be done, the tape is rolled back and that particular portion is rerecorded. Sometimes the discussions on how to handle opinion or information become arguments. The rerecording and associated arguing necessary to produce a twenty minute program might take well over an hour.

On September 16, 1958, a tape recorder was brought to the North American Service studio, and the authorities granted a request that everything that went on in the studio during the production of "Moscow

Mailbag" be recorded. The following items are taken from the recording made at that time. These are the questions in the order in which they were discussed:

1. Tell me about a summer resort here in the Soviet Union where the average person spends his vacation.
2. When large or small improvements or construction take place and it is necessary to move houses, perhaps even villages, from the way, what provisions are made to rehouse and relocate the displaced persons?
3. What is the program for super highways throughout the Soviet Union?
4. Does your planning include possible needs for 30, 40, or 50 years ahead when blueprints are drawn today, particularly for highways?
5. What part does the teaching of dialectical materialism play in your education setup? Is this philosophy widespread, and is it taught to members of the armed forces?
6. In exactly what way is Marxist-Leninist philosophy introduced into schoolrooms?
7. Is there much interest in western newspapers and magazines among students, and is such paper matter sold or subscribed to by libraries?
8. Are hotdogs and hamburgers, typical Canadian and American snacks, popular in the USSR?
9. What is to be done to make Siberia a great producing area?
10. If, as you have previously said, "rock-and-roll" is not very popular, what types of music are popular, and would you please play typical favorites?
11. Do you think that the differences in political thinking between the USSR and the United States can be resolved without war?
12. What do you think about the way in which China's petition to be admitted to the United Nations has been treated?
13. How many national parks are there in the USSR?
14. Requests for music.

We might note the light and noncontroversial nature of questions 1 to 4. Questions 5, 6, and 7 are controversial and demand careful handling, and relief is provided by more lightness and simple reporting in questions 8, 9, and 10. Questions 11 and 12 carry the propaganda punch of the program, and in answering number 12, especially, the panelists carefully tried to build an impressive case against American policy on the China issue. Tension is again relaxed by question 13, as well as by the requests for music which concluded the program.

Language usage in foreign broadcasts has changed greatly during the past decade. For example, there has been a noticeable decline in the use of inflammatory and belligerent language. During the Korean War, Radio Moscow would often address its American listeners as "treacherous war mongers," then expect sympathetic attention to a Russian point of view in the next paragraph. By 1961, however, such viciously "loaded" terms were rarely employed in the North American Service, and when violent language is to be found, it is explicitly applied to a few men in Washington who are allegedly leading the American people along a tragic course.

The use of more moderate language has been accompanied by changes in phonetic style and greater informality of address. British speech has been eliminated from the broadcasts, as have all regional dialects of the United States except "general" American. Radio Moscow appears to have adopted as guides to correct pronunciation speech standards that are used by American radio networks. Slang and colloquialisms are used abundantly, contractions are frequent, and most of the performers use direct forms of address. The personal pronouns, "I," "you," and "we," which the Service used rarely on the air prior to 1952, are now routinely injected into the programs. Announcers make frequent personal references, telling about their homes, families, hobbies, and habits. This broadcasting style makes them appear as radio "personalities" rather than as disembodied voices.

Today a frankly experimental approach to international broadcasting is appearing in the North American Service. Issues that were formerly taboo are now treated in open discussion. The prevalence of atheism in the USSR and the basic differences between Soviet Communism and the democratic system in capitalist states are examples of subjects that the performers at Radio Moscow are willing to tackle. Staff members seem to enjoy answering the "hottest" questions their listeners direct to them. They also fill requests, such as playing "The Star Spangled Banner" magnificently recorded by a Moscow orchestra.

DOES ANYONE LISTEN?

Radio Moscow is naturally interested in the size of its audience and the type of American listener who tunes in on its programs. This, of course, is a difficult research task, and thus far the staff has employed only crude techniques. One method they use is to encourage the audience to request program schedules for the North American Service. Along with a recent program schedule they enclosed the following note:

TO ALL LISTENERS:

If you have any specific questions about life in the USSR, which you would like answered in one of our feature programs or by mail;

If you have any questions or comments on Soviet-American relations or other international problems, which you would like to offer as topics to be discussed in our broadcasts;

If there is any particular music you would like to have played at your request—

Don't hesitate to let us know.

Please mention which Service you listen to: the North American or the Pacific Coast.

You will receive advance notice on when to listen to the answer to your request.

Reception reports are always welcome. If QSL is requested, don't forget to mention in your report such essentials as: day and hour of reception, waveband and megacycles, items of program heard.

Color postcards with views of Soviet cities are enclosed in all letters from Radio Moscow as a souvenir.

Our mailing address is:

> RADIO-MOSCOW
> MOSCOW, USSR

In another attempt to elicit listener response, the station enclosed the following letter with its printed program:

Dear Listener:

We will be much obliged if you take the trouble to answer the following questions:

1. How often do you listen to Radio-Moscow and at what time?
2. What do you enjoy in our programs and what don't you like?
3. Is there anything pertaining to life in the Soviet Union that you would like to have described in our programs?

Please fill in your answers on this questionnaire and mail to RADIO-MOSCOW, MOSCOW, USSR.

Thank you in advance, we are

> Yours Sincerely,
> RADIO-MOSCOW

Radio Moscow has also made at least two attempts to assess listenership through contests and the awarding of prizes. The first was the by-product of a special program called "International Quiz," which was broadcast early in 1957. The listener was given nine questions (three each day) dealing with Soviet accomplishments and Soviet-American relations. A similar program in the spring of 1958 was the

"40th Anniversary Quiz," in celebration of the Bolshevik revolution. Listeners who sent in the correct answers received substantial prizes, including books, stamp collections, phonograph records, and reproductions of paintings from various galleries. It was anticipated that the mail response to these quiz programs would give Radio Moscow at least some idea of the location of their most interested auditors.

We in the United States probably have no more precise information than the Russians concerning the popular response to foreign broadcasts. To estimate the impact of the North American Service upon American listeners we obviously need to know who listens. This information is not available at present, nor is it likely that studies or surveys will produce reliable data in the foreseeable future. Using questionnaires and interviews, American specialists have attempted to study the listening and viewing practices of the domestic radio and TV audience, but the results have not been entirely satisfactory. Certainly such a bold question as "How many hours a week do you listen to Radio Moscow?" would probably yield less than frank answers from American interviewees.

For these reasons we can only speculate about the size, nature, and listening habits of the audience reached by the North American Service. Since effect can only be estimated in terms of a known audience, it will be useful to pull together the scraps of evidence we have in an effort to identify the audience as best we can. Our speculation will be aided somewhat by the fact that the reception of Soviet broadcasts is influenced by technical considerations and requires special types of listening equipment. Such factors as program scheduling and American listening and viewing habits also serve to limit the potential audience for the North American Service.

What technical factors help us to define a probable audience? Obviously, before an individual can become a listener to Radio Moscow he must have access to a shortwave radio receiver. Although home radios in the pretelevision era frequently had "shortwave bands" as well as the "broadcast band," the shortwave feature in radio receivers has received less emphasis in recent years. Table model receivers dominate the market, and small radios are less likely to be multiwave than are the large "console" radio-phonograph combinations. Moreover, attention has shifted from shortwave to frequency modulation, especially since the development of "good music" FM stations. A dual purpose receiver tends to be "AM and FM," with only one broadcast band, rather than "broadcast and shortwave" as was frequent before television became popular. In the light of these facts, it is probable that only a small proportion of the American people have receivers capable of picking up programs beamed from the North American Service.

Even if an American home has a shortwave receiver, further technical difficulties make listening to Radio Moscow unlikely. The shortwave section of a dual-purpose receiver is usually not as powerful or as well designed as the part made to receive the "broadcast band." Because it is not used frequently, the shortwave instrument is typically not well maintained and is often out of alignment—factors that influence performance more adversely than is the case with the longer wave "broadcast band." For these reasons the shortwave section of the usual home receiver is an inefficient mechanism. Add to this the fact that the signals from Moscow are weak and frequently almost buried in interference, it would appear unlikely that any significant amount of regular listening to Radio Moscow takes place in American homes using home-type radio receivers.

Shortwave listening over great distances is strikingly unreliable when compared with the reception of nearby domestic broadcasting stations. Because of what the radio ham terms "atmospherics," the station that the listener desires to hear may "fade out" for days at a time, or it may simply deteriorate into unintelligibility during a single program. "Interference" is much more annoying on the short wave than on regular broadcast frequencies, for electric razors, household appliances, and electric gadgets of all sorts raise hob with shortwave listening. In fact, an urban listener may find that his home location makes satisfactory shortwave reception virtually impossible.

Another irritating feature of shortwave communication lies in the fact that shortwave reception is worst in winter, best in summer. Since time for listening and the inclination to do so are usually greater in winter and less in summer, the curious citizen may be somewhat frustrated in his attempt to keep track of "what Radio Moscow is saying these days."

In most locations in the United States, regular listening to the North American Service can be accomplished comfortably and satisfactorily only if the listener has a communication-type receiver attached to a shortwave antenna that is located outside his living quarters, away from sources of electrical interference. Even with this fairly rare combination, an auditor is able to tune in one of the North American Service channels clearly enough for easy listening approximately one evening in three, and during the winter, reception may be impossible for as long as a week at a time. Thus, even with the best equipment, the American listener must be persistent and steady in his listening habits if he is to hear enough of Radio Moscow to understand what the programs are about.

Besides these technical considerations, other factors probably limit Radio Moscow's American audience. The programs from Radio Moscow are beamed to the United States from five in the evening until midnight (CST)—when many Americans are comfortably settled in their chairs watching TV. FM and AM radio also compete with Radio Moscow for possible listeners. The people who own and use the best equipment for shortwave listening are radio amateurs, or "hams," but these technicians may not be especially interested in political issues or in sustained listening to international programs such as those beamed through the North American Service. Those who question this observation are invited to monitor conversations among the "hams" on shortwave and to note the proportion of time devoted to discussions of political matters or international affairs.

In view of these technical and cultural considerations, the number of regular American listeners to the North American Service is probably very small. Since listening involves a considerable amount of effort, the faithful listener is likely to require special motivation, an interest in propaganda analysis, or an interest in Soviet life and policy. It may be that the people who exhibit a keen interest in the USSR are the central targets of the North American Service. Whether the Russians have accurate estimates of the size of this group or the nature of its membership is, of course, an important question that at the moment cannot be answered. In any event, foreign broadcasts by the Soviet Union are designed, as is the system of domestic radio and television, to serve the needs of the regime and to support its foreign policy in every intricate detail.

9

SPECULATIVE GLANCES INTO THE FUTURE

Robert T. Holt
John E. Turner

Robert T. Holt is an associate professor of Political Science at the University of Minnesota. He has traveled and studied in eastern and western Europe and in French North Africa. He is the author of Radio Free Europe *and* Strategic Psychological Operations and American Foreign Policy *(with Robert W. van de Velde).*

For biographical sketch of Professor Turner, see Chapter 1.

Although the ordinary citizen feels the impact of East-West relations upon his daily life, he really knows very little about the Soviet Union—its people, its politics, and its problems. This lack of information, combined with an understandable anxiety about Soviet policies, naturally encourages speculation (and sometimes wishful thinking) about the future of the Russian dictatorship. With slightly less certitude than the Marxists, many westerners have made forecasts concerning the trends of Communist development, and, like the Marxists, they have often been inaccurate in crucial aspects of their predictions.

POPULAR VIEWS ABOUT THE SOVIET FUTURE

During the past 40 years several contradictory notions have become widespread in the West concerning the type of society that might ultimately emerge in the Soviet Union. Some people believe that the

207

"humanistic" and "democratic" tenets of Marxian philosophy will gradually prevail over the harsher features of the dogma, and that the dictatorship will eventually mellow, evolving into a liberal socialist democracy. Others prophesy that the Russian people will one day unite in rebellion against their Communist masters and overturn the dictatorship that has held them in subjection for so long. A third group, made up of those who assume that the Soviet system is static, hold out no hope for change in the dictatorship, either because the regime's controls are too tight to be dislodged, or because the Soviet system represents a continuation of the Tsarist past; the worship of centralized authority, they believe, is a feature of the Russian "national character" that is likely to be projected far into the future. Each of these "crystal ball" forecasts of future Soviet development is sufficiently interesting and is endorsed by enough advocates to merit brief examination.

Evolution toward Liberal Socialist Democracy

Those who envisage the gradual transformation of the Soviet system into a liberal form of democratic socialism tend to base their hopes more on faith than on persuasive evidence. This brand of wishful prophecy was dramatically illustrated by an American Secretary of State at a press conference in 1957. It was a "working hypothesis" of American policy, he stated, that the type of dictatorship existing in the USSR and Communist China would "never prevail" and that "the kind of government which is responsive to the will of the people and which admits diversity and freedom of thought and expression is the government which has the future ahead of it." He went on to say: "I am confident that [the trend toward freedom in the Communist world] is a basic truth. Certainly it is an assumption that I think must be made by anybody who believes in the American tradition." A working hypothesis about socio-political change in the USSR is scarcely realistic when it is formulated not from an analysis of the Soviet Union itself, but from a commitment, however sincere, to the "American tradition."

But even if one examines the "Russian tradition," he will find slight cause for optimism. The liberal democratic movement, which showed signs of vigor in the latter decades of the nineteenth and the opening years of the twentieth centuries, was never given sufficient opportunity to sink deep roots. The prevailing ideology and established political practices in both the Tsarist and Communist systems have provided only narrow scope for individual initiative, and the citizen's welfare has usually been subordinated to the designs of the community and the state. Whether governed by Tsarist officials or Communist rulers, the ordinary individual has been permitted little voice in the formulation of public policy. Far from subjecting their leaders to open criticism, the Russian masses have tended to bow before them in submission, worshipping them as infallible demigods. When one realizes that advanced democratic systems in the West have been developed gradually through centuries of education and experiment, he can hardly expect democratic forms cast in the western image to emerge quickly in Russia—a country whose people have never become acquainted with free elections and have had virtually no experience with the "give and take" of truly representative assemblies.

Those who hope that the liberal features of Marxism will eventually be accorded greater emphasis in Soviet Russia occasionally seek an analogy in the history of Christianity. Christian theology, they point out, has been used to support inquisitions, crusades, the divine right of monarchs, and colonial rule, but in more enlightened form it has been brought to the aid of movements for political freedom and economic reform. Just as the canons of Christianity have underwritten widely differing forms of political legitimacy, so also might the doctrines of Karl Marx be employed in due time as ideological underpinning for a more democratic system in the Soviet Union. This analogy appears less convincing when one compares the power of a traditional autocracy, legitimated in part by Christian teaching, with the overwhelming might of a modern totalitarian state which seeks to impose its single belief system upon every inhabitant and which employs advanced scientific techniques to enforce its will. The patterns of social change are extremely complex, and ideology is only one component interacting with other forces in the society. But even if one accepts the superficial comparison, it is well to remember that more than two centuries elapsed before the main stream of Protestant thought shifted its support from forms of absolutism to democratic government.

The gradual transformation of the Soviet dictatorship into a democratic system will be difficult, if not impossible, to achieve, for most rulers who wield enormous power are unwilling to relinquish or even to share that power voluntarily. The Communist leaders, having won command of a vast empire, exercise greater influence than any other political group in history. Men of this stripe are unlikely to yield their position without an internal struggle or the intervention of external force, especially since they are persuaded by their doctrine that they have a legitimate claim to power. By the same token, an opposition party—so essential to the operation of democratic government—would probably not be tolerated and would be regarded as an heretical clique seeking to propagate false beliefs. The emergence of a "loyal opposition" within the framework of the Communist Party itself will also be difficult, since the Party has always prided itself upon its monolithic solidarity, and members who deviate in any way from the official line have usually been condemned for their "factionalism" and branded as disloyal.

Overthrow of the Regime by Mass Rebellion

That the Soviet people will eventually rebel against the dictatorship is a belief often found in the West, especially among segments of the American population. Perhaps some Americans look back with pride to the founding of our own nation, when the colonists, suffering much less oppression than the Russian people, revolted against the mother country and won their freedom from one of the most powerful nations in the world. Others possibly regard the French Revolution or the 1917 revolutions in Russia as the models upon which to base their expectations. In any event, they eagerly await the day when the Russians will rush to the barricades and strike a successful blow for freedom.

The hope that violent revolution will overthrow the Communist regime and usher in a democratic system represents a form of romanticism which grossly underestimates the strength of the Soviet state and the men who govern it. Successful mass revolt against a highly organized state has been rendered impossible by the technological developments in armaments during the last century. Because of these changes, the men who control the instruments of coercion hold a tremendous superiority of power over the general population. At the time of the American Revolution, the New England minuteman with his hunting musket held a weapon that was virtually as effective as the gun of the British redcoat. But the Soviet citizen today has no weapons that can effectively match the tanks, machine guns, and artillery of the Red army and the police.[1] The defeat of the Hungarian "freedom fighters" in 1956 indicates once more that the age of barricade revolution against a well-armed government has passed. Revolts of this sort were slated for failure shortly after the invention of the first machine gun.

Indeed, advanced technology and brutally efficient methods of organization have provided the Communist rulers with the means for detecting and uprooting opposition long before it becomes an open threat. Alert police and anonymous informers, comprising an intelligence system that reaches into the most remote corners of Soviet life, operate in such a way that the potential rebel becomes isolated, unable to establish

---

[1] A revolution stands some chance of being successful if a split develops within the army and army leaders take sides. Such a split is most unlikely, however, since the Party imposes tight controls over the armed forces.

contact with other dissidents who might share his views. With these obstacles to effective communication, it becomes virtually impossible for dissenters to search each other out and to coordinate their activities in any promising form of resistance, which, in any case, would be quickly snuffed out by the massive power of the regime.

Even if an organization of dissidents were to emerge in the shadows of the underground, there is no guarantee that plots to overthrow the regime by violence would win widespread support among the Soviet masses. More than four decades of Communist rule have left a deep imprint on the population. For most of the people the years before the revolution are little more than a childhood memory or a section in their history lessons, and they have had direct experience with only the Communist form of social organization. From early youth they have been targets for the regime's vast propaganda effort—in the schools, in the youth organizations, and through the various forms of mass communication. The great investment in the programs of indoctrination has paid off, for apparently most citizens, especially the younger people, accept the basic values of Soviet society, even if they frown upon the use of force.

This does not mean, however, that the USSR is free from tensions and "gripes." There is still widespread dissatisfaction with the inadequate supplies of consumer goods and with the poor quality and high cost of some of the goods that are available. Many students are frustrated by the rigid curriculum which does not permit them to enroll in courses outside their specialty, and they resent being assigned to jobs after graduation. Some writers strongly object to the Party's stringent controls over their work, which is usually judged according to its "ideological purity" and "social utility," not on the basis of its literary merit. It is important to remember, however, that the hostility generated by these deficiencies is not directed against the essential features of Communist organization. Discontended consumers, for example, do not advocate the abolition of state ownership as a means of increasing the supply of commodities; students do not demand university curricula based upon an American model; and the artists are not at this juncture ablaze with revolt against the power structure of the Communist elite. Undoubtedly some elements of Soviet society would like to see modifications in the system, but, when measured alongside the expectations of many westerners, the changes would be relatively minor.

That many Soviet citizens, despite their grievances, are nevertheless committed to the collectivist values of the system is suggested by much of the current research on the USSR. This interpretation becomes somewhat more vivid, however, as the western visitor converses with with his Russian hosts. In this real-life setting, he soon realizes that Soviet citizens view their society from a set of assumptions entirely different from his own—that certain values considered to be universal by many westerners are probably not understood and certainly not accepted in the USSR.

Take, for example, the case of the young lady who has been trained to teach English in a Russian secondary school. She possesses a driving curiosity that leads her to read provocative books and to converse with foreign visitors about subjects that would draw stern frowns from the guardians of ideological purity. One of the books she has recently read is John Gunther's *Inside Russia Today*. Now this work is obviously not circulated in the Soviet Union with the blessing of the ministry of culture, for many of Gunther's observations concern matters that the official censors seek to withhold from their people. In response to a general question about what she thinks of the book, the young teacher replies: "I have learned many things about my country that I did not know before—things that are not very favorable. And yet I believe these reports to be true!"

Admittedly, then, the regime is imposing strict censorship, which this intelligent, inquisitive young lady might be expected to abhor. Further questions designed to lead her subtly to this realization have little effect, however, and finally she asserts with frankness and obvious embarrassment: "Do you know what Gunther's book proves? It proves that there are American spies in the Soviet Union! If there were no spies, how could an American journalist learn about things that are known only to a few top leaders of the Communist Party?" She then proceeds in sincere tones to justify the existence of censorship, which prevents the Soviet people from knowing about many developments in their own country. She is actually defending the type of official controls that render democratic government impossible.

One might anticipate that the reading of a book on the Soviet Union by an American author would stimulate critical thought among the young people. But as new facts about their country clash with values that have been inculcated through intensive indoctrination, the results are often quite different from what many westerners expect. In this young lady, at any rate, the cardinal beliefs of the Soviet system have taken root and she adroitly defends them.

A free-wheeling discussion with a group of Russians—a rare occasion, but exciting when it occurs—illustrates even more strikingly the degree to which the assumptions of a dictatorial regime are accepted by ordinary citizens. A verbal engagement of this sort usually covers a wide range of touchy subjects: the landings in Suez and Lebanon, Soviet intervention in Hungary, the Communist purges, and unemployment in capitalist countries. Before the discussion has gone very far, someone invariably raises the question of race relations in the United States. "How can America call herself a democracy when Negroes are barred from some schools?" "How many Negroes have been lynched in your country?" Since many Russians have heard of Little Rock, they recount events in that unfortunate city to drive home their contention that democracy in the United States is a sham. When discussing the race issue, of course, an American is not on his strongest ground, but he attempts to explain that his country is trying to resolve a difficult problem through the democratic procedures of a federal system, and that these methods, while seeming to be pitifully slow, are nevertheless achieving some results.

When he sees that this line of discussion is making little impact, the American visitor attempts to throw the burden of argument to his Russian friends by asking, "What would you do if a large section of your country has a history of racial segregation, and prejudice has become deeply rooted in the culture? Would it not take time to solve such a difficult problem?" The answer comes quickly and crisply from a young electrical worker: "In the Soviet Union we would do two things—we would make a law and then we would shoot anyone who disobeys it!" With eloquent simplicity he summarizes the most repugnant features of the Soviet system: the will of the dictator, enunciated by decree, is to be enforced if necessary by generous portions of police terror. No Russian who hears the young worker's response is stimulated to question the propriety of this approach.

No Change in the Dictatorship

Sensitive to the absence of a strong democratic tradition in Russia and aware of the overwhelming power at the command of the dictatorship, many westerners have concluded that there is no possibility of change in the Soviet system. Unfortunately, those who take this position usually place no time span on their forecast, and, like their Marxian foes, they tacitly claim an ability to predict the course of historical development. But whereas the Marxist dogmatically prophesies a predetermined pattern of economic and social change, they foresee no change at all. Such a conclusion is based on the assumption either that a modern totalitarian dictatorship is entirely static or that no change is significant unless it involves a movement in the direction of liberal democracy.

This assumption merits closer examination, for an oversimplified approach to the complexities of the Soviet system runs the risk of engendering fatalistic attitudes in the popular mind. Such attitudes overlook some of the potential weaknesses of dictatorial rule and render more difficult the formulation of flexible policies by the West. To assume that Soviet society is static is to ignore important patterns of change that have developed in nearly all industrial societies, whether democratic or nondemocratic. Such an assumption also disregards events in Russia since Stalin's death—an era that has produced no democratic upsurge but has nevertheless brought important developments regarded by most people as unthinkable a few years before they occurred. Many of these changes, of course, reflect the problems that confront a dictatorship as it strives to become an industrial and military giant. These are the problems that will receive our attention during the remainder of this chapter.

THE STYLE OF "KHRUSHCHEVISM"

In order to gauge the undercurrents of change in post-Stalin Russia, it will be useful at the outset to review the characteristic methods of governance that prevailed under Stalin.

1. There was a complex network of distinct but interlocking bureaucracies—the Party apparatus, the economic administration, the police empire, the military establishment, and others—each of which was responsible ultimately to Stalin. The lines of jurisdiction were dimly marked, and the agents of each hierarchy infiltrated the ranks of the others, reporting valuable information to Stalin and his henchmen at the top. The supreme leader often shifted his reliance from one group to another, reshuffling the power formations at will so that no single bureaucracy would become completely dominant. The Party apparatus itself was under the close scrutiny of the police, and in the closing years of Stalin's rule the central organs of the Party, as well as its representative bodies in the lower echelons, did not meet regularly.

2. The regime relied excessively upon raw coercion and terror as instruments of control. Stalin's reign was marked by stringent measures to insure labor discipline, the exercise of arbitrary powers by the police, the periodic introduction of wholesale and brutal purges, and the extermination of literally millions of people so that the regime's social and economic objectives could be realized and its power preserved and consolidated.

3. Great emphasis was placed upon the development of heavy industry at the expense of the agricultural and consumer segments of the economy. The advances in heavy industry resulted in an imbalanced economic system, and the tendency to assign a low priority to consumer interests adversely affected the living standard of the bulk of the population.

4. There was extreme centralization of political and economic decision-making in Moscow. In the political sphere, the provincial Party organizations were merely the handmaidens of the central authorities, whose decisions they were expected to carry out to the letter. In the economic realm, a myriad of industrial ministries sprang up in the capital—huge, horizontal monopolies that directed the operation of their respective industries throughout the entire USSR, no matter in what section of the country the plants happened to be located. The authority of the plant manager was limited, and the regional Party officials had little voice in decision-making in industry, although they played an important role in agriculture.

Even though there has been no significant modification in the basic power structure, Khrushchev's methods of rule, as we have seen, differ in several important respects from Stalin's. Since 1953 the men in the Party apparatus have gradually reasserted the Party's authority over such powerful bureaucracies as the police (since Beria's downfall), the economic administrators (since industrial reorganization), and the military forces (since Zhukov's demotion). The Party has also compelled the artists to recognize its leading role (although they are less rigidly controlled than they were under Stalin), and it has instituted a wholesale reform of the educational system. The Party organization itself has been revitalized, and the lower representative assemblies and the central organs now meet with greater regularity. The program of economic reorganization has given local Communist leaders increased responsibility over the industrial plant. Khrushchev's reliance upon social pressure as a means of controlling delinquent behavior has likewise expanded the role of the Party units. Khrushchev, in other words, rules the country in large measure by controlling and manipulating the Party hierarchy; activities at all levels of social interaction are carefully scrutinized by the appropriate Communist secretary and his assistants.

Although the post-Stalin era has certainly not been free from terror, the use of physical coercion has been more restricted and much less obvious than was the case under Stalin. Rather than relying largely upon the police and the ordinary courts to enforce compliance, the Khrushchev regime has substituted "administrative pressure" wielded by factory managers, and social pressure, exerted through such agencies as the voluntary police detachments, the antiparasite assemblies, and the comrades' courts. While the ordinary citizen appears to have less fear of the police than he once had, he is now confronted by the wrath of his peers—which is of course appropriately organized by local Party units.

Another distinguishing feature of post-Stalinist rule can be seen in the greatly increased emphasis upon the production and distribution of consumer goods. The Soviet housewife can purchase her wares from a wider assortment of commodities in the shops, and the regime is making available large numbers of apartment dwellings, although the construction is poor and the supply is still far from adequate.

Perhaps the most significant change instituted by Stalin's successors has been the reorganization of industry on a republic and regional basis. Many of the industrial ministries in Moscow have been broken up and their responsibilities turned over to the republic governments and the regional economic councils. Although a stable relationship between the economic control of Moscow and that of the regions has not yet been achieved, regional Party officials now have somewhat more influence in the economic affairs of their regions, plant managers have a slightly expanded range of administrative discretion, and consumers may be able to express their preferences a bit more effectively, since the economic officials in the regions are closer to consumer pressures than were the industrial ministers who resided in Moscow.

While these features of Khrushchev's rule provide an interesting contrast with Stalin's, the question naturally arises as to whether the changes are likely to constitute a permanent part of the political landscape. Are the recent developments simply a by-product of the struggle for succession that may be modified or reversed as Khrushchev, or his successor, becomes more firmly entrenched in the Kremlin? Are these changes merely the personal preferences of the present leader that are likely to disappear when he passes from the scene? Such questions, of course, cannot be answered except in highly speculative and tentative form, but we can perhaps lay the groundwork for speculation by examining briefly some of the possible reasons for the changes in post-Stalin Russia.

On political grounds, several considerations help to explain the policies of the Khrushchev era. Khrushchev's strength is based primarily upon the Party apparatus, while that of his opponents was linked with the other bureaucracies. In order to make himself secure, Khrushchev needed not only to remove his present rivals from the contest but also to reduce their bases of support so that future challenges to his power would be less likely. While the authority of the police could be diminished without serious consequences to the regime, this was hardly possible in the cases of the military establishment and the economic bureaucracy. The best that Khrushchev could do here was to reduce their political effectiveness by placing the two hierarchies more firmly under the Party's control.

This strategy is perhaps best illustrated by the program of economic reorganization. The officials in the industrial ministries in Moscow constituted an important power bloc, and most of them probably had close attachments with Malenkov, Molotov, Kaganovich, and other rivals of Khrushchev. Under the new program, Khrushchev attempted to disperse this grouping of officials by assigning them to administrative posts throughout the widely scattered regions of the USSR. In locales more remote from Moscow and under closer supervision by Communist functionaries, the industrial administrators have suffered a noticeable decline in political influence. By the same token, functionaries in the Party apparatus have gained greater leverage in the economic sphere.

Political considerations also account in part for the decreased reliance upon terror as a major mechanism of control. Stalin's use of arbitrary and brutal methods had created deep resentment among the Soviet people, and it was important for the new rulers to dissociate themselves as much as possible from the harshness and austerities of the past. Any Soviet leader responsible for leading his country through a period of international uncertainty could hardly forget the mass defections at the time of the German invasion—a memory probably kept alive by rebellions in some of the satellite countries, disturbances among the Soviet prison population, and unrest in the universities. Should a serious international crisis develop, Stalin's successors would have to count upon the loyalty of their people, and attempts to advertise themselves as a more humane regime were partly designed to assuage the bitterness among the masses and to appeal for popular support.

Although these political considerations help to account for the policies of the post-Stalin era, they are not compelling enough in themselves to warrant the conjecture that the changes will be permanent. With his power consolidated and his position secure, Khrushchev could begin to juggle the various bureaucracies, introducing a style of rule reminiscent of Stalin's. If he decides to pursue far-reaching policies that encounter resistance (comparable, for example, to Stalin's program of forced industrialization), he might find it desirable to rely more heavily upon harsh, coercive techniques.

Mixed with the political factors are important economic motivations that help to explain Soviet policies in the decade following Stalin's death. According to this analysis, many of the changes represent a partial accommodation of the system to the organizational requirements of a rapidly maturing industrial society. If this interpretation has any validity, it may provide some clues to possible courses of Soviet development in the future.

POWER VS. PERFORMANCE: CONFLICTING PRESSURES

The developments in post-Stalin Russia suggest an important dilemma that confronts the leaders of a large-scale dictatorship. The regime is concerned on the one hand with preserving its own power, but, on the other, it is faced with the problem of building the industrial and military strength of the state so that it can compete with the advanced technologies of rival countries. While these goals do not appear to be so much at variance during the initial stages of industrialization, the difficulty of reconciling traditional power relationships with industrial demands becomes more apparent as the society matures and advances to higher levels of complexity. Readjustments of this sort can assume many forms and may be so gradual as to go undetected for long periods of time. It is impossible, in other words, to forecast either the direction or the success of the adaptation. But however much Communist rulers try to forestall developments they do not themselves initiate or control, it would be misleading to assume that the Soviet system is completely insulated against the impact of industrialization, the perplexities of urbanism, and contact with other cultures. Such phenomena have helped to generate long-term change in nearly all industrial societies, and there is no reason to believe that the USSR is immune to their influence. In erecting an industrial and military fortress, the Soviet rulers may be compelled to introduce policies the unintended consequences of which might be seen decades later in new socio-economic patterns, favorable or unfavorable from the western point of view. Thus, over a long span of time, the regime may be vulnerable to conflicting pressures: at one extreme it becomes concerned with safeguarding its privileged position, which may require the maintenance of a Stalinist (or "classical") type of totalitarian rule; and at the other extreme it is sensitive to the demands of advanced technology, a pressure that tends to pull the system *in the direction* of technocratic "managerialism." The implications of this dilemma will become clearer as we discuss the potential demands of a maturing industrial society.

The Characteristics of "Classical" Totalitarianism

As we have seen, the classical type of dictatorship patterned on the Stalin model emphasizes the preservation of the political elite. The dictator operates through a network of bureaucracies that overlap in structure and function. The system is thus marked by *multiple* chains of command, and it is possible for the dictator or his cohorts to intervene at any point in a given hierarchy, bypassing important officials along the way.

The bureaucracies in this system have two characteristics in common:

1. There is designed ambiguity in the jurisdiction of each office or post, and while a functionary will know some of the duties he is expected to perform, he can never be certain how far his authority extends. For example, the "job descriptions" of the factory manager and the Communist secretary in the plant are not explicitly laid out, so that it is difficult for the Party official to know at what point his orders to "check" factory operations invade the province of "management." This deliberate fuzziness of obligation is often extended to the ordinary citizen through such devices as the rule of analogy which exposes him to criminal prosecution even though he has violated no specific statute. An individual thus may be reprimanded or arrested for doing what he did not realize was forbidden, or for neglecting what he did not know was obligatory. Without well-defined spheres of competence, the administrative official may suffer from feelings of insecurity and is likely to perform his duties cautiously, handling only those matters that are clearly required and leaving the peripheral problems for someone else to resolve.

2. Significant power relationships tend to be personal in character. This means that personal allegiances to powerful or potentially powerful leaders become crucial, and loyalty is often ranked ahead of efficiency and merit in evaluating an individual's performance. The existence of these allegiances makes it easier for the dictator to bypass the formal chain of command and intervene in the operations of a bureaucracy at any point in the hierarchy.

This entire system is justified, as we have seen, by an official ideology that is exclusively interpreted by the ruling elite—ultimately by the dictator himself. No citizen in the society can effectively base a claim upon the doctrine, since the authorities can manipulate its meaning to suit their purposes.

The pattern of organization in the classical totalitarian dictatorship has often been compared with that of an army under the control of a powerful general who chooses his own general staff and operates through a system of rigidly structured subordinate commands. This analogy, however, is misleading; the essential features appear more in contrast than in comparison. The Stalin-type dictatorship is characterized, as we have noted, by multiple chains of command rather than the single line of authority that is the ideal in the modern military organization. Moreover, the duties and responsibilities attached to specific offices in a modern army are definitely outlined and the sphere of competence of any office is ideally regarded as inviolate. But the bureaucracies in a classical totalitarian dictatorship are designed to facilitate the bypassing of formal chains of command by those at the top. The dictator can, for example, use his hierarchy of police agencies to intervene in the operations of the Party or governmental bureaucracies, or he can employ the military hierarchy to invade the jurisdictional realm of the police apparatus. It is also possible for him to circumvent a given chain of command by utilizing the network of personal connections and allegiances. Such actions can be justified and sanctified by reinterpretations of the official creed.

Organizational Requirements of a Mature Industrial Economy

Although it is difficult to compile a definitive list of requirements for operating an advanced industrial order, the economic bureaucracies of highly developed industrial countries have some distinctive features or tendencies that appear to be relatively independent of the particular cultures in which the forms of economic organization have been developed.

A mature industrial economy is characterized by an advanced technology, a high capital-manpower ratio, and high levels of productivity and production. Organizationally it is dominated by what is sometimes called the "super-firm," which is vast in scope and which develops a complex, highly ramified bureaucracy. In this system there is a unified chain of command and a clearly defined "managerial" division of labor, with explicit job descriptions for every role. Duties, responsibilities, and authority are assigned primarily to offices in the organization rather than to individuals.

In the super-firm, great emphasis is placed upon rationality and efficiency. Thus high priority is given to long-range planning, centralized control over capital expenditures, and adequate rewards for job performance. There are limits, however, upon the degree of rationality that can be achieved if attention is restricted to the *internal* organization and operation of the firm itself. For this reason there is a tendency for the super-firm to seek to control its environment. In a relatively free economy, for example, this tendency is manifest in such practices as price-fixing agreements, lobbying, and contributions to political organizations.

The super-firm is also characterized by complex patterns of recruitment and by an emphasis upon "in-service training." These training programs are designed not only to increase managerial and technical skills but also to produce a certain kind of orientation to the firm. In other words, institutional devices are developed to produce what Americans sometimes call the "organization man." One might even argue that there is fostered a type of value system or "ideology" that stresses an individual's dedication to the firm and that emphasizes rationality and efficiency as high-priority goals.

With the introduction of the early five-year plans, the USSR developed its version of the super-firm in the form of huge industrial ministries, which were frequently reorganized in an attempt to make them more efficient and to thwart the emergence of group loyalties. These vast horizontal monopolies proved to be relatively effective organizations for the rapid development of the economy during the initial stages of industrialization. As the economy began to mature, however, these industrial combines tended to become less effective means for organizing the economic life of the country. Indeed, it can be argued that the distinctive features of Stalinist rule were inappropriate for continued rapid growth during the more advanced phases of industrialization.

The difficulty of applying Stalinist methods of organization and control in a maturing economy can be seen more clearly if we compare the kinds of decision-making problems that existed in the 1920s and 1930s to those that were paramount in the 1950s and 1960s. During the first two decades of Communist rule the fundamental economic needs of the country were fairly obvious. A basic iron and steel industry had to be developed; an aluminum industry could be given much lower priority. The railroad system had to be greatly improved and expanded; a network of major intercity highways could be delayed. The location of some deposits of high-grade iron ore and coking coal was known, and these had to be quickly linked with the few manufacturing centers by adequate transportation facilities. It did not take a highly trained economist to decide which of a relatively few types of steel had to be produced. Political decisions to neglect agriculture and to keep consumer goods production at minimal levels could be made without seriously hampering economic growth.

But by the 1950s economic decisions in the Soviet Union had grown far more complex. As the economy matured, the number of products that needed to be produced increased enormously. Not a few kinds of steel, but many kinds in proper proportion had to be scheduled for production. New industries like plastics and electronics had to be developed. The problem of how to distribute investment resources among the various industries and among factories within the same industry became much more difficult. Moreover, industrial production was spreading to far-flung sections of a vast country (rather than being concentrated in a few centers like the Moscow region and the Donbas), making it harder to integrate the economies of widely dispersed areas. Equally important, agriculture and the production of consumer goods could no longer be neglected without serious implications for economic growth.

Ordinarily these kinds of economic problems can best be resolved by giving more discretionary authority to technical experts who are competent to make rational decisions, that is, to trained economic managers. Merely to bring technically competent people into the traditional Stalinist framework, however, is probably not sufficient. For the experts to perform adequately, changes need to be made in the structure of economic organization, perhaps somewhat on the model of the "ideal" super-firm. Indeed, some Soviet economists themselves have indicated the need for a structural reform of their economic system.

Although the changes in post-Stalin Russia undoubtedly stem from a combination of circumstances and developments, some of the reforms may represent concessions to the organizational requirements of a mature economy. The program of economic reorganization, to be sure, has robbed (at least temporarily) many industrial administrators of the political power they once wielded and has deprived them of a voice in economic decision-making at the top level. But in other respects the Khrushchev regime has bowed to economic pressures and has recognized the importance of the economically and managerially competent. In the administrative decentralization of Soviet industry, for example, regional economic officials and individual factory managers have been granted a somewhat wider range of discretion in determining *how* what is to be produced shall be produced. Equally significant has been the extensive discussion permitted among Soviet economists on the need for objective criteria for measuring efficiency so that investment resources can be allocated in the most useful way.

The reduction in the use of raw coercion and terror and the expansion of consumer goods production may also be regarded in part as concessions to the demands of a maturing economy. In the initial stages of development, an economy that is poor in capital goods can undertake certain gross projects through the use of slave laborers who work with picks and shovels. The situation changes, however, when power shovels and bulldozers become available. Scarce and expensive machinery cannot be entrusted to a slave laborer, who may be tempted to destroy the equipment as an act of revenge against his masters even though it costs him his life. When mammoth earthmoving machines are put to use on a wide scale, it is inefficient to waste manpower on pick-and-shovel projects, especially of the slave labor variety, which require large numbers of custodial personnel. In the post-Stalin period, some Soviet officials have pointed out that their forced labor camps were economically unprofitable—a viewpoint that helps to explain why the prison population has been diminished.

The imperatives of economic growth are also an important factor in the decision of the new Soviet rulers to increase the supply and variety of goods available to the consumer. If the Soviet Union is to catch up with the United States in industrial production, there must be an increase in labor productivity per man hour. In addition to removing the most glaring inefficiencies from the system of economic planning, two major techniques can be employed to increase productivity. The first is to expand the supply of labor-saving machinery. Since the USSR, however, has always invested huge amounts of capital in the production of such equipment, it is doubtful that a significantly larger proportion of the country's resources can be earmarked for this purpose. The second technique is to stimulate the labor force to work harder and more efficiently. From the beginning the Communist rulers, in an effort to encourage workers to produce more, have resorted to methods that can best be represented by the age-old symbols of the stick and the carrot.

At various times in Soviet history, severe punishment has been handed out for even minor breaches of labor discipline, such as tardiness, absence from work, or changing jobs without permission. While an unskilled worker might be kept on the job by physically coercive methods, the skilled technician usually does not respond well to this kind of pressure. Moreover, for the regime to dismiss or harshly treat a worker as an "example" to his fellows may be an acceptable form of sanction when labor is cheap and an individual can be trained for the job in a short time. But the man who has undergone several years of training cannot be easily replaced and the costly investment in his training cannot be easily written off. In an advanced technological system, the use of the stick to discourage inefficient practices tends to become self-defeating.

The changing requirements for the effective use of the carrot to stimulate worker productivity is even more challenging for Stalin's successors. Since the early years of the industrialization drive, the Soviet rulers have employed a vicious system of monetary incentives based upon piecework wages, with bonus payments for the overfulfillment of production quotas. The incentive system applies for both managers and workers, although it is with the latter that we are chiefly concerned in this discussion. While this system had its limitations under Stalin, it was a factor in stimulating the industrial work force, a significant proportion of which was recruited from rural areas and was not accustomed to the routine and discipline of the factory. In general, under the Stalinist formula levels of living remained low and consumer goods were in short supply. A failure to meet production quotas would not simply mean that a worker would be unable to secure luxury goods; it might seriously reduce his ability to provide adequate food and clothing for himself and his family.

At times during the past decade, however, the traditional system of monetary incentives has shown signs of losing its effectiveness. The evidence for this is indirect rather than direct. The sixth five-year plan had to be scrapped because production fell miserably short of the targets set by the planners. This could have been partially due to the fact that the targets themselves were set unrealistically high and because, as we pointed out earlier, the cumbersome bureaucracies in the huge industrial ministries could not efficiently cope with the increasing complexities. Another important contributing factor might well have been that worker productivity did not increase at the expected rates.

The policy of "consumerism" may be viewed in part as an attempt to increase worker productivity. In the 1950s there was a general increase in the levels of living in the Soviet Union. Workers could live without bonus payments, and the higher-paid piecework laborers discovered that the goods they wanted to buy were not available in the shops. As it became easier to purchase basics of life, matters of style and taste began to become a relevant consideration for more and more consumers. Certain consumer goods, particularly those of low quality and tasteless design, became a glut on the market; other goods were in high demand and very difficult to purchase. In this situation some workers had less motivation to fill and overfulfill their quotas. The goods they wanted were not available. The government's record of devaluation of currency and confiscation of savings gave them little motivation to accumulate funds for future purchases.

In this situation, workers might tend to opt for leisure time. Rather than working so hard in the factories to earn money they had little use for, they might wish to save their time and energy for low cost recreation. In such circumstances productivity would suffer.

If the piecework system were going to continue to stimulate labor productivity, more goods of the types consumers wanted would have to be made available. In order to buy these goods, the workers would have to work harder and productivity would increase. But this whole approach required some shift in capital investment away from heavy industry and into consumer goods industry. Khrushchev probably did not adopt Malenkov's program of "consumerism" either because he pitied the toiling masses who had so long been deprived or because he feared the direct consequences of their unfilled demands. More likely, he did it because he had little alternative, if he wanted to increase productivity and maintain the high growth rates in the economy.

If the major departures from the pattern of Stalinism that Khrushchev initiated in the 1950s can be looked upon partially as concessions to the demands of a maturing economy, can we make some predictions about how these demands will manifest themselves in the coming decades? It is difficult to say anything positive, but there are two developments that seem unlikely. The increasing discretionary authority of the economic managers should not be hailed as the first stage in a "managerial revolution," which will end with the managers capturing the basic political power of the society. Whatever increasing authority they obtain is most likely to remain in the economic sector of the society. Nor should the requirements for rationality in economic order be construed as likely to lead to the development of a democratic polity. There are a number of forms of political organization that are compatible with a mature industrial economy. Some are democratic, others are dictatorial. The argument here is mainly that the outstanding characteristics of Stalin's dictatorship are not very compatible with the organizational and operating demands of a mature industrial economy.

The point that deserves careful reflection is this: while the Stalinist model may be satisfactory for a society that is laying the groundwork for industrial development, such a system may prove inadequate for an economy that is moving into the advanced stages of industrialization. In the decades ahead the regime will probably be tempted to go in the direction of a Stalin-type dictatorship, but if it does, it may have to pay a price in terms of economic efficiency. On the other hand, the Soviet rulers may yield to the pressure to rationalize their system in order to meet the requirements of a mature industrial order, in which case they may be opening the door to changes they would prefer to avoid. This is not to say that either of these developments *will* occur. It is more likely that the regime may oscillate between these two tendencies through a series of makeshift policies designed to meet momentary needs. Indeed, tendencies towards "recentralization" of the economy since 1959 illustrate the serious dilemma confronting the Soviet rulers. Although the regime may decide that a measure of decentralization is necessary to enhance efficiency at the regional level, such a policy creates serious problems of interregion integration. To solve this problem, it is necessary either to let market forces manifest themselves and serve as a partial basis for interregion allocations of resources or to tighten the controls of the central authorities in Moscow. The latter course, however, may lead to an overly complex system of bureaucratic planning and inefficient direction that become the basis for a return to decentralization.

We have already outlined the kinds of pressures that tend to draw the Soviet leaders away from the classical patterns of Stalinism. But there are also some pressures that may tend to pull the system back in the direction of Stalinism. The most important of these is the self-interest of the top elite who have a conspicuous stake in the system and who seek to maximize their power. These men can be expected to resist developments that might permit any other group to evolve into a position of relative autonomy. They may be reluctant over long periods of time to share power with economic managers who possess skills and interests they lack. If Khrushchev felt himself threatened politically by a coalition of managers or by a group of subordinates in the Party, he might be tempted to increase the power of the police and to turn them against his rivals in the Party or the economic bureaucracy.

The official ideology may also serve as a brake against the development of an independent corps of economic managers. The belief system has always glorified the worker more than the manager, and its equalitarian theme probably still has some mass appeal and is not congenial with the sharp, hierarchical divisions of labor inherent in the bureaucracy of the super firms. The official ideology also legitimates the Party as the repository of "truth" and justifies the authority of political leaders to make basic decisions in every area of society. Although the regime conveniently manipulates the dogma to meet specific situations, the use of proletarian doctrine to justify long-term managerial control distorts it virtually beyond recognition.

The continued existence of the cold war may constitute another pressure towards the classical form of dictatorship. Foreign policy considerations are often influential in the areas of economic decision-making. The sale of cheap crude oil to western Europe, for example, or the shipment of machine tools to underdeveloped countries might further the interests of the USSR in the international field, but such actions may require a commitment of resources that would not be sanctioned by an administrator concerned with increasing the efficiency of the economic machine at home. As long as competition with the West (or with the East) remains intense, the Soviet political leaders may be interested in maintaining strict controls over the economic bureaucracy in order to insure flexibility in adjusting the economy to the requirements of foreign policy.

OTHER CATALYSTS OF CHANGE

Change in any society is a complex phenomenon, precipitated by intricate combinations of forces. Our discussion thus far has emphasized the incompatibilities between the classical Stalinist dictatorship and the demands of a mature industrial order as a potential source of change in Soviet society. The problems of a rapidly developing economy, however, and the policies designed to meet them could have additional implications for the Communist system over a time span of several generations, and these problems deserve brief consideration.

As any society grows more complex, its operation requires highly technical knowledge that is within the grasp of specialists but beyond the understanding of ordinary politicians. The USSR recognizes the need to train increasing numbers of these specialists for positions of responsibility in the system. Practitioners of this type are likely to develop a markedly different outlook from that of the traditional political leaders. They have been trained to perform in a professional role, and their interests probably tend to be focused upon the achievement of relatively concrete goals, such as the expanded production of steel, the design and construction of more housing units, the improvement of educational standards, and the development of adequate legal codes. To some of the specialists, a dogmatic ideology that was useful during the fanatical stages of the movement may have less appeal than a more flexible and pragmatic set of beliefs. As they face the challenges of their daily work and associate with colleagues who are interested in relatively sophisticated ideas, they may look upon the tedious and threadbare propositions of the official creed as dull and unsatisfying, to be accorded little more than ritualistic observance. Indeed, professional people who become habituated to standards of objective inquiry and scientific demonstration in their regular work may eventually be tempted to transfer this critical outlook into areas of social and political life. The growth of skepticism among such important and articulate groups might gradually weaken the force of the doctrine by which the Communist leaders lay claim to legitimacy.

As the practitioners are given more authority over technical matters, they naturally tend to become the judges of their own needs, thereby widening their spheres of competence. Indeed, some day-to-day decisions may have to be made by functional staffs when there is not sufficient time for adequate consultation with responsible Communist officials. This means that segments of the technical intelligentsia, from the very nature of their work, move farther from the restraining arm of the political authorities and become increasingly difficult to control.

At the present time, of course, the specialists operate under the watchful eye of local and regional Party secretaries, who are situated in factories and serve on economic councils to make sure that Communist directives are properly carried out. These functionaries, however, usually lack the technical competence of their professional colleagues and could easily become lost in esoteric discussions or be swamped by the flood of detailed paper work. Under these circumstances there may be a tendency for the ordinary Party secretaries to become little more than the ambassadors of management in their negotiations with higher Communist officials. If this occurs, the Party's controls over the technical intelligentsia are correspondingly weakened. Thus, to be effective in the jobs assigned to them, the Party secretaries need some degree of technical competence. The Soviet rulers, apparently recognizing this problem, have recently instituted programs to give the necessary training to subordinate Communist officials, and in some cases have moved technically trained managers into posts that handle the Party's organizational affairs. In either event there is the possibility that a managerial outlook will gradually be diffused into the Party's ranks, reducing the effectiveness of the organization as an instrument of control by political leaders.

In the past the Party has been fairly successful in absorbing professional people of all types into the power structure. It has sought to make them reliable Communists who are willing to place their talents at the regime's disposal. As the Party is compelled to open its doors more widely to these specialists, however, the character of the Communist elite may gradually undergo change, and new outlooks may eventually be injected into the centers of power. Should this occur, the fanaticism of Communist doctrine may become somewhat tempered by the pragmatic approach of the professional man.

As the need for professional competence increases, the specialists may come to desire a degree of autonomy that they feel is dictated by the requirements of their calling, and they may increasingly chafe under the restraints imposed by the Communist rulers. Economists or creative artists, for example, may reach the point where they require wider areas of autonomy if they are to meet the standards of their professions. In their clash with Party leaders, they may be able to hold their ground by insisting that only by following the advice of the specialist can the Party achieve its objectives—an argument that is being increasingly made with some effectiveness in the USSR. When the regime reasserts its authority, these specialists may be tempted to question the propriety of the political arrangement and to challenge the doctrine upon which it rests. The integrity of one's specialty thus becomes a competing master, and if the practitioner is prevented from applying his professional standards, he may become contemptuous of his political superiors and search for ways of escaping their controls.

In training and utilizing the specialists needed to operate a modern industrial state, the Soviet rulers can be expected to encounter difficulty in keeping the intelligentsia isolated from the outside world. Since the regime cannot ignore the scientific studies carried out in other lands, foreign publications will have to be imported into the USSR and technicians will have to be sent abroad periodically to keep them abreast of developments in their fields. This means that more and more of the intelligentsia will be exposed to alien influences that give them a less distorted picture of the non-Communist world. The specialists who will have greater access to foreign publications or be selected for travel abroad are drawn from the articulate elements of the society, the people who are likely to be the most susceptible to new ideas and alternative values. Increased contact with other cultures may have some impact upon the ideological solidarity of the Soviet system, since the spread of knowledge about the West will make it more difficult for the regime to invent "enemies," to exaggerate the virtues of Communism, and to mold the official brand of citizen.

The problem of consumer needs also has important implications for the future of the Soviet system. Prolonged scarcity of consumer items not only affects the program of monetary incentives but also develops frustrations among the population that can be more hazardous for the regime than intellectual unrest. Since Communist appeals are based upon the promise to improve living standards, the rulers cannot afford to ignore the requirements of consumers indefinitely. As they increase the supply of consumer goods, however, the material wants of the people tend to expand even more rapidly. A family that moves into a new apartment, for example, suddenly becomes interested in buying furniture and kitchen appliances. As the supply of men's overcoats becomes more plentiful, a man may come to desire a special type of overcoat. A foreign visitor to the USSR encounters many young people who look forward to the day when they can live in better surroundings, wear attractive clothing, eat fine food, and even own an automobile. If their society develops more "consumer consciousness," the Communist leaders may find it increasingly difficult to shift suddenly from policies of "consumerism" to programs of austerity and sacrifice. To the extent that this occurs, the political leaders become somewhat restricted in their freedom to maneuver.

The process of social change may be accelerated if succession crises resembling the post-Stalin struggle become more frequent. This is, of course, a distinct possibility in view of the relatively high age-bracket of the current Soviet leaders. By the time Stalin had won his contest for supremacy, has was only fifty years old. Khrushchev, on the other hand, was sixty-three years old by the time he had consolidated his control, and most of his established colleagues in the Presidium are already in their mid-fifties or even older. It is likely, therefore, that Khrushchev will not be able to rule as long as Stalin did and that the candidates to succeed him will not be young men.

More frequent power struggles naturally involve some risks for the system. Such crises tend to disturb the equilibrium of existing power blocs, bringing the vicious competition more into public view and widening the opportunity for functional specialists to bid for recognition. As the contest develops, the grievances of the population become more visible, indicating to the new rulers the popular desire for relaxed controls and improved living conditions. The first struggle for succession was marked by a continuation of the "new economic policy," the second by "the thaw." If these periods present any clues for predicting the policies to be followed during future struggles for succession, they suggest that the leaders can be expected to assume a more liberal posture and temper the harsher policies of the dictatorship. Concessions of this sort are often hazardous for an autocracy, for they may bring renewed hope for the disaffected, who sense that their leaders are vulnerable and can be pressured into further relaxations.

Struggles for succession invariably lead to the denunciation of former Communist heroes, which tends to cast doubts about the alleged infallibility of the Party's leadership. Leaders who were once portrayed as virtuous, dedicated men may come to be perceived as mere politicians engaged in a self-seeking struggle for power.

Increased education, greater contacts with western societies, and more frequent power struggles appear to support in several respects the kinds of institutional adaptations that are demanded by a mature industrial order. If forced to make a positive statement about the most likely developments in the next few decades, we would hazard a guess that the top political leaders will gradually loosen their direct control over some sectors of the society. There will probably be a continuing but uneven increase in the discretionary authority of the economic managers to administer their affairs at the regional and local levels, and this increasing autonomy may gradually spread to professional people in other areas of the system. But we do not look upon these developments as containing the seeds of a democratic order. (Or if they do, the seeds will be a very long time in maturing.) The top political elite will not let the developing autonomy of professionals in their spheres of competence become the basis for a legitimate opposition. Khrushchev and his successors will jealously maintain their monopoly of power to make the decisions that determine the priorities in every realm of the society and will refuse to allow the development of any institutions through which they could be held accountable for their decisions.

This image of the near future in Soviet society should be of some comfort to the citizens of the Soviet Union. The overtly oppressive and most resented features of Stalinism are not likely to be with them for prolonged periods. Their standards of living are likely to rise to levels that were inconceivable a decade ago. But the image we have of the Soviet future should be of little comfort to citizens in the free world. We anticipate the continuation of a dictatorship, but one that is more coldly rational than that of Stalin, and that will enjoy wider support from its citizens. Unless the antagonisms between China and the USSR split the Communist world apart and the Soviet Union is forced to seek rapprochement with the West, we shall be faced in the international arena with a stronger and more effective competitor, a more willing perhaps, but a tougher negotiator than the one we have known since the end of World War II.

SUGGESTED READING FOR FURTHER STUDY

From among the many important studies of the Soviet system, the contributors to this volume have selected those works that will be especially valuable to the lay reader. A number of them may be obtained in paperback form. The studies cited in "The Future" have influenced the thinking of the authors of the concluding chapter, who desire to acknowledge their debt.

Soviet Government and Politics

ARMSTRONG, JOHN A., *The Politics of Totalitarianism*, New York: Random House, 1961. The most recent, specialized study of the Russian Communist Party, covering the period from 1934 to 1960.

BRZEZINSKI, ZBIGNIEW K., *The Permanent Purge*, Cambridge, Massachusetts: Harvard University Press, 1956. An account of the development of the Soviet purge, emphasizing the Great Purge (1936–1938) and describing the purges that have taken place since Stalin's death.

FAINSOD, MERLE, *How Russia Is Ruled*, Cambridge, Massachusetts: Harvard University Press, 1953. A detailed, scholarly study of the entire Soviet system, including a penetrating analysis of the nature and role of the Party, the governmental system, the methods of political control, and the strains and tensions in certain areas of Soviet life.

MCCLOSKY, HERBERT, and TURNER, JOHN E., *The Soviet Dictatorship*, New York: McGraw-Hill Book Company, 1960. An analysis of the Soviet system in its historical and cultural setting, including a treatment of Communist ideology, the Party, the governmental framework, and the instruments of political and social control in the economy, mass communications, and the arts.

MOORE, BARRINGTON, JR., *Soviet Politics—Dilemma of Power*, Cambridge, Massachusetts: Harvard University Press, 1950. An exciting study of the changing ideas and policies of the Communist rulers in the decades following the Bolshevik revolution.

SCHAPIRO, LEONARD, *The Communist Party of the Soviet Union*, New York:

Random House, 1960. An outstanding history of the Party from its origin through the major political struggles of the post-Stalin period.

Soviet Geography

COLE, J. P., and GERMAN, S. C., *A Geography of the USSR*, London: Butterworths, 1961. An up-to-date, systematic geography of the Soviet Union, with noteworthy emphasis upon the economy and population.

OXFORD REGIONAL ECONOMIC ATLAS, *The U.S.S.R. and Eastern Europe*, New York: Oxford University Press, 1956. An important reference for those interested in the physical geography, agriculture, forest reserves, mineral and industrial resources, transportation, ethnography, and trade patterns of the Soviet Union.

Soviet Economy

BERLINER, JOSEPH, *Factory and Manager in the USSR*, Cambridge, Massachusetts: Harvard University Press, 1957. A study of some of the "types" who become factory managers and of the problems they encounter in performing their tasks.

CAMPBELL, ROBERT W., *Soviet Economic Power*, Cambridge, Massachusetts: The Riverside Press, 1960. A penetrating analysis of Soviet economic growth, the problems of planning, and the incentive system.

GRANICK, DAVID, *The Red Executive*, New York: Doubleday and Company, 1960. A study of the "organization man" in Soviet industry, which analyzes the problems of operating the factories and controlling the bureaucracy, making fruitful comparisons with the western world.

NOVE, ALEC, *The Soviet Economy*, New York: Frederick A. Praeger, 1961. An excellent study of the economic system, which describes the organization of industry and agriculture, identifies the problems encountered by factory and farm managers, interprets the current discussion of "economic laws" that is taking place among Soviet economists, and appraises the ability of the Soviet system to deal with a maturing economy and competition with the West.

SCHWARTZ, HARRY, *Russia's Soviet Economy*, Englewood Cliffs, N. J.: Prentice-Hall, Inc., 1954. An encyclopedic survey of the economy, including treatment of economic development, the organization and growth of industry and agriculture, transportation and communication, trade and finance, and economic relations with the outside world.

Soviet Agriculture

Comparisons of the United States and Soviet Economies. Papers submitted by panelists appearing before the Subcommittee on Economic Statistics, Joint Economic Committee, Congress of the United States. Part I, "Agriculture," pp. 201–318, Washington, D.C., September 1959. An analysis of agricultural structure and growth, prices and costs, and production policy.

Economic Aspects of Soviet Agriculture. Report of a Technical Study Group, Washington, D.C.: United States Department of Agriculture, May 1959. Report of a 12,000-mile study tour by professional agricultural economists of the U.S. Department of Agriculture.

JOHNSON, D. GALE, and KAHAN, ARCADIUS, *The Soviet Agricultural Program: An Evaluation of the 1965 Goals,* Santa Monica, California: The RAND Corporation, Memorandum RM-2848-PR, May 1962. An item-by-item examination of Soviet progress in "reaching and surpassing" the United States in agricultural output.

LAIRD, ROY D., *Collective Farming in Russia,* Lawrence, Kansas: University of Kansas Social Science Studies, 1958. A succinct account of the major structural changes in collective farms under Khrushchev.

Soviet Science and Technology

CHRISTMAN, RUTH C., *Soviet Science,* Washington, D.C.: American Association for the Advancement of Science, 1952. A symposium, with contributions from nine experts on Soviet science, which surveys a number of fields and contains some pertinent observations on the difference between western and Soviet approaches to scientific endeavor.

JORAVSKY, DAVID, *Soviet Marxism and Natural Science, 1917–1932,* New York: Columbia University Press, 1961. A detailed analysis of the changing effects of Marxian ideology and Soviet politics on the natural sciences during the first fifteen years of Communist rule.

VUCINICH, ALEXANDER, *The Soviet Academy of Sciences,* Stanford, California: Stanford University Press, 1956. A well-documented analysis of the organization of the Academy and its place in Soviet social and economic life.

Soviet Education

BEREDAY, GEORGE, Z. F., BRICKMAN, WILLIAM W., and READ, GERALD H., *The Changing Soviet School,* Boston: Houghton Mifflin Company, 1960.

Best general description of preschool, primary, secondary, and special education in the USSR.

BEREDAY, GEORGE Z. F., and PENNAR, JAAN, *The Politics of Soviet Education*, New York: Frederick A. Praeger, 1960. A description of the content and methods of Soviet education, teacher training, techniques of Party control, and class tensions.

DEWITT, NICHOLAS, *Education and Professional Employment in the USSR*, National Science Foundation, Washington, D.C.: Government Printing Office, 1961. A massive study of Soviet education, especially useful for its treatment of professional training, academic personnel, and the employment of professional and specialized manpower.

Soviet Youth

BURG, DAVID, "Observations on Soviet University Students," in Pipes, Richard, *The Soviet Intelligentsia*, New York: Columbia University Press, 1961. An interesting essay on a subject about which little is known.

FISHER, RALPH, *Pattern for Soviet Youth*, New York: Columbia University Press, 1959. An elaborate history of the *Komsomols*, one of the youth organizations of the Communist Party.

Soviet Radio and Television

INKELES, ALEX, *Public Opinion in Soviet Russia*, Cambridge, Massachusetts: Harvard University Press, 1958. The best available study of mass communication in the USSR, including the press, cinema, radio, and TV.

The Future

BAUER, RAYMOND A., INKELES, ALEX, and KLUCKHOHN, CLYDE, *How the Soviet System Works*, Cambridge, Massachusetts: Harvard University Press, 1956. A study of the informal adjustive mechanism in the Soviet system, with special emphasis on the popular attitudes of particular socio-economic groups.

HOLT, ROBERT T., *Radio Free Europe*, Minneapolis: University of Minnesota Press, 1958. An analysis of the changes in the satellite countries during the post-Stalin era.

INKELES, ALEX, and BAUER RAYMOND A., *The Soviet Citizen*, Cambridge, Massachusetts: Harvard University Press, 1959. A unique and scholarly study based upon interviews with émigrés, which analyzes social stratification and mobility, patterns of family life, and popular attitudes toward the regime.

MOORE, BARRINGTON, JR., *Terror and Progress USSR*, Cambridge, Massachusetts: Harvard University Press, 1954. An insightful sociological study of the politics and problems of industrialization, with an interesting chapter on "Images of the Future."

ROSTOW, W. W., *The Dynamics of Soviet Society*, New York: W. W. Norton and Company, 1953. An analysis of Soviet society which provides a synthesis of the most important research findings on the USSR, with an emphasis on patterns of change and development.

INDEX

Academy of Sciences, 121, 133–134
Agricultural reforms, see Reforms, post-Stalin
Agriculture, current objectives of, 96–99
  future potential, 115–117
  incentive for production, 107–111
  machinery, 102
  and politics, 111–115
  resources of, 99–107
  see also Collectivization
Adamov, Joe, 199–200
"Agitprop," 186
Analogy, rule of, 25, 219
"Anti-Party faction," 18

Beria, Lavrenti, 1, 14
Bulganin, Nicolai, 17

Capital goods, 69–71
Capitalism, features of, 74
Change, political
  democratic potential, 208–210
  improbability of, 213–215
  popular views of, 207–214
  revolutionary potential, 210–213
Centralization, economic,
  and political change, 214–227
  problems of, 220–221
  see also Reforms, post-Stalin
Cities, growth of, 35–38
  outlying, 54–59
  see also Moscow
Coercion, physical, 8–9, 214, 222
Collective leadership, 30
Collectivization, agricultural, 92

Communication, mass media, 9–10, 185–196
Communism
  economic characteristics of, 75–77
  political characteristics of, 6–14
Communist Party, ideology, 6–8
  as instrument of control, 11–12, 84, 111–115, 125–129, 186, 216
"Comrades' Courts," 26
Control, machinery of, 11–14
  see also Communist Party; Coercion
Counseling, vocational, 149

Decentralization, economic, 29, 81–83, 216–217
Delinquency, juvenile, 171–177
Democracy, characteristics of, 7–8
De-Stalinization, (see Reforms, post-Stalin)
Dictatorship, characteristics of, 7–8
"Doctors' Plot," 15
Doctrine, (see Ideology)

Education, and indoctrination, 10
  classroom procedures, 152–154
  and economic plan, 140
  Khrushchev's critique of, 139–142
  polytechnical, 148–149
  science, 122, 133, 145–146
  social studies, 146
  US and USSR compared, 161–162
  vocational, 142, 146–147
  see also Higher education; schools

Economic decentralization, (see Decentralization, economic)

Economic growth, determinants of, 66–73
future trends, 88–89
rates of, 63–66
US and USSR compared, 64–66

Economy, organization of, 79–85
problems of, 80–85
requirements of, 220–227
see also Agriculture; Reforms, Post-Stalin

Factory managers, 83–84, 222
Farms, (see Kolkhoz; Sovkhoz)
Food consumption, 91

Geography, 36, 99–100
Gosplan, 80
Great Purge, (see Purge)

Higher Education, 155–161
admission standards, 156–157
counseling, 158
degrees, 161
examination, 157–158
number of students, 155–156
scholarships, 159

Hooliganism, 175–177
Housing, 50–52, 57–58

Ideology, Communist, 6–8, 119, 141, 180–181, 207–208, 225
Incentives, 223–225
Indoctrination, 9–11, 162, 164–167
Industrial regions, 36–37
Institute of Metallurgy, 127
Institute of Scientific and Technical Information, 122

Kaganovich, Lazar, 14, 17, 18
Kamenev, Leo, 4–5
Kapitsa, Peter, 128
KGB, (see Police)
Khrushchev, Nikita S., 1, 14, 16, 18–19, 24, 30, 52, 63, 88, 113, 136, 143, 144, 147, 214–218
Kolkhoz, 93

Komsomols, 26, 27, 139, 151, 164, 166–168, 178
Kremlin, 41–42
Kruprianov, Victor, 199
Kulaks, 4

Labor, slave, 223
Legal reforms, (see Reforms, post-Stalin)
Lenin, Vladimir ("Nikolai"), 2–3, 6, 149
Leningrad, 55
Literacy, 140
"Little Octobrists," 164
Lysenko, Trofim, 126, 131

Malenkov, Georgi, 1, 15, 16, 17, 18
"Managerial revolution," 225
Manpower, 67–69, 149
Market, in agriculture, 110
substitute for, 85–88
Medicine, 126, 135
Mendeleev Institute, 122
Mikoyan, Anastas, 14, 19
Molotov, Vyacheslav, 1, 17–18
Moscow, countryside, 53–54
expansion of, 47–51
industries, 45–47
slums, 44–46
suburbs, 51–53
urban renewal, 42–44
"Moscow Mailbag," 199–201

"New Soviet Man," 168

Party Control Committee, (see Control, machinery of)
Physics (see Sciences)
Physiology (see Sciences)
Planning, economic,
after decentralization, 81–82
in mature economy, 220–227
problems of, 77–79
Pioneer Palace, 165–167
Police, 8–9, 13–14
Power struggle,
post-Lenin, 2–5
post-Stalin, 14–20

"Proletarian myth," 6
Psychology (*see* Sciences)
Purge, 5, 9

Radio, control of, 186
  diffusion exchange, 193
  equipment, 192–193
  foreign broadcasting, 196–206
  listening audience, 195–196
  number of sets, 193
  programming
    children's, 194–195
    drama, 194
    educational, 195
    music, 194
Radio Moscow, North American
    Service
  listening audience, 202–205
  objectives of, 198
  programming, 198–202
  technical problems, 204–205
Reforms, post-Stalin
  agricultural, 93–96
  in the arts, 27–28
  economic, 21–23
  legal, 23–27
Reforms, educational (*see* Education; Schools)
Resources, natural, 66–67
Rudin, Sergei, 199

Sadovaya, 42
Samarin, Alexander, 126
School, "Complete Secondary General Education, Polytechnical, Labor," 143
School, "Incomplete General Education, Polytechnical, Labor," 142
School, Urban or Rural Technical, 143
School, for Working or Rural, 143
Schools, boarding, 144
  curriculum reform, 145
  examinations, 152–153
  four-year, 140
  for the gifted, 144
  reorganization, 142–145

Schools (*Continued*)
  seven-year, 140
  ten-year, 141, 146
Sciences
  astronomy, 131
  biology, 131
  chemistry, 130–131
  electronics, 131
  mathematics, 130
  medicine, 131
  meteorology, 131
  oceanography, 131
  physics, 129–130
Science, future potential, 135–137
  reasons for rapid development, 120–125
  regimentation of, 125–129
  self-criticism, 132–135
Secretariat, 3
"Show trials" (*see* Purge)
Social change, catalysts of, 227–231
  and consumerism, 229–230
  and education, 230–231
  and foreign contracts, 229
  and power struggles, 230
  and professional autonomy, 227–229
Sovnakhoz, 82–83, 86–87, 93
Sputnik, 119, 124, 128, 138
"Spiv," 174–175, 177
Stalin, Joseph, 1, 3–6, 13, 126–127, 135
"Stilyaga," 172–173, 177
State bureaucracy, 13–14
Super-firm, 220, 221

Tamm, Igor, 128
Technikum, 143, 147
Television, control of
  equipment, 190–19
  listening audience
  programming
    educational, 18
    feature, 188
    films, 189
    line telecasti
    news, 187
    quiz shows, 18

Terror, (*see* Coercion)
Totalitarianism, characteristics of, 218–220
Trotsky, Leon, 4–5

Universities (*see* Higher Education)

Village, peasant, 38–40
Virgin lands, 90–91, 95
Voice of America, 173

Wage system, 222–226 (*see also* Workday unit)

Workday unit, 93, 94

Young Pioneers, 151, 164–167
Youth, cynicism of, 180–182
    characteristics, 168–170
    Golden, 171–172, 177
    political ideas of, 179
Young Communist League (*see* *Komsomols*)

Zhdanov, Andrei, 125
Zhukov, Marshal Georgi, 13, 18
Zinoviev, Gregory, 4, 5